THIRTEEN HANDS

THIRTEEN

HANDS

and Other Plays

**Departures & Arrivals
Anniversary (co-written with Dave Williamson)
Fashion, Power, Guilt and the Charity of Families
(co-written with Catherine Shields)
Thirteen Hands**

CAROL SHIELDS

Vintage Canada

VINTAGE CANADA EDITION, 2002

Published in Canada by Vintage Canada, a division of Random House of Canada
Limited, in 2002. Distributed by Random House of Canada Limited, Toronto.
Vintage Canada and colophon are registered trademarks of Random House of
Canada Limited.

National Library of Canada Cataloguing in Publication
Shields, Carol, 1935–
    Thirteen hands and other plays / Carol Shields.

Anniversary co-written by Dave Williamson; Fashion, power, guilt and the charity
of families co-written by Catherine Shields.

Contents: Departures & arrivals—Anniversary—Fashion, power, guilt and the charity
of families—Thirteen hands.

ISBN 0-679-31210-2

I. Williamson, Dave, 1934–   II. Shields, Catherine, 1962–   III. Title.
IV. Title: Anniversary. V. Title: Departures & arrivals. VI. Title: Fashion, power,
guilt and the charity of families. VII. Title: Thirteen hands.

PS8587.H46T453 2002   C812'.54   C2002-901638-X
PR9199.3.S514T453 2002

Cover and text design by CS Richardson
Printed and bound in Canada

www.randomhouse.ca

2 4 6 8 9 7 5 3 1

To Agnes Sigurbjorg Peterson (1905–1994)
and to Clarence Allden Shields (1911–1984)

Contents

Preface

Before becoming a playwright, I was a novelist, and one who was often impatient with the requisite description of weather or scenery or even with the business of moving people from room to room. I was more interested in the sound of people talking to each other, reacting to each other or leaving silences for others to fall into. Always while writing I felt a quickening of interest when a patch of dialogue was about to erupt in my novels. I noticed, too, that the books I loved to read were full of human speech.

I was an avid theatre-goer in the sixties and seventies, and was greatly attracted to the experimental theatre of the time. I remember once seeing a play in which not one word was spoken, and another play whose script was improvised by the actors as they went along. I liked rough theatre with episodic structures, theatre that was richly theatrical, theatre in which one never knew from one minute to the next what was going to happen.

Departures and Arrivals was my first attempt at a full-length play. It has seen a number of incarnations, beginning its life as a musical set in an airport and culminating in a dramatic script comprising twenty-two vignettes. It was originally written for six actors (three men and three women), but in its many productions as many as 150 actors have taken part. What interested me in the play was the way in which our lives are heightened and enlarged when taken within the frame of public spaces—airports, train stations, public streets—so that we all become, in a sense, actors. The circular theme of departure and arrival has been, and continues to be, a theme in all my work, as does the fusion between the real and the surreal, the naturalistic and the fantastic.

The early development of *Departures and Arrivals* led me to an almost holy respect for directors and actors, and a delighted satisfaction in seeing a single play take so many creative curves. The play's structure is open so that separate scenes can be omitted or re-shuffled, and geographical references regrouped as required.

I wanted to write a play that an audience would enjoy. As a writer I did not feel it was my task to shock, shame and punish those who had bought tickets to my play. I wanted to ignite in them moments of recognition and toss out a handful of provocative questions at the same time. The central proposition of drama is not what happens. It is who are we and how do we see ourselves.

My friend David Williamson and I often discussed this matter, and we decided to write a play, *Anniversary*, within a very tight, self-assigned box. Was it possible, we asked ourselves, to haul out one more time that single-set domestic drama of discontented suburbanites? Two acts. A middle-class living room. Real time. Two couples and a fifth character thrown in to help stir the conversation. *Anniversary* was the result. A talky play.

The play is built on a triple narrative irony. One couple in the play are married and pretending to be close to separation. Another couple, who are separated, are pretending to be married. The third and overriding irony is that the separated couple are still emotionally together, while the married couple have already emotionally separated. We like to think this play operates, as all good theatre does, on a subversive level; it mocks its own confines, confronts its own familiarity and redeems the idea of comic pleasure through painful recognition.

Fashion, Power, Guilt and the Charity of Families is a musical play written with Catherine Shields. A mother and daughter, we were both interested in the ambivalence felt toward families, the drive we all share to find or create some kind of family—and the equally strong desire to escape the family's fury. We began the play by giving voice to the notion that if the family didn't exist, it would have to be invented—and this felicity led us away from a strictly naturalistic approach.

Family is the most universal of our institutions and the most mysterious and private in its workings. It seemed important to interrogate the basic assumptions about the nuclear family by placing abstract commentary margin-to-margin with the ongoing life of a "real" family, and bring music and drama edge-to-edge in order to open that question as far as it would allow.

Our characters are a mother, a father, a son and a daughter, and, in addition, we created Character Five, a woman actor who plays a number of roles and who provides the outsider's perception of the drama that every family sets up. We have reinforced this family-as-theatre sense in the newly revised script of the play that appears here.

For many years I've been interested in the lives of women, particularly those lives that have gone unrecorded. The last twenty or thirty years have seen, in literature and in theatre, the partial redemption of women artists and activists. But one group seems consistently overlooked, a group who, for historical reasons mainly, were caught between movements: "the blue-rinse set," "the white glove brigade," "the bridge club biddies." There were (are) thousands of these women, millions in fact. I am reluctant to believe that their lives are wasted or lost. Something important goes on around a bridge table, a place where many women have felt not only safe but brilliantly alive. It is altogether possible to believe that feminism found its early roots in just such gatherings.

Thirteen Hands, a musical play for four women actors, attempts to valorize those lives. (The play has been produced with eight and even twelve actors.) Two principal patterns of human behaviour play against each other: continuity and replacement.

Continuity is represented by the multi-generational range of the play and by the way women create and preserve history in their stories.

Replacement is the inevitability that all people face; in this play new faces appear around the table; a wife replaces one who dies, mothers are replaced by daughters and granddaughters. In the play, the four founding members of the bridge club are all, one by one, replaced, but there is an ever-present yearning—expressed in the final scene—to return to that moment when the four original members sat down at a table in the early years of the twentieth century and began their lives. The game of bridge is used literally and metaphorically in the play, and it is hoped that this doubleness is strengthened by the fact that the word *bridge* never appears.

Conflict in this play lies not between generations or between one woman and another, but between the differing social constructs that balance and assign the worth of a human life.

I have felt greatly honoured by the many productions that have flowed from these four play scripts. The collaborative aspect of theatre has given me an almost inexpressible gift of happiness. I remember that on the first day of rehearsals for *Thirteen Hands* at Prairie Theatre Exchange in Winnipeg, forty of us stood in a circle on the stage: director, actors, stage managers, carpenters, designers, all of them committed to taking a piece of writing on a page and blasting it into a third dimension. And this they proceeded to do.

— Carol Shields

DEPARTURES & ARRIVALS

CAROL SHIELDS

Departures and Arrivals was workshopped in draft form in 1983 by the Manitoba Association of Playwrights, directed by Bob White, and first produced in 1984 by The Black Hole Theatre at the University of Manitoba, under the general direction of Chris Johnson, with music by Rob Matheson.

Playwright's Note

The play's structure (twenty-two vignettes) is intended to be open so that separate scenes can be omitted to meet time requirements or reshuffled to suit the demands of an individual director. The scenes are not distinguished in the text, and directors should feel free to adjust the stage directions and transitions between scenes.

The play is designed so that the many parts can be taken by six actors, three men and three women. Costumes are minimal: a hat, a coat, a prop and so forth. In addition to the six actors, there is an offstage public address (PA) voice, which announces flights and provides connections. (In the Black Hole production, this voice was an onstage presence, an actor/musician who also provided musical accompaniment on an electric piano.)

Although the play is not a musical, some form of musical connection (organ, piano, flute, etc.) helps to join the separate scenes.

It is my hope that all the elements of the play will contribute both to a cyclical sense of arrival and departure, and to the human appreciation of the public place—be it airport, train station or city street—as a venue for the theatrical sense that enlarges ordinary lives. It is also my hope that the play will realize a fusion of the real and the surreal, the naturalistic and the fantastic. This is a comedy with edges.

Cast
Six characters make up the cast, three men and three women. The play is designed so that each character plays several roles. In addition, there is an off-stage voice. The different roles of the play can be taken by other actors, if desired.

Setting
The play is set in a large international airport. There are standard benches, potted plants, a luggage chute and a coin-operated phone booth to one side.

Act One

Scene: the foyer of an airport. There are two stairways side by side at centre stage, one marked Departures, the other Arrivals. To one side is a revolving platform for suitcases with a chute to feed it. At the other side is an automatically opening door to the outside. The foyer has a bench or two, a public telephone and one or two information desks. Other furniture or equipment is brought on as needed.

At rise, a single piece of luggage, a small exotic vanity case of green, pink and silver, goes around on the platform several times. An airport CLEANER *walks across the stage with a big push broom; he turns and recrosses.* PA *announcements give flight arrival and departure times. Strobe lighting on stage. People—six actors coming on stage and then exiting and reappearing in different costumes—*WOMAN IN SILK DRESS, MIDDLE-AGED MAN, YOUNG MAN, ELDERLY WOMAN, WOMAN OF THIRTY, MAN IN BROWN SUIT, WOMAN IN BROWN SUIT, MAN IN SWEATER, WOMAN WITH SHAWL *and* MAN WITH BRIEFCASE—*enter from various corners carrying suitcases, wheeling trunks, pushing luggage carts, etc. Music, organ or electric piano, and strobe lights stop; spotlight on one person while others freeze.*

WOMAN IN SILK DRESS

[Addresses the audience.] I'm off to London. London, England, that is. I always go to London at this time of year. When I'm in London I always stay at the St. Irmine's, and when I'm at the St. Irmine's, I always have kippers for breakfast the first morning. But I never have a sense of déjà vu. Or maybe I have, but I don't know it.
[Strobe lights again; people continue to move, then freeze.]

MIDDLE-AGED MAN

I'm in sales. Computers. Plastics. About 6.8 percent of my life is spent airborne. Does that amaze you? Does that give you pause?
[Lights, music, people moving.]

YOUNG MAN

[Dabbing eyes.] I don't want to leave. Not really, not wholeheartedly. This

wasn't my idea, this move. But what can I do? On the other hand, I didn't want to come, either.

[Lights, music, people moving.]

ELDERLY WOMAN

Who knows what's going to happen when you get into an airplane. This may be my last scene of reality, that ashtray over there full of butts, that PA voice all stuffed with smiles. Who really knows?

[Lights, music, people moving.]

WOMAN OF THIRTY

I wonder, do I look different? I mean, inside I'm the same person, but, well, not the same person. I mean, does it show? Is he going to . . . guess? Does he have the sensitivity to guess? So okay, I've let him down in a sense, but in another sense I've reached out. Oh, hell, if he notices I'll just say I'm coming down with the flu or something.

[Lights, music, people moving.]

MAN IN BROWN SUIT

I'll miss you terribly.

WOMAN IN BROWN SUIT

Me too.

MAN IN BROWN SUIT

It's never easy. Saying goodbye.

WOMAN IN BROWN SUIT

Agreed.

MAN IN BROWN SUIT

It's pain. Anguish.

WOMAN IN BROWN SUIT

Right.

MAN IN BROWN SUIT

Until tomorrow then.

WOMAN IN BROWN SUIT

Tomorrow.

[Lights, music, people moving.]

MAN IN SWEATER

I'm off to Omaha. Spelled O-m-a-h-a. Change planes at Minneapolis. Why Omaha? A good question. Because it's somewhere else, that's why. It's not here.

[Lights, music, people moving.]

MIDDLE-AGED MAN

Wonder if she'll notice I've been working out. Six months of weights, a mile before breakfast, she'd better notice. All this new muscle tissue. I mean, if she doesn't notice, she's gotta be blind or something.

[Lights, music, people moving.]

WOMAN WITH SHAWL

This happens to be my fifth Club Med holiday. Yippee. That first time in Peru, my girlfriend and I, we stayed in our room all night and cried. But later? We really got into it. In a way. You know?

[Lights, music, people moving.]

MAN WITH BRIEFCASE

I'm an MP. So okay, that's a dirty word these days. But take a look at this ticket. Tourist class. Get a load of that. Register that. Remember that. Think about that.

[Lights, music, people moving.]

YOUNG WOMAN

[Shouting.] Don't forget to write. Or telephone. Every week. Twice a week. Oh God. You promised, don't you forget it.

[Lights, music, people moving.]

MAN

[To WOMAN.*]* So tell me, what is it you really want?
*[*WOMAN *whispers something inaudible in his ear.]*
Yeah, well.
[Lights, music, people moving.]

WOMAN IN GYPSY DRESS

God, I could die, I'm so happy . . . I can't stand it. This is my home. My
turf, my place. I never thought I'd get back here. I could . . . I could kiss
the ground . . . I wonder if . . . no, I couldn't . . . or maybe . . . why not?
*[She stoops and kisses the ground. Lights change; people wander off leaving
only a young* PEOPLE-WATCHER *on a bench at centre stage. She eases her
backpack onto the bench and places it beside her. She is in her early twenties,
dressed with a moderate smartness that suggests she has recently left the stu-
dent life and is about to begin the real thing. Her random thoughts are either
read by voice-over or said by her. She holds a book on her lap, but looks
around the empty stage continually, furtively, appraisingly, touching her face,
her body scarcely moving—the ultimate people-watcher. This very long solilo-
quy can be divided into two alternating voices coming from two young
women who look very similar, identically dressed but unaware of each other,
suggesting they are the same person, trading perspectives.]*

PEOPLE-WATCHER

God! *[Pause.]* If I had one wish . . . this bench! *[Pause.]* Why can't they have
soft chairs in airports? . . . Good thing I brought a book . . . to pass the
time . . . A book can be your best companion, that's what Miss Newbury
used to say back in sixth grade. Miss Blueberry we called her behind her—
[Looks around.] Hmmm, he's attractive . . . for his age . . . nice necktie . . .
looks like he keeps in shape, probably jogs or something, tennis maybe,
with that tan—but green socks! His wife maybe bought them for him, or
his mother, or one of his kids . . . if he has kids, which he probably does.
He's as old as Dad . . . well, almost . . . but green! And that looks like the
Financial Post under his arm. You'd think if he reads the *Financial Post*, he'd
know about green socks, yeech . . . at least they're dark green. *[Pause.]* Two
hours is a long time. One hundred and twenty minutes.*[Pause.]* My new

watch looks great, makes my wrist look sort of thin, kind of casual, but not too casual. I've really changed this year. My life's really . . . well . . . I'm older this year, more in control, sort of—a year ago I'd be sitting here worrying about how I looked and all that, and now I look like . . . like . . . someone who's . . . sort of got it together. *[Pause.]* Here I am, reading *Crime and Punishment*, Dostoevsky. A year ago I'd be flipping through some magazine, just flipping through . . . *Flipping.*

Oh, gross, too many chains. Some people are so unaware of what they look like—gross!

If I had one wish I'd—oh! I love it, *I love it*, she's so . . . everything matches, shoes, suit, blouse, sort of—what do you call that look?—monochromatic . . . She's so pulled together, probably spent a week planning what she'd wear on the plane, laying it all out on the bed. *[Pause.]* Wonder what her bedroom looks like. Lots of mirrors, I bet, track lighting, silky bedspread . . . It's neat, everyone in the world has a bedroom . . . or part of a bedroom, every last person . . . I wish I could go up to that man over there in the white pants and say, "Hey, what's your bedroom like?" Or that girl with the chains, "What's *your* bedroom like? I mean, have you got wallpaper or what? Have you got a four-poster maybe or . . ." God, I really liked that Japanese bed of Bobby's, that mattress thing, not that I'd buy one, but now and then . . . and if I decide to get a place of my own and—ugh, no, spare me, give *moi* a break, bedroom slippers in the airport! . . . *Embroidered* bedroom slippers, *gold* embroidery. *[Pause.]* She must be a hundred years old.

They must notice it, people must notice how they're getting older and older—like we're all getting older. Right the minute you're born, you start getting . . . your skin gets older and your fingernails get older, even your eyebrows get older, and when you breathe out, you're *breathing out old breath*. If only they didn't have to dress like that. Why can't someone tell them, those old-lady coats with one giant button in the middle. He's sort of interesting . . . maybe a little macho . . . machismo . . . macho-mio. *[She rolls the word around in her mouth.]* I think he's looking at me—he is! What would happen if he wandered over here and sort of looked down and said, "Hey, not only are you an attractive woman, but you're reading *Crime and Punishment*, my favourite book," or something along those lines . . . and I'd say, "Well, I sort of, you know, I'm into the Russians at the moment . . ." or maybe . . .

[Looks around.] If I had one wish, I'd wish I was really gorgeous, only not dumb. I'd be able to talk about politics and stuff, nuclear disarmament . . . that time I got a B+ on my essay on Argentina and Mr. Griffiths wrote "lively and provocative." [Pause.] That poor kid, I know just how he feels, you can tell he hates his haircut, the way he's holding his head, all stiff like a robot. Do I ever know how he feels—if I get in line behind him, I could say something nonchalant like, "Hey, do you mind if I ask who cuts your hair? You look great," something like that . . . or I could say, "Look, not to worry, it'll grow out, that's one thing about hair." Ha, that time Mom gave me the home perm and I had to wear a scarf to school for a week while the frizz settled down—a soft perm it was supposed to be—I probably thought the whole world was looking at me and all the time everyone was just worrying about how they looked, that's the way people are. If I started all of a sudden vibrating right here in the airport, no one would come running up and say, "Hey, why's this woman suddenly vibrating?" They wouldn't . . . they probably wouldn't even notice, or, if they did, they'd just say, "Well, she probably vibrates all the time, that's the way she is."

At least I don't look like *that*. She probably thought it looked nice on the hanger or something, or maybe it was a present . . . That time Bobby and Marcie gave me that sweater with the bumblebee stitched on the front, a pink bumblebee with little sparkles. *[Looks around.]* I don't believe it, they're kissing . . . like they don't even notice there's anyone else around—I wish . . . Oh, my God, he's probably leaving. Maybe he got transferred . . . or maybe she's the one who's leaving, that looks like her luggage, not his, white vinyl. She's not crying, tell me she's not crying. Tears. Tears in an airport—they really, really love each other, you can tell. *[Pause.]* If only . . . oh, how I long, how I long— *[Staring.]* Is that plastic or leather? Could be leather . . . no plastic . . . or maybe . . . leather—now that's Mr. Weird! He must've got the conditioner mixed up with the shampoo. He's so conditioned, he's about to explode, talk about thick hair—to think I used to walk around blowing bubble gum like that, what a goof, and thinking I looked so cool in my denim jacket when I looked like—what a cute little kid . . . I remember being just that size and my mouth came up to the counter like that . . . *He's licking the edge of the counter*—I was that size for years and years and I used to . . . lick the counter . . . Did I really?

Droopy! Are they ever droopy. How do they get that droopy? From not wearing a bra probably. It makes you feel droopy just looking at them drooping away—that man with the tennis racquet, I wish he'd come over here and start a conversation . . . Don't tell me he's with that other guy . . . Oh no! They're not . . . they're maybe . . . together . . . The story of my life. *[Pause.]* If I had one wish . . .

*[*PILOT *and* FLIGHT ATTENDANT *enter and freeze.]*

Now he's sensational, it's the uniform . . . very, very nice . . . and those eyes . . . Pilots make more than eighty thou a year, more than stockbrokers, that was in *Time* magazine . . . That must be a stewardess he's talking to— only they don't call them that anymore, what do you call them? *[Pause.]* Flight attendants. They look like they've really got it together, relationship-wise, like they're really in sync, like their hearts are beating at the same rate or something—I can feel my heart beating. When I think of all the hearts in this airport! . . . We can't see them, we can't hear them, but they're all thumping away, *kaboom, kaboom, kaboom*, hundreds of them. Oh God, I feel so lonely sitting here . . . I can't stand it. Maybe a cup of coffee or something . . . *[She gets up and puts on her backpack.]* . . . maybe a muffin, something sweet, a chocolate bar. *[Pause.]* If I had one wish . . .

[The PILOT *and* FLIGHT ATTENDANT *appear in four contretemps scenes throughout the play, standing always in the same very tight spotlighted space at stage front. The lighting and musical background separate these contretemps from the other reality of the play, evoking the "soap-operish" or "true romance" aspect of the airport. Organ music might help underline the melodramatic content. The two characters appear suddenly, and are just as suddenly blacked out.]*

PILOT

How 'bout a movie?

FLIGHT ATTENDANT

Afraid not. Not tonight.

PILOT

A drink then. A quickie?

FLIGHT ATTENDANT

I'm terribly sorry. I'd like to but—

PILOT

But you're busy. Is that right?

FLIGHT ATTENDANT

I suppose you might . . . yes. That's it. I'm afraid . . . I'm busy.

PILOT

And you're busy tomorrow night, right?

FLIGHT ATTENDANT

Well, yes.

PILOT

And next weekend?

FLIGHT ATTENDANT

Look, I'm sorry, but—

PILOT

Let me tell you what I sense. I sense we're . . . now how can I put this? . . . I sense we're drifting apart.

FLIGHT ATTENDANT

We hardly know each other, how can we drift—

PILOT

But we were starting to . . . know each other. Didn't you feel it? That night at the Japanese restaurant? Don't tell me you didn't feel anything.

FLIGHT ATTENDANT

It was—

PILOT

It was magic. Say it. Two people with everything in common, their lives enmeshed.

FLIGHT ATTENDANT

Well—

PILOT

And now you're all of a sudden tied up every night of the week.

FLIGHT ATTENDANT

I wish I could explain, but—

PILOT

But what? There's gotta be a reason.

FLIGHT ATTENDANT

There is.

PILOT

Well, then?

FLIGHT ATTENDANT

There's a reason, but, well, I think you might find it hard to accept.

PILOT

I see. It's something about me that you find—

FLIGHT ATTENDANT

No, it's about me. And really about you, too. I can't explain.
[Pause.]

PILOT

I see. I see.

[Light snaps off on PILOT *and* FLIGHT ATTENDANT. *Two couples enter from opposite sides. The two women,* JANICE *and* RACHEL, *are seeing their husbands,* JIM *and* ROBERT, *off on a plane which is being announced by the* PA *in the background.]*

PA

Flight 89 now boarding at Gate 2. Flight 89 for Toronto now boarding.

JANICE

[To JIM.*]* Now promise you'll phone Alice if you get a chance.

JIM

I'll try. I said I'll try. But there're going to be meetings all day—

JANICE

She'd love to hear from you. She always loves it when—

JIM

And meetings in the evenings. Plus sales seminars. Plus two official lunches and a banquet—

JANICE

She's the only sister you've got. If she ever found out you went to Toronto and didn't call—

JIM

I'll try. I said I would, didn't I?

JANICE

I know she'd appreciate it. Five minutes. It'd mean the world.

RACHEL

[To ROBERT.*]* Good luck. It'll go fine.

ROBERT

Look, will you take the car in for a lube job while I'm away?

RACHEL

I'm sure there's nothing to be nervous about. It isn't as if they're calling you into Main Office to—

ROBERT

And tell them to do a good job this time. The last time they gave it to some jerk who didn't know the hell what he was doing—

RACHEL

Let's see. Thursday night, Flight 450. I'll be here.

ROBERT

You can tell them I was not pleased. Not at all pleased.

PA

Flight 86 now boarding, Flight 86 now boarding. Step lively for Flight 86.

JANICE

Give Alice my love.

ROBERT

And get them to check the goddamn muffler.
*[*JIM *and* ROBERT *go up the Departures steps, one a little ahead of the other.* JANICE *and* RACHEL *go over to a booth that sells flight insurance. There is a smiling* ATTENDANT *behind the booth.]*

ATTENDANT

[To JANICE.*]* Can I help you?

JANICE

[To RACHEL.*]* I believe you were first.

RACHEL

No, you were first. I'm in no hurry.

JANICE

Well, that's very kind.
[To ATTENDANT.*]* I'd like the one-million-dollar policy.

ATTENDANT

If you'll just fill in this form.

RACHEL

I'll have the million-dollar policy, too. That's the one I always get.

JANICE

I do, too. It seems a little silly, I know, but Jim, that's my husband, travels
an awful lot.

RACHEL

So does Robert. And it's not silly at all. It's common sense.

JANICE

I can't help worrying about him.
*[The two women continue their discussion standing near the insurance booth
or, perhaps, sitting on a bench.]*

RACHEL

I'm an awful worrywart myself. If Robert knew I worried the way I do, he'd
probably stop flying. He doesn't even know I buy insurance when he flies.

JANICE

My Jim doesn't either. He'd think I was morbid. He'd think it was a waste
of money. He thinks flying across the country is safer than driving down
Portage Avenue.

RACHEL

Isn't that amazing! You won't believe this, but Robert says exactly the same thing.

JANICE

Jim would think I was downright neurotic if he knew I bought insurance every time he went up.

RACHEL

I never let on to Robert. I buy the million-dollar policy every time.

JANICE

Me too. I have for years.

RACHEL

What a coincidence.

JANICE

You have to think about how you would manage. If.

RACHEL

You sure as hell do.

JANICE

Lots of women have been left standing with just the change in their purse. They don't think ahead.

RACHEL

They don't think it will happen to them.

JANICE

Well, I know better. I know the statistics. I read that article, in *Newsweek*.

RACHEL

It only makes sense. If you spend enough time in the air—

JANICE

—your number's bound to come up.

RACHEL

Exactly.

JANICE

It's a responsibility, taking out insurance, that's how I look at it.
[Pause.]

RACHEL

The way I look at it, say I get the full million. I'd put half of it in short-term investment certificates, shopping around, of course, for the best interest rate—

JANICE

Oh, you have to shop around.

RACHEL

—and one-quarter into government bonds—you can't go wrong there.

JANICE

That's what I'd do, government bonds.

RACHEL

And the remaining quarter I'd sink into a good energy stock. I figure that way I'd be getting a decent tax break.

JANICE

I think I heard Jim saying something about the energy market being risky.

RACHEL

Robert says the same thing, but that's crazy. Energy's the future.

JANICE

You'd probably have a house to maintain, too.

RACHEL

Well, I've thought about that, and you know, I think I'd . . . you know, if something . . . happened . . . if Robert, you know . . . I think I'd put the house up for sale.

JANICE

Really? You think that's wise?

RACHEL

What I picture is one of those new condos on Wellington Crescent.

JANICE

Wonderful view from some of those condos.

RACHEL

And look at it this way. When you want to go away in the winter, you just shut the door . . . and go!

JANICE

We don't usually go away in the winter. Once we went to Bermuda but—

RACHEL

Winter's Robert's busiest time, so we don't get away either. But if I was on my own, I'd—this probably sounds batty—but I've always wanted to see Australia. And New Zealand.

JANICE

Not me. I'd head back to Bermuda. Those beautiful beaches! Jim thought they were all out for his money, but I—

RACHEL

Well, if you went into a condo . . . like me . . . you could get away to Bermuda any time you liked. Just shut the door.

JANICE

I think what I'd do is subdivide.

RACHEL

Subdivide?

JANICE

The house, I mean. I mean, if Jim . . . if . . . well, I've had this idea for years.
All I need is the second floor for my personal use. I'd have to close off the
stairs and . . . of course I'd have to get a really good architect. But it's a big
house. I figure I could get four apartments out of it easily.

RACHEL

Why not? Maximize your income. And you'd have your own little apartment.

JANICE

I think I might do it in tones of gold and green.

RACHEL

Nice. Very nice.

JANICE

I'd probably want to refurnish, too. You know, go in for something lighter.
Wicker maybe. We have all this heavy furniture from Jim's mother's side,
and well, it would be a terrible wrench parting with it—

RACHEL

An emotional wrench.

JANICE

But if Jim's . . . not here . . . and I know he'd want me to be comfortable.

RACHEL

I think Robert feels the same. When your life alters radically, you have to
make radical adjustments.

JANICE

One thing for sure is I'd buy a waterbed.

RACHEL

What a good idea! They say they're wonderful for your back, but Robert thinks—

JANICE

Jim says they make him seasick, *gurgle, gurgle* all night. We had one in our hotel in Bermuda and I loved it. It was a funny thing, but I had the most wonderful dreams in that bed. And I mean wonderful. The kind of dreams I haven't had since . . . I don't know when.

RACHEL

In that case, I think you should definitely go ahead and get the waterbed.

JANICE

And I'd have a very good reading light put in. Jim hates it when I read in bed—

RACHEL

So does Robert, he makes a great big fuss, says the light keeps him awake. And I love to read.

JANICE

So do I. But Jim—

RACHEL

As a matter of fact, I think I'd probably go back to university.

JANICE

Really!

RACHEL

Well, once I move into the condo and invest the money from the insurance,

I'll have to have something to do. I mean, I can't spend all my time travelling around Australia and New Zealand.

JANICE

So you'd get a degree?

RACHEL

I'd have to do that first. But then—

JANICE

Then?

RACHEL

Then . . . this may seem weird . . . but I thought I'd go into social work.

JANICE

Social work! That sounds fascinating.

RACHEL

Robert always says social workers are a bunch of do-gooders, but—

JANICE

But . . . if Robert wasn't here . . .

RACHEL

I think I have it in me to help people.

JANICE

I think what I'd do is open a china shop. A sort of boutique, you know. Just very, very good things.

RACHEL

You could have a bridal register.

JANICE

Oh, I'd have to have a bridal register. I know times are bad, but—

RACHEL

—but people are still getting married. And you'd have the money to invest.

JANICE

And I think I have a good business head even if Jim says—

RACHEL

The world of business is fascinating.

JANICE

Full of fascinating people.

RACHEL

And it's not entirely . . . well . . . not impossible . . . that you . . . or I . . . might meet someone. In the business world, I mean. Anything could happen.

JANICE

A man you mean?

RACHEL

Well, something like that. If someone comes along, well, why not?

JANICE

You mean . . . you might remarry if . . . if your husband . . .

RACHEL

Well, people aren't meant to be alone.

JANICE

That's what Jim always says. His sister, Alice—

RACHEL

We all need companionship. I think we owe it to ourselves.

JANICE

But remarriage?

RACHEL

Maybe not remarriage. Maybe just a . . . you know . . . a relationship.

JANICE

A relationship. That might be an interesting thing to . . . I think . . . maybe
. . . I might consider a relationship as well.

RACHEL

[Walking off.] If . . .

JANICE

[Walking off in opposite direction.] Yes, if.

PA

Ladies and gentlemen, those bound for ordinary and exotic destinations,
please board. This is the final call.
*[Suitcases roll down the chute, and in a minute all six people come and go,
down the Arrivals stairs. They pick up their cases and exit, leaving only the
silver case and two identical white bags going around. Lights change.* ALPHA
and BETA, *dressed identically and looking androgynous, start to reach for the
bags, then pull back, exchange looks, and then let the cases go around again.
They repeat this two or three times, each finally taking one.*

*I've seen this played very broadly, and it doesn't work. Playing it absolutely
straight preserves what the scene is about, which is not sexuality but the hidden
core of innocence.]*

ALPHA

Coincidence.

BETA

Yes. It is.

ALPHA

I've never seen . . . one . . . like mine before.

BETA

I haven't either. I thought mine was . . . the only one . . . the only one there was.

ALPHA

That's what I thought, too.

BETA

It's not that I haven't looked. I mean . . . I really have . . . looked . . . but I've never seen—

ALPHA

To tell you the truth, I'd given up looking.

BETA

So had I. I was resigned.

ALPHA

Goodness!

BETA

What is it?

ALPHA

How can we be sure . . . well, that this is yours and . . . this is mine?

BETA

We could always . . .

ALPHA

Always what?

BETA

Well, I was going to suggest . . . I don't want to intrude on . . . to be overly personal, but I was going to suggest—

ALPHA

Please go ahead. Don't be shy.

BETA

Well, I was going to suggest that . . . we . . . open them.

ALPHA

Oh, I never open mine. Never.

BETA

I don't either. At least I never have before.

ALPHA

I don't think I could. I'm awfully sorry.

BETA

Have you had yours . . . for a long time?

ALPHA

Well, come to think of it, it has been a long time. In fact—

BETA

I've always had mine.

ALPHA

You get so you're attached. *[Laughs.]* It's not easy . . . I mean . . . it's hard to think of not having one.

BETA

I know just what you mean.

ALPHA

I don't even like . . . to let anyone else . . . touch mine.

BETA

That's how I feel. But the truth is, well—

ALPHA

Well?

BETA

The truth is . . . no one's ever touched mine.

ALPHA

Oh. In my case—

BETA

Yes, go on. You can tell me.

ALPHA

Well, the fact is, no one . . . no one's ever *wanted* to touch mine.

BETA

No one?

ALPHA

No one.

BETA

Maybe—

ALPHA

Yes?

BETA

Maybe you'd let me . . . touch it.

ALPHA

Oh, I don't know.

BETA

Just a little, you know, just a little pat.

ALPHA

Well, I don't suppose . . . why not?

BETA

[Touching case.] There.

ALPHA

Oh.

BETA

That wasn't so bad, was it?

ALPHA

No. Not at all. I . . . liked it. I enjoyed it.

BETA

That's good.

ALPHA

Would you like me to . . . give yours . . . just a little pat?

BETA

Do you think you could?

ALPHA

[Touching case.] There. And there.

BETA

Thank you. Very much.

ALPHA

You're welcome.

BETA

I've got an idea.

ALPHA

What?

BETA

No, never mind. Forget what I said.

ALPHA

Please.

BETA

Well, I just thought . . . now if you don't like this idea, all you have to do is—

ALPHA

I'll like it. I promise.

BETA

Well, what if I gave you mine . . . and you gave me . . . yours?

ALPHA

I . . . I . . .

BETA

I hope you don't think—

ALPHA

What I was going to say is . . . I think that would be wonderful.

                                        BETA
Really?

                                        ALPHA
Really.

                                        BETA
Well, here you are.

                                        ALPHA
And here you are.

                                        BETA
Thank you.

                                        ALPHA
Thank *you.*

                                        BETA
Are you going this way?

                                        ALPHA
Yes, as a matter of fact—

                                        BETA
[Offers arm.] Well, why don't we—

                                        ALPHA
We might as well.
[They exit. Three REPORTERS *carrying cameras enter at a run and take up
positions at bottom of the Arrivals stairs. A number of pieces of matched red
luggage comes down the chute. They are followed an instant later by a greasy
backpack.]*

PA

Ladies and gentlemen, will you kindly clear the area for the arrival of an important personage.

REPORTER ONE

Where the hell is she?

REPORTER TWO

You sure her flight's in?

REPORTER THREE

That's gotta be her luggage.

REPORTER ONE

Gee, that's a lotta luggage for one day in this town.

REPORTER THREE

I didn't want this assignment. I wanted to cover the Agricultural Support Talks.

REPORTER ONE

You did?

REPORTER THREE

Some real interesting stuff coming up today on wheat quotas. And oats. Maybe even barley!

REPORTERS

[In unison.] Here she comes. One, two, three, ready.
[Flashbulbs go off. At the top of the Arrivals stairs is large voluptuous movie star, MISS HORTON-HOLLIS, *vulgarly dressed. She does several poses as cameras go off.]*

MISS HORTON-HOLLIS

That'll have to do, fellas.

REPORTER ONE

Would you mind answering a few questions, Miss Horton-Hollis?

MISS HORTON-HOLLIS

I've got four minutes and I'm willing to talk about anything except my relationship with Warren Beatty—

REPORTER TWO

That's completely kaput, right?

REPORTER ONE

Is it true you're in therapy, Miss Horton-Hollis?

MISS HORTON-HOLLIS

Psychic reconstruction, unmasking the self so you can find the true core of being that—

REPORTER THREE

[Scribbling.] Core of being? Could you comment on that please?

MISS HORTON-HOLLIS

I'm talking about the amalgam of the absence and the presence. The intersection of innerness and outerness.

REPORTER TWO

How do you spell "amalgam"?

MISS HORTON-HOLLIS

The coming together of otherness and ethos, nature and anti-nature, the chicken and the egg—

REPORTER ONE

Neat.

MISS HORTON-HOLLIS

All life, you see, is a question of arrivals and departures. Of going through gateways.

REPORTER THREE

Gee, that's right. When you stop to think.

MISS HORTON-HOLLIS

You travel out as far as you can go—

REPORTER ONE

Far out!

MISS HORTON-HOLLIS

Then you turn your face 180 degrees and retrace your steps.

REPORTER THREE

[Excited.] Like . . . like . . . like life's kind of like, sort of, you know, a cycle . . . and the custom's officer sort of symbolizes, well, you know, he sort of represents—

REPORTER ONE

About this thing with Warren Beatty, you say it's definitely over. We heard there was a chance of—

REPORTER THREE

[To others.] This person is on a quest to the centre of being, and you slobs want to talk about some Tinseltown romance.

REPORTER ONE

All I want to know is, is it on or off?

MISS HORTON-HOLLIS

Off. But talk to me tomorrow.

[She descends, goes through the doors; an aide appears and carries her luggage. The REPORTERS *keep snapping.]*

REPORTER THREE

And to think I almost went to the Agricultural Support Talks. That's the problem with stereotypes, fellas, we get bounced on our heads every time. *[A young* POET *bounds into view and down the stairs, picks up the backpack turns and faces the* REPORTERS.*]*

POET

If you'd like a statement, gentlemen . . .

REPORTER THREE

[After a pause.] You got a statement?

POET

I'll be brief. The verse is dead. The line is dead. And be sure to get this— get your pencils ready, gentlemen—the word is dead.

REPORTER ONE

And you are?

POET

It's in the press release. Poet on the road. Man with a message.

REPORTER THREE

The message again is—?

REPORTER ONE

I took a course in poetry once. The prof said all great poetry was about—

POET

The poem is about the poem is about the poem is about—

REPORTER THREE

Wait a minute, I can't write that fast.

POET

And now, if you'd like one more picture—

REPORTER THREE

Thank you.

[He takes the picture; the blinding flashbulb blacks out the stage for an instant. The POET *and* REPORTERS ONE *and* TWO *go out through the automatic doors, leaving* REPORTER THREE *on stage.]*

REPORTER THREE

[Addressing the audience.] There's something I'd like to share with you out there. It's about the rich and famous. I meet quite a few of them in my line of work. You know, there's a saying that if you stand here, right here, at the information counter, long enough, the whole world passes by. No kidding, it's true. I've seen it happen. But that's not what I want to say to you. What I want to say is that the rich and famous, well, they're just like you and me. Inside I mean, like deep down, like they've got feelings. They've got bad taste in art, some of them. They applaud in the wrong places at the symphony. They get struck by lightning. They get hives. Hernias. Corns on their feet, know what I'm saying?

[Behind REPORTER THREE *a tall, splendidly dressed* SHEIK *appears.]*

If it isn't the fabulously wealthy, the near-legendary, the practically mythical . . . *[confides to audience]* Travelling incognito, of course, but get a load of that ruby ring. Excuse me, folks.

[He hurries after the SHEIK *who exits through the automatic doors. As they leave, a* TELEPHONER *enters and goes to the pay phone.]*

TELEPHONER

[Dials.] Mom? Yes, it's me. No, it's not Andy, it's Bob. Must be a bad connection. I said, it's me. It's Bob. Bobby. No, I'm not kidding, it's me. I'm right here in town. Out at the airport. I'm on my way to Calgary. No, a business trip! Well, I was going to write and let you know, but I'm only here for

a twenty-five-minute stopover and I didn't want you coming all the way out from the house just for—what? No. No, Mom. I haven't seen Andy lately. Well, this is a big city, and I just haven't seen him for a couple of months or so. No, he looked fine, I thought, same old Andy. I'll tell him, Mom, but you know he was never one for letters. I'll just tell him to give you a phone call, okay? Anyway, Mom, I just wanted to let you know Irene and the kids are fine. Sandy's just had his birthday. We took all the kids in the neighbourhood over to McDonald's and they had a ball. You should have seen Sandy all surrounded by—what? No, not that I know of, Mom. I don't think so, Mom. No. Mom? Well, look, Mom, I can't just call him up and say, do you have a girlfriend? I know he's my brother, but Jesus, Mom. Why don't you write him and ask him then? *[Pause.]* And what did he say? Oh, I think you worry too much, Mom. Irene says . . . Irene! My wife. She says Andy isn't ready to settle down. Well, thirty-two's not exactly over the hill and when the time comes—you've *got* grandchildren, Mom. You've got Sandy and Missy and Muffy and they all send you hugs and kisses, Mom. The last thing Muffy said at the airport—it was the cutest darned thing— she said, "Tell Grammy I lof her a lot." He's . . . yes . . . as far as I know, Mom. Yes, the same address. No, he hasn't moved. What makes you think he's moved? Yes, I think so, the two of them. Well, I don't know, Mom. How can I tell what kind of influence he has on Andy, you can't lump all interior decorators together—I'll try. Okay. I promise, but he's a big boy, I can't tell him how to run his life, but I'll have a talk . . . I can't this week, Mom. Because I'm on my way to Calgary. We're opening a new branch and . . . Mom, I know you worry. Look, you're getting all worked up for—he's happy, he's got his life. Well, he's probably happy. Well, he could be. No one's happy all the time. Jesus! I gotta go. I really . . . bye Mom.

[He exits. PA *makes an announcement, the specifics of which are inaudible.]*

PA

Eight [inaudible] has been delayed due to [inaudible]. Attention all passengers on flight [inaudible]. Because of [inaudible] we will be delayed for two hours, and passengers are asked to [inaudible].

[A FRENCHMAN *dressed in a European style enters. He speaks with a French accent.]*

FRENCHMAN

Zut! Two hours. This is a *catastrophe.* I am expected. I am anticipated.
[A BRITISH MATRON *enters, speaking with a British accent.]*

BRITISH MATRON

But this is intolerable. Not to be tolerated. Surely they don't expect one to tolerate—
[A woman, DOROTHY, *enters. She is young but already matronly.]*

DOROTHY

Oh dear, what next? First the handle of my suitcase breaks? Just snaps in two? And now?
[A young JOCK *enters, a beer-drinker sort.]*

JOCK

Hey, this's gotta be—I mean, we put a guy on the moon, but we can't put a—
[An elderly POLITICIAN *enters.]*

POLITICIAN

This is an outrage. The committee will hear about this. Heads will roll. I intend to file a formal report.

DOROTHY

A refund maybe?

FRENCHMAN

And *apologie* perhaps, no?

BRITISH MATRON

Shocking inconvenience.

JOCK

Yeah, sort of like, shocking.

POLITICIAN

I'm going to insist on a meal voucher.

FRENCHMAN

Or a drink *peut-être*.

BRITISH MATRON

Sherry! A dry sherry.

DOROTHY

Gee, a cuppa coffee would sure go down.
[A FLIGHT ATTENDANT *enters with a tray of Styrofoam cups.]*

FLIGHT ATTENDANT

My apologies, ladies and gentlemen, for the delay. The airline has authorized, I am happy to say, a cup of coffee for each and every inconvenienced passenger.

POLITICIAN

Well, I should hope so.

JOCK

Hey, great!

FRENCHMAN

Magnifique.

BRITISH MATRON

Splendid.

JOCK

Hey, you know something, there's nothing—nothing!—like the smell of coffee.

DOROTHY

That's for sure.

FRENCHMAN

Ah, ça sent bon!

POLITICIAN

Fresh brewed aroma.

FLIGHT ATTENDANT

The best smell on this earth.
[All raise their cups and drink; a short silence follows.]

FRENCHMAN

Well . . . there are some peoples, and I believe I am one, who hold the opinion that the best smell in the world is—

BRITISH MATRON

Yes?

FRENCHMAN

It is only my opinion, of course, but perhaps you have on occasion walked
through a virgin forest, no? Early in the morning. After a little fall of rain.
[Sniffs deeply.] It is, how you say, the perfume of nature, the aroma of the
earth, an experience that is unrivalled in this world.

JOCK

Yeah, man.

BRITISH MATRON

Speaking personally, I can't help remembering—now I expect this is going
to sound absurd—but I do distinctly remember, from my childhood, the
smell of liver and bacon frying.

POLITICIAN

I beg your pardon.

BRITISH MATRON

This was during the war years, you understand, a time of courage and
deprivation. We had strict rationing, so many ounces of meat per week. A
difficult time, you have no idea, but we came to appreciate small things.
Humble things. And one day, a cold, damp day, January, I believe, I
returned from my school. I was twelve, thirteen, a child really—

FRENCHMAN

But it is children who appreciate the—

BRITISH MATRON

I let myself in the door and at once was struck by a veritable gale of sen-
sation. Liver and bacon. My mother stood in the kitchen with a meat fork
in hand. She was like, like a priestess. And from the smoking fry pan beside
her came a smell that has always seemed to me to be supreme in the world
of smells. A kingly smell. I don't expect any of you to understand but—

JOCK

[Sincerely.] I guess it's like you kinda hadda be there, eh?

POLITICIAN

[Clears throat noisily.] My father was a man of simple but severe tastes. A
traditionalist in the finest sense. We were far from being affluent and made
do with countless small economies. But a single luxury was permitted: my
father's white shirts were sent out to be laundered. Seven shirts every week.
No, on second thought, it was six, he made his Friday shirt do for Saturday
as well. Wonderful man. Well, as a boy, I was given the task of fetching his
shirts. The laundry—they no longer exist, not the same—was tiny, crowd-
ed, steamy—and the smell! How can I describe it?

BRITISH MATRON

The smell of cleanliness.

FLIGHT ATTENDANT

Scorched cotton.

DOROTHY

Starch? Bleach?

FRENCHMAN

I know also this heavenly smell.

JOCK

Hey, me too, in a way.

POLITICIAN

That smell held both the security of the present and the possibility of the future. Tradition and dignity. Comfort and order. The finest smell in the world.

JOCK

I kinda know what you mean, but—

POLITICIAN

But what, my boy?

JOCK

I mean, yeah, clean smells are great, but sometimes, well, it's hard to describe, but—

BRITISH MATRON

Try.

JOCK

Well, it's like I've played a little hockey, well, a lot of hockey, like I started when I was, jeez, I must've been four years old, something like that. My dad took me down to the rink and signed me up and there I was, thinking I was going to be a star, playing for the Blackhawks or something—

FRENCHMAN

It is a most interesting game, this hockey.

JOCK

Yeah, well, a lotta kids, when they grow out of their skates, they take 'em to this second-hand place, but my dad, he saved my old skates, he's kind of—

DOROTHY

Sentimental?

JOCK

Yeah, like that, sentimental. Anyway, he's got this cardboard box down in the basement full of my old stinky skates, little bitty ones this long, right up to the size twelves I wore when we won the provincials—well, all I can say is, the smell of old ice skates is just about, well, it's the smell of all smells.

FLIGHT ATTENDANT

You know, what I love is the smell of a party, going to a party, when you first get there. You stand in the hall, and it's partly cold and partly warm and you can smell all the boots lined up there, and there's a kind of chip-and-dip breeze blowing in from the living room, and cologne and aftershave—

DOROTHY

Once . . . once—
[DOROTHY pauses. The others prompt and encourage her to continue.]
Well, my husband? He travels a fair amount? He's a, you know, a consultant? He goes all over the place, all over the world? And, well, usually he comes home with this suitcase just chock full, just bulging with dirty socks and underwear and stuff? I open it up and, whew! Well—
[She pauses and the others prod her once more.]
Well, last year he went to Mali? That's in Africa? Where they speak the French language.

FRENCHMAN

That is true.

DOROTHY

Well, he got home and I opened his suitcase, expecting I'd see the same old bunch of dirty underwear? Only, what I didn't know was . . . he'd had it all washed there in the hotel? They wash stuff by hand, he said, and hang it on the bushes in the back of the hotel to dry. I couldn't believe it, what my nose was smelling. It was . . .

BRITISH MATRON

[Wisely.] The smell of purity.

FRENCHMAN

Fresh linen, nothing like it.

DOROTHY

No, no, it wasn't that. It *was* that, and more? I buried my nose in all those clean, white, folded-up clothes, and what I was smelling, I realized all of a sudden, was Africa. *[Pause, looks from face to face.]* I could smell . . . Africa!

JOCK

Excellent, hey, that's—

BRITISH MATRON

[Dreamily.] The smell of cold metal, water pipes, and swings in the park. Doorknobs.

POLITICIAN

A nice new newspaper when you open it, nothing can beat—

FRENCHMAN

Or an old newspaper—

JOCK

Peanut butter when you first open it, that second when you zip the top off—

FRENCHMAN

Anything you have to work hard to open. It smells best when you have to work at it, getting the cork out of the—

JOCK

Someone with a new haircut smells great; they smell sort of crisp-like. Like you know that haircut hasn't been slept in yet, nothing bad's happened to it.

DOROTHY

Wallpaper paste?

FLIGHT ATTENDANT

Christmas tree ornaments when you bring them down from the attic—

POLITICIAN

But the best smell—are you listening?—the best smell is a combination of smells. Like . . . like brandy and wet wool, like when you come in from being heroic—

BRITISH MATRON

[Dreamily again.] Boiled cabbage and cooking gas.

JOCK

Erasers, wow! With lockers and dirty jeans.

FRENCHMAN

And what I find so, so marvellous, is that each of us, we each have a smell that is all our own.
[A sudden silence falls; each of the six stiffens and contracts and stares upward.]

PA

Flight [inaudible] for [inaudible] is now ready to board. Will passengers for [inaudible] please go to Gate [inaudible].

FLIGHT ATTENDANT

If you will follow me, please—
[All rise from the bench and follow her; conversation begins again, random and overlapping.]

POLITICIAN

Popcorn. An old-fashioned bowl of—

BRITISH MATRON

When you polish a fine piece of furniture—

JOCK

Coffee, boy, a fresh cuppa coffee sure—
[Exit all. Enter PILOT *and* FLIGHT ATTENDANT *in their second "true-romance" contretemps, spotlighted, same position as in the first contretemps.]*

PILOT

Well, hello!

FLIGHT ATTENDANT

Hello.

PILOT

I know.

FLIGHT ATTENDANT

You know what?

PILOT

About it. I know all about it. Everything there is to know, I know.

FLIGHT ATTENDANT

It?

PILOT

Why you're so busy every night.

FLIGHT ATTENDANT

Oh.

PILOT

I don't see how you expected me not to find out about something like this
. . . keep *this* a secret from me.

FLIGHT ATTENDANT

I didn't want to hurt you. I knew you wouldn't be able to understand.

PILOT

How could I not understand?

FLIGHT ATTENDANT

That night in the Japanese restaurant. Do you remember?

PILOT

As if I could ever forget that night.

FLIGHT ATTENDANT

Do you remember, we were talking, everything was going so—and then
you told me what you thought about women who . . .

PILOT

Go on.

FLIGHT ATTENDANT

About women . . . training for their . . . pilot's papers. About women having no place in the air.

PILOT

In the cockpit is what I said. The cockpit.

FLIGHT ATTENDANT

Exactly.

PILOT

You're the best flight attendant working for this airline, and now suddenly
you want—

FLIGHT ATTENDANT

This is something I've always wanted.

PILOT

But why?

FLIGHT ATTENDANT

This is my dream. I was hoping . . . hoping you might share it with—

PILOT

Why did it have to come to—just when—why must you—
[Lights snap off. They exit as a middle-aged MAN *and his* DAUGHTER, *a
young woman, enter.]*

MAN

You've got a few minutes, honey.

DAUGHTER

I know.

MAN

Unless you'd rather go through now.

DAUGHTER

Not unless . . .

MAN

Unless what?

DAUGHTER

I mean, you know, there's no need for you to stick around. These farewells are so . . . phoney. No one knows what to say. Well, maybe they do, but they don't say it.

MAN

I think you're right. Why is that, I wonder. We talk and talk, and then, at the last minute, we act as though we're scared of each other.

DAUGHTER

We think we have to say something big. Something important, that's the problem. And it's hard to think of important things, we just think of dumb things.

MAN

Like, did you pack your winter coat? Do you have your money in a safe place? Do you, by the way? Your money?

DAUGHTER

For heaven's sake, Dad—

MAN

And what about your down jacket? Vancouver's not all that balmy.

DAUGHTER

You see what I mean?

MAN

I suppose what I should do is give you some advice.

DAUGHTER

Advice?

MAN

Fatherly advice. But I guess the last thing you want is advice.

DAUGHTER

That's not true. I think I'd like some advice. Something primal and wise from the great treasure house of age.

MAN

I'm not sure I can live up to that.

DAUGHTER

Just shoot.

MAN

You mean it?

DAUGHTER

Why not?

MAN

My golden opportunity. Do you know, in your twenty-two years you've never asked me for advice?

DAUGHTER

Did you ever ask *your* father for advice?
[Pause.]

MAN

Only once.

DAUGHTER

Well, here's your chance. Give me some advice. I won't promise to take it. Just to listen.

MAN

I suppose that's something.

DAUGHTER

Well, then?

MAN

The problem is—

DAUGHTER

[Mocking.] Reluctance overtakes him. The subject is too delicate to broach.

MAN

No, it's not that. I guess I'd have to think about it a little more.

DAUGHTER

What you're saying is, you don't have any advice for me.

MAN

You sound disappointed.

DAUGHTER

You know something, I am.

MAN

I guess I do have a question at least.

DAUGHTER

Well, I suppose that's better than nothing.

MAN

Okay, here it comes. Are you sure he's the one?

DAUGHTER

Listen, I thought you were going to ask me something new. Not just, "Is he the one?" You and Mom have been asking me that for three weeks steady.

MAN

I know. But now I'm really asking. It's just you and me, you and your old man, and we've got six minutes before you get on that plane, and you can still cash in your tickets, and you can put through a phone call or send a fax if that's easier, or—

DAUGHTER

Look, give me a break—

MAN

I mean, you say you're sure, but—

DAUGHTER

Let me ask you a question. What exactly do you mean by that little word, *sure?*

MAN

I mean, do you feel it? Do you feel that absolute certainty that there's a future—

DAUGHTER

Well, shit, when it comes right down to it, there's not an awful lot anyone can be a hundred percent sure of. I could crash on that plane for instance. You could have an accident just driving home. We can't even be sure of the next five minutes. Some crazy could come along and toss a bomb at us—

MAN

Listen, I'm asking you, do you, from time to time, have doubts?

DAUGHTER

Well, sure, I've got the odd little doubt now and then, everyone has
doubts—

MAN

It's a big step. I've seen lives ruined because people get locked into things
they're not sure of.

DAUGHTER

You don't like him. Is that it? I mean, basically, is that it?

MAN

My liking him or not liking him is immaterial.

DAUGHTER

What exactly is it about him? Is it because he didn't send me a Christmas
present? Big deal. He doesn't believe in Christmas presents. He thinks that's
a lot of pagan bullshit.

MAN

Look, there are three more minutes, so I'm going to try this on you once
more. Are you sure?

DAUGHTER

You're trying to wear me down.

MAN

I love you, that's all.

DAUGHTER

I love you, too. I just wish—

MAN

What?

DAUGHTER

I wish you'd get it through your head that things are different now. Say it doesn't work out. It's not like it was in your day. You don't have to stick it out forever. You don't have to spend the rest of your life paying for it.

MAN

Is that what you really think?

DAUGHTER

I'm just saying, if. That's a big if. I'm not saying it's not going to work out.

MAN

You do feel pretty sure then?

DAUGHTER

How sure was Mom when you got married?

MAN

She was sure.

DAUGHTER

I'll bet she was. Well, those days were simpler in a way.

MAN

I won't ask you again.

DAUGHTER

Is it because he works out in a health club?

MAN

I was sure, too.

DAUGHTER

Is it because he sells computers? We can't all—

MAN

We were both sure, your mother and I.

DAUGHTER

We've opted for an entrepreneurial society, and someone has to—

MAN

We were engaged for almost three years. That's what people did then. So they'd be sure.

DAUGHTER

He talks to me about computers, takes me into his world. That's what's important in a relationship—

MAN

When we got married it was forever. That's why we had to be so sure. Or else—ah, but you aren't listening to me, are you?

DAUGHTER

I'm listening, I'm listening. But I guess . . . I guess I've got a question for you. Why in God's name have you and Mom stuck it out all these years?

MAN

I said—

DAUGHTER

And whatever you tell me, please, please don't say it was for my sake.

MAN

We naturally felt—

DAUGHTER

Because I couldn't bear that. It would break my heart if I thought—

MAN

Your mother and I—

PA

Flight 411 boarding for Vancouver at Gate—

MAN

I suppose it's just that your mother and I believed—

DAUGHTER

Listen, Daddy, you don't have to stick it out any longer. Look at me, I'm twenty-two years old. I've grown up, I'm off on my own. You don't have to hang in there for the rest of your—

MAN

There've been lots of good times—

DAUGHTER

How many? One good time? Two good times?

MAN

A few, a few.

DAUGHTER

A few isn't enough. No one should settle for a few good times. Believe me, I'm not about to settle for—

MAN

You're going to miss your plane.

DAUGHTER

I know. I have to go.

MAN

And I never gave you any advice.

DAUGHTER

[Shrugging.] Well, did your father give you any advice when you got married? *[Pause.]*

MAN

He did give me some advice, yes. It was the only time, I think, he ever did.

DAUGHTER

And did you take it?
[Pause.]

MAN

Yes. I did.

DAUGHTER

I can just guess what kind of advice he gave you.

MAN

Sweetie, you've got one minute.

DAUGHTER

I think he took you aside and said, "Son, you've got to do the honourable thing."

MAN

Look, you've—

DAUGHTER

He said, "You got this lovely sweet young girl in trouble, and you've got to do the honourable thing and make her your wife." *[Pause.]* I've known for years. Ever since I could add and subtract. So you did the honourable thing, didn't you? Oh, Daddy.

MAN

Those were different days.

DAUGHTER

And look what you got. You were noble and honourable and you got nothing.

MAN

I got you, sweetie.

DAUGHTER

That's pretty corny. That's bullshit.

MAN

Maybe it is. But maybe it's true. You know, if things don't work out . . . you can always come back. We'll be here.

DAUGHTER

But you don't have to be here. You haven't been listening to a word I've said, have you? I just said—

MAN

And I just said, we'll be here. Just keep that in mind. In case.

DAUGHTER

I've got to go.

MAN

[Calling after her.] Be happy. Be kind to each other.

DAUGHTER

Hey, that sounds like advice. Thanks.

MAN

[Calling.] You're welcome. It's free.
[They exit. A woman of about sixty, MRS. KITCHELL *of Rosy Rapids, comes to centre stage. She settles herself on a bench, loosens her coat, checks her watch, pulls out her knitting from her bag, which is on the floor.]*

MRS. KITCHELL

[Addressing audience directly.] I'm early. *[Fishes in her bag for a pattern.]* Quite early. As a matter of fact, I'm two hours early. My father was the same, always early, only of course he travelled by train. He worked for Timothy Eaton's, a buyer in ladies' shoes, did quite a bit of gadding about, here and there, always off some place. He liked to get down to the station in plenty of time. "You never know," that's how he put it. Meaning, you never know what could happen.

I was up at six-thirty this morning. Had my breakfast, *[fishes in her bag]* Bran Flakes, then a cup of tea. *[More fishing.]* Mr. Skelton picked me up at eight sharp. Lovely new car he has, even smells new. I said, "This is awfully nice," and he said, "What are neighbours for?" He's got a way with words. I said, "Not many neighbours would get up at this ungodly hour." Well, he took me all the way into Red Bluff, right to the bus station, and said, "Well now, you sure you're going to be okay, crossing the drink on your own?" and I said, "I sure am."

I was in plenty of time, even had time for a cup of coffee. The girl at the counter said, "Well, well, I hear you're going all the way over to England, Mrs. Kitchell," and I said, "That's right, you heard right." *[Rummages in her bag, takes out a tape measure, measures knitting, replaces the tape measure.]* I said to her—I think she was one of the Swanson girls, the youngest—I said, "I guess you know I'm off to visit my brand new grandson, six months old." "Is that right?" she said, and *[pause]* gave me a look.

Well, the bus finally came along and we got into the city just about noon, and I said to myself, guess I'll pop over to Penney's. I always like to look around Penney's, even if I don't buy, only this time I did buy—some more wool—and then I caught my bus out to the airport and here I am. *[Holds up the sweater.]* Almost done. These teensie weensie sleeves are the devil. It's for little Moe. Moe! What a name. When I got out here to the airport, I had to go over to the counter there and show my ticket—it's my daughter's husband who got the idea in the first place, oh, some time ago, of sending me a plane ticket and talking me into coming over for a visit. We've never met, my son-in-law and myself, but we had a nice chat on the long distance. He's got money, that's one thing, plenty of money, well that goes without saying. He had to say everything twice because of his accent. "Allo Meesus Keetchell." Also he's got a lot of family feeling, that's something. Susan says they all do. And he wanted his little Moe to meet his grandma.

[Confidentially.] His full name is Mohammed. Now here's a very interesting fact. What is the most common first name in the world? A good question for a quiz program. You'd probably think John or Bill or Jim, but no, it's Mohammed. That's on account of all the Mohammedans have to name their first sons that particular name. It's a rule like the Catholics used to have, calling their first girls Mary, Mary Gladys or Mary Grace, or what have you. When Susan sent the birth announcement, she said, "Now Mother, be sure to put it in the local paper." Well, I did just what she said, but I didn't put the name in. I just said, "A little son born to Dr. and Mrs. B. Khazzi. Mrs. Khazzi is the former Susan Kitchell of Rosy Rapids," and so on. Well, the phone half rung off the wall, everyone wanted to know what they were going to call it, but I just kept mum. I wasn't about to tell the whole world my daughter had a baby named Mohammed, but after a time I kind of dropped the hint that Susan had nicknamed the baby Moe. Mr. Skelton, he's the only one who knows about the name Mohammed, and he says it's a real nice name. Well, I wonder if . . . of course he'll have dark hair, I expect that, even with Susan being so fair.

My husband, Sam, was dark-haired, that would be the Russian side of his family. My own family didn't know what to think when I married someone with Russian blood and a farmer to boot. But Susan took after me. I had a feeling when she went over to England for her trip that something would happen, that she'd meet someone foreign. A premonition, that's the word for it. But I didn't think this, that she'd marry . . . Susan says he's real modern though, doesn't wear the cloth thing on his head. If she'd stayed home she might have married Larry Kingman who has the Macleod store, or rather his dad does. *[Pats bag.]* Larry sent her a nice wedding present, all wrapped up so nice. Looks like a nice coffee pot to me, electric maybe. Poor Larry. Looks a little, well, down in the mouth these days. Says it's a late wedding gift. *[Pats parcel.]* Says it's a sort of remembrance—so she won't ever forget him. He's a nice boy, clean living. Well, you can't run your

children's lives for them. If they want to marry someone, they're going to
. . . At least we believe in the same god—more or less, that is.

[Three young BASKETBALL PLAYERS *in sports sweats enter while* MRS.
KITCHELL *is talking. One of them sets a zippered bag beside her, opens it and
takes out a basketball. The three of them begin pitching it about. They dribble and move about the stage, sending the ball flying over her head. She ducks
once or twice, then picks up her bag and moves to another bench. The three
of them sit on a bench and pick up copies of the sports page as* MRS. KITCHELL
continues.]

As I was saying, it took getting used to. My Susan—she was in 4-H,
you know—well, I couldn't imagine, the same bed and all . . . but I suppose if you turn out the light . . . Sam used to turn out the light, he was
very thoughtful that way. But sometimes in the summertime . . . you
know how long it takes for the sun to go down in the summertime . . .
some of the time a little light crept in through the curtains. Well, what
he liked to do, well, was unbutton my nightie and then he'd, well . . .
suck on my bosom. It seemed like a real strange thing for a grown-up
man to do, but years later I read in *McCall's* magazine or maybe in the
Digest that it's something men . . . something they like to do. Well,
sometimes when it was summer and the light was getting in through the
curtains, I would look down and see that black hair of Sam's, rough
black hair, the Russian side, and he'd be sucking and sucking. I could see
every strand of his hair so clear. I could count them almost. It was a long
time ago. I've gone all saggy here, *[touches breasts]* but once, well once, a
long time ago I used to think, Sam and I, we're the only two people in
the world who know about . . . these. *[Touches breasts again.]* And now
I'm the only one.

[A woman OFFICIAL *briskly approaches* MRS. KITCHELL. *She is dressed in an
official airline uniform.]*

OFFICIAL

Are you Mrs. Kitchell of Rosy Rapids? The lady who's going on Flight 223
to Heathrow this afternoon?

MRS. KITCHELL

Why, yes, that's me.

OFFICIAL

I'm awfully sorry, Mrs. Kitchell, but I have some rather disappointing news for you.

MRS. KITCHELL

Why, what on earth—?

OFFICIAL

Nothing serious, nothing to worry about. Just an overbooking. It happens all the time.

MRS. KITCHELL

Overbooking? Now is that when there are more people than—

OFFICIAL

—more people than there are seats. That's it, and we're really awfully sorry—

MRS. KITCHELL

You mean I won't be able to go?

OFFICIAL

All it means is that you're able to go tomorrow instead of today.

MRS. KITCHELL

Tomorrow? But I was up at six-thirty and Mr. Skelton very kindly drove me all the way into Red Bluff to catch my—

OFFICIAL

We'll be happy to put you up at a nice hotel tonight.

MRS. KITCHELL

But my daughter's expecting me. And little Moe.

[Another WOMAN *joins them. She is slim and white-haired and wears boots, blue jeans and a jean jacket.]*

WOMAN

Wait a minute. Wait a minute. What's going on here? Why exactly has this particular person been bumped, if you don't mind my asking?

OFFICIAL

It's just routine. The plane to Heathrow's overbooked.

WOMAN

And why is it suddenly overbooked? It wasn't overbooked yesterday when I made my reservation.

OFFICIAL

Things happen.

WOMAN

What kind of things? It doesn't by any chance have anything to do with *[gestures at* BASKETBALL PLAYERS*]* those animals?

OFFICIAL

This happens to be the National All-Star team. They'll be playing in London, England, tomorrow night, representing all of us, you and me and Mrs. Kitchell here.

WOMAN

Balls. Everyone knows there are five players on a basketball team.

OFFICIAL

Oh, they never travel together. Think what would happen . . .

WOMAN

[To MRS. KITCHELL*]* How long have you had your booking?

MRS. KITCHELL

Well, now, let me think. My daughter's husband—he's quite well to do, a doctor—he sent me a plane ticket last . . . I think it was last July. Just after little Moe was born.

WOMAN

Hear that? This woman has had her ticket since July. And these greasers come along and flex their muscles and wave their little flag, and all of a sudden they're on and this passenger is off.

OFFICIAL

We'll be happy to notify Mrs. Kitchell's relations in England and—

WOMAN

Listen to me, Mrs. Kitchell. Don't let them do this to you. You know why they chose you to bump? They said to themselves, "Let's check the passenger list and find us a little old lady." It's called an LOL, little old lady. LOLs are pushovers. They cave in without a fight. Because LOLs have spent their lives giving in. Always accommodating, always making sure they don't make a fuss. Giving in to fathers, giving in to husbands, giving in to children. Now is that true or is it not true?

MRS. KITCHELL

Well, I don't know—

WOMAN

When an LOL is faced with a direct question, she says, "Well, I don't know."

OFFICIAL

I think you should know that these young athletes are going to represent our nation.

WOMAN

And who does Mrs. Kitchell represent? Let me tell you, ladies and gentlemen.

[The scene now takes on the tone of a revival meeting; the three BASKETBALL PLAYERS *begin to sway slowly in unison.]*

Mrs. Kitchell here represents the LOLs of the world. Now let me tell you loud and clear that we are not talking about some tiny, piddling fraction of the universe, no ma'am. We are talking about one-sixth of the human race. Do you know how many LOLs are walking around? Look on the buses of the cities of the world. Look into the hospital wards, look into the shabby rooms of boarding houses—

BASKETBALL PLAYERS

[In unison.] Gee, we don't see all that many little old ladies around.

WOMAN

That's because they're little, remember?

BASKETBALL PLAYERS

[In unison.] Hey, that's right.

WOMAN

And when exactly did the little old ladies get little? They weren't little *young* ladies. In the beginning they were full-sized human creatures. But what happened? Well, I'll tell you what happened. They were told to keep their voices down. They were told to keep their feet together, to keep their hands on their laps, to hold their elbows in, to keep their eyes lowered, to keep their chins tucked in, to keep their heads modestly bowed, that's how they got little. And that's not all.

MRS. KITCHELL

What else? What else?

WOMAN

Some of them got so little they got to be invisible. The Eskimos put their little old ladies on ice floes and set them adrift. We put ours in chimney corners and hand them a pair of knitting needles and say, "Be quiet, you."

They're voiceless. They've got no guts, but I ask you, is it their fault they've got no guts?

MRS. KITCHELL AND OFFICIAL

No, no, no.

WOMAN

Their guts were taken away over the years, bit by bit, inch by inch. They were too fragile for sports, they were too dizzy for math, they were too unclean for church, they—

MRS. KITCHELL

There was this one woman preacher last summer in Rosy Rapids—

OFFICIAL

Tokenism.

WOMAN

Their boyfriends say, "Give over." Their husbands say, "Lie back." Their sons say, "When's dinner?" They go to restaurants and they get a table by the washroom.

MRS. KITCHELL, OFFICIAL AND BASKETBALL PLAYERS

Yes, yes, that's right. *[Etc.]*

WOMAN

No one brings them a wine menu. All they get is a stinking pot of tea.

MRS. KITCHELL

Sometimes a nice pot of tea can—

WOMAN

They join a political party and they get put on the coffee brigade. They go on trips sometimes, but—have you noticed?—they never go on journeys.

MRS. KITCHELL, OFFICIAL AND BASKETBALL PLAYERS

Yes, right on, bravo, amen. *[Etc.]*

WOMAN

They go out to get a job and people say, "Hey, you can't do anything or you would have done it by now. Where have you been, little old lady?" I'll tell you where they've been. Look at Mrs. Kitchell from Rosy Rapids here. She can't even stand up straight. She's so used to making herself agreeable and grateful and nice nice nice nice that she's just faded away. And now she's being asked to give up her seat on a transatlantic jet. She was going to visit her daughter and her brand new grandson—

MRS. KITCHELL

[Throws her arms open, making a public confession.] His name's Moe. It's short for Mohammed. And he's a real sweetie pie, he's just the cutest bundle of—

WOMAN

Mrs. Kitchell was going to visit her little grandson, taking him this sweater she's made with her own hands. The LOLs are the makers of garments, the healers of family wounds—

MRS. KITCHELL

Why, that's true.

BASKETBALL PLAYERS

[In unison.] It's not our fault. We were just following orders.

OFFICIAL

Mrs. Kitchell, you're going to have your seat. You're going to be in London, England in eight hours with little Moe in your arms.
[BASKETBALL PLAYERS sway and hum.]
You're an LOL and that's something to stand up and be proud of.

WOMAN

Come with us, Mrs. Kitchell. It's time to board.

OFFICIAL

It's time.

[MRS. KITCHELL *jams her knitting needles into her bag, more precisely into the gift-wrapped parcel on top. Leaving her bag on the floor, she is hoisted up by the* BASKETBALL PLAYERS *and carried out in procession style. An airport* CLEANER *enters with a push broom and crosses the stage, turning and recrossing. He pauses when approaching* MRS. KITCHELL*'s knitting bag. He listens, and the audience can hear a ticking sound getting louder and louder. He touches the bag and peers in. The ticking gets very loud. He removes the parcel, unwraps the coffee pot and takes off the lid. A music box begins to play, replacing the ticking, a merry tune that gets louder and louder as the airport* CLEANER *stares at it. Darkness; curtain. End of Act One.]*

Act Two

At rise, the same setting, some time in the vague future. The stage is empty except for the luggage platform going slowly around, still carrying the green, pink and silver case. A young airport CLEANER *crosses with push broom, then recrosses. He encounters a* LADY *on her hands and knees advancing across the stage, running her hand across the floor as though looking for something.*

CLEANER

Excuse me. You lost something, lady?

LADY

What d'ya think?

CLEANER

If it's your contact lenses, give up. People all the time lose their contact lenses, but no one ever finds a contact lens, that's a fact. You ever hear anyone say, "Hey, I've found this contact lens—"?

LADY

It's not my contact lens. My contact lenses are here.
[She points to her eyes.]

CLEANER

Earrings then? Let me tell you, it's a lost cause. Someone finds an earring, they put it in their pocket. Especially if it's gold. People aren't crazy.

LADY

I don't wear earrings. I don't believe in earrings. Earrings are not a part of my belief system.

CLEANER

You lost a dime or something? Then, listen, it's not worth it, crawling around this dirty floor for a dime. Hey, let me give you a dime, what the hell.

LADY

You think I care about money?

CLEANER

Hey! I get it. What you've lost. It's something metaphysical.

LADY

What d'ya know! How'd you guess?

CLEANER

I work in an airport. You know what an airport is? *[Mimicking the voice of* Dragnet*'s Joe Friday, he quotes from the radio show* Grand Central Station.*]* "It's the crossroads of a million private lives; a gigantic stage on which are played a thousand dramas daily."

LADY

Yeah?

CLEANER

People coming. People going. Departures. Arrivals. Get it? It's an equation of the absurd. Going cancels out coming, see? And that means . . . no one's going anywhere.

LADY

Hey!

CLEANER

We're all standing still. Like you and me here. We're powerless.

LADY

What about space travel? What about our astronauts?

CLEANER

Interesting question. The answer is we've given up on this world. We gave it a few million years and it didn't work out, so now we have to move on. It's our last chance to express our will.

                                CLEANER
That's it. That's what I'm looking for. My will. My freedom not to act.

                                CLEANER
Give up, lady. You're in the hands of the historical dynamic. You can't do a blessed thing but move along.

                                LADY
I refuse to believe that.

                                CLEANER
Don't believe then.

                                LADY
I don't believe we always have to rush toward some theoretical destination, departing, arriving, going in circles. I can choose—

                                CLEANER
What?

                                LADY
I can choose nothing. Stillness. I can just—*[sits in lotus position]* I can just *be.*

                                CLEANER
Well, that's a real nice thought but sentimental if you don't mind my saying so. Didn't you know that sitting still is boring?

                                PA
Ladies and gentlemen. This is our last and final and ultimate call for non-travelling passengers. This is our zero-hour call.

CLEANER

Lady, you're going to miss your plane.

LADY

The only plane I recognize *[strokes floor]* is the plane of the inner consciousness.

CLEANER

I wouldn't give you odds on the inner consciousness. It can land you in hot water. See that couple over there? They're sad, real sad. A case in point. *[Lights focus on* PILOT *and* FLIGHT ATTENDANT *in the same position as in their previous contretemps. The lighting is perhaps a trifle more lurid, the music more lurid as well.]*

PILOT

Oh! Hello.

FLIGHT ATTENDANT

Hello.

PILOT

I suppose I . . . I should say . . . really should say . . . congratulations.

FLIGHT ATTENDANT

You've heard then? My first solo. All alone up there. Just me and the clouds and the great big unforgiving sky.

PILOT

What I can't understand . . . someone like you, especially someone . . .

FLIGHT ATTENDANT

It went beautifully. My supervisor gave me full marks. In three weeks I'll have my exams and then—

PILOT

Then?

FLIGHT ATTENDANT

Maybe . . . maybe we could . . . you know . . . when the time comes . . .
we could maybe . . . celebrate?

PILOT

Celebrate?

FLIGHT ATTENDANT

My treat. Dinner maybe. That Japanese place—

PILOT

I'm . . . er . . . pretty busy these days.

FLIGHT ATTENDANT

And nights, too?

PILOT

I wish things had been . . . different.

FLIGHT ATTENDANT

Different? Ah, I see. Well.

PILOT

Well.
[They exit; a number of people cross the stage with suitcases.]

PA

Eight 492 for Los Angeles has been delayed. Passengers are asked [inaudible].
[Passengers with suitcases line up at a desk, perhaps the same one that func-
tioned as the insurance booth in Act One. At end of the line is a YOUNG
WOMAN *and* YOUNG MAN. *She carries a backpack; he is wearing a business*
suit. As they speak, others freeze.]

YOUNG WOMAN

Excuse me?

YOUNG MAN

Me?

YOUNG WOMAN

Is this . . . can you tell me . . . is this the right line?

YOUNG MAN

I hope so.

YOUNG WOMAN

Long. It's long, isn't it?

YOUNG MAN

I've been standing here five minutes and it hasn't budged.

YOUNG WOMAN

Oh, excuse me. Sorry.

YOUNG MAN

Sorry?

YOUNG WOMAN

I knocked you. With my backpack.

YOUNG MAN

Don't mention it. Never felt a thing.

YOUNG WOMAN

Will you look at this crowd. Wonder if it ever slows down.

YOUNG MAN

Doubt it. I travel a lot and I've hardly ever seen a really quiet airport. I mean *really* quiet.

YOUNG WOMAN

Modern life.

YOUNG MAN

You say something?

YOUNG WOMAN

Modern life. Hustle? Bustle?

PA

Flight 492 for Los Angeles has been delayed and will now depart at 9:05.

YOUNG WOMAN

Oh, no, that's my flight. 9:05. That's two whole hours from now.

YOUNG MAN

You really are early.

YOUNG WOMAN

What about you? Which flight are you?

YOUNG MAN

L.A. Same flight.

YOUNG WOMAN

Oh . . . so you're kind of early, too.
[Pause.]

YOUNG MAN

Well, I like to be early.

YOUNG WOMAN

Oh.

YOUNG MAN

I didn't intend to be this early but . . . well, my girlfriend, she dropped me off. She had an early appointment at work, so . . .

YOUNG WOMAN

Did you see that? That man up there. He just barged in front of that lady there.

YOUNG MAN

You have to wonder at guys like that.

YOUNG WOMAN

"A" types. *A* for aggressive.

YOUNG MAN

K for klutz.

YOUNG WOMAN

I don't know, people like that. I did this course last winter. Different personality types, you know? Some people can't help themselves. Basically they're insecure and afraid of the world, but they like to push people around.

YOUNG MAN

I guess my girlfriend's a little like that. Very aggressive. If she were here, she'd be up there in front demanding to know why we're late.

YOUNG WOMAN

Could be engine trouble. Or weather.

YOUNG MAN

Uh-uh, not with that blue sky. Look through the doors there. It's going to be one great day, not a cloud in sight.

YOUNG WOMAN

Well, just that little one.

YOUNG MAN

Where? Oh, yeah. Well, at least there's no wind.

YOUNG WOMAN

Could be the pilot's sick. There's this South American flu going around.

YOUNG MAN

You're telling me. My girlfriend, has she been sick! Had to take a day off work. That's how I knew she was really sick.

YOUNG WOMAN

You know, I used to want to be a pilot. Isn't that crazy? Talk about being unrealistic.

YOUNG MAN

I don't know. Things are changing. My girlfriend? She's the office manager. Instead of taking dictation, she does the dictating.

YOUNG WOMAN

She's still stuck in an office though.

YOUNG MAN

Exactly! That's exactly the point I was making the other day and—

YOUNG WOMAN

We talk about taking charge and all that, but do we ask ourselves what we really want?

YOUNG MAN

Never. Well, hardly ever. Only, in my case, I think I know, sort of.

YOUNG WOMAN

You know what you want? What? But, hey, I guess I really shouldn't ask. I mean, if it's personal.

PA

Passengers for Flight 492 to Los Angeles are advised that departure time is now 9:05.

YOUNG MAN

No, I don't mind you asking. I believe people should ask questions if there's something they really want to know. Otherwise—

YOUNG WOMAN

So what is it? What do you want?

YOUNG MAN

Well, it's a little hard to describe. But let me ask you this. Have you ever tasted goat's milk?

YOUNG WOMAN

Goat's milk?

YOUNG MAN

Or, listen, have you ever eaten goat's cheese? Lots of times in restaurants you get these little chunks of this white cheese in your salad?

YOUNG WOMAN

Oh, yeah, sure, I know.

YOUNG MAN

That's goat's cheese. Usually. There's nothing like it. Goat's cheese is terrific. Texture, flavour, you name it.

YOUNG WOMAN

So you want to get in the business? The goat's cheese business?

YOUNG MAN

There's a future in it. I've shown my girlfriend some market projections, but she's—and you can also make a very nice goat's milk soap. Good for the skin. Excellent for the skin.

> YOUNG WOMAN

But doesn't it—?

> YOUNG MAN

I know what you're going to say. Doesn't it smell? People always think goats smell. They think of goats and they hold their noses.

> YOUNG WOMAN

You mean it's not true? You mean goats smell good?

> YOUNG MAN

It's the kind of smell you get used to. You almost get so you like it. And the other thing is that goats have excellent dispositions. They're independent, proud animals, but they can also be affectionate with human beings.

> YOUNG WOMAN

Gee, I didn't realize—

> YOUNG MAN

I hate to see any species maligned.

> YOUNG WOMAN

That can happen. I happen to know—

> YOUNG MAN

I'm not saying the goat business doesn't have problems. Let's just say it presents a small growth industry with varied possibilities.

> YOUNG WOMAN

So. You've made up your mind. You're going into the goat business.

YOUNG MAN

Well, no. I doubt it. It's unlikely, all things considered.

PA

Passengers for Kansas City, Flight 91, may now board at Gate 12. Passengers for Kansas City [inaudible].

YOUNG WOMAN

Sorry, I didn't hear what you were saying.

YOUNG MAN

I just said, just because you want to do something doesn't mean it's necessarily going to happen.

YOUNG WOMAN

I know what you mean. Oh, brother, do I ever know what you—

YOUNG MAN

Like things . . . things get in . . . they get in your way.

YOUNG WOMAN

Let me guess. Your girlfriend doesn't go for goats.

YOUNG MAN

Hey, you're very intuitive.

YOUNG WOMAN

Well, I took this night class last winter—

YOUNG MAN

It's not just goats. It's the lifestyle she can't handle.

YOUNG WOMAN

It would be a major change. But sometimes a major change is what we need. A good hard kick, if you know what I mean. As a matter of fact, the reason I'm going to L.A. is—

YOUNG MAN

She's always lived in a large city—

YOUNG WOMAN

Your girlfriend?

YOUNG MAN

She thinks nature means walking around a park looking at the grass. She thinks flowers come in borders. Borders! That's the way they grow, she thinks, a bunch of little pansies in a row.

YOUNG WOMAN

I always think that—

YOUNG MAN

Concerts, museums, art galleries, she's used to having it all. As a matter of fact, that's where we met, at the art gallery.

YOUNG WOMAN

It's hard to meet people in a big city. I've really—

YOUNG MAN

There was this big exhibition. Modern sculpture. A guide was taking us around, a bunch of us, and there was this woman carved out of stone with a big hole in her body, right in the middle, and the guide said—

YOUNG WOMAN

It was easier to meet people in our parents' day. My folks, believe it or not, met at a bridge party. Imagine meeting someone at a bridge party nowadays—

YOUNG MAN

Anyway, the guide said the hole in her body meant there was a sense of incompletion in all human encounters—

YOUNG WOMAN

My grandparents, they met each other at a prayer meeting, a Wednesday night prayer meeting. Can you imagine, it's Wednesday, say, and someone says to you, "Hey, let's go to a prayer meeting," and—

YOUNG MAN

Then, after the tour was over at the art gallery, she and I went to this little place for coffee—

YOUNG WOMAN

Some people recommend singles bars but—

YOUNG MAN

—and right away we seemed to have a lot in common—

YOUNG WOMAN

And as a matter of fact, one reason I signed up for this evening course last winter was so I might maybe meet—

YOUNG MAN

But now, after six months, I don't know if we have anything in common at all. I mean, I think of that woman with the hole through her stomach and I, well . . . I start to wonder.

YOUNG WOMAN

I see.

YOUNG MAN

It's like, like I've got a hole, in me, but she doesn't even notice.

YOUNG WOMAN

[Puzzled.] Exactly.

YOUNG MAN

Lately we seem to be fighting all the time. Last week she came right out and accused me—I could hardly believe this—of being selfish. I mean, I'm the one—well, that's one reason I thought I'd get away for a week. I saw this seat sale and—

YOUNG WOMAN

So did I. Just couldn't resist. I just had to get away, and well, you know what they say about travelling—sometimes you meet—

YOUNG MAN

Once she threw a plate at me.

YOUNG WOMAN

A plate!

YOUNG MAN

A plate . . . with butter on it.

YOUNG WOMAN

Violence doesn't solve a thing, but sometimes—

YOUNG MAN

Another time she locked herself in the bathroom and stayed in there—

YOUNG WOMAN

Withdrawal. Common pattern for delaying stress. That's one of the things I learned last winter at this—

YOUNG MAN

I mean, in our relationship, I'm the one who vacuums. Did my father ever vacuum? And not only that—

YOUNG WOMAN

What?

YOUNG MAN

Well, I was going to say, I'm the one who takes the sheets down to the laundromat.

YOUNG WOMAN

That's where I've seen you!

YOUNG MAN

Where?

YOUNG WOMAN

I knew you looked familiar!

YOUNG MAN

Yeah?

YOUNG WOMAN

Saturday mornings? Around ten-thirty? That laundromat at Dover and Twenty-fourth?

YOUNG MAN

What d'ya know!

YOUNG WOMAN

You're usually using machine number three. Drinking coffee out of a paper cup? Cream. No sugar.

YOUNG MAN

Right!

YOUNG WOMAN

And you're usually buried in a paperback. Last week it was . . . I think it was—

YOUNG MAN

The War of the Last Planet. Now that's a very interesting thing. I never read sci-fi, never touch the stuff, except in the laundromat—

YOUNG WOMAN

I think . . . yes, I'm sure of it . . . once I asked you if you had four quarters for a dollar. For the dryer? And you said no.

YOUNG MAN

I did?

YOUNG WOMAN

You didn't even check in your pockets. You didn't even look up from your book. You just said no.

YOUNG MAN

Well, I never carry a lot of change on me.

YOUNG WOMAN

No, it wasn't that.

YOUNG MAN

Maybe—

YOUNG WOMAN

You just didn't want to take the trouble.

YOUNG MAN

Maybe it was some other guy. I don't remember—

YOUNG WOMAN

Of course you don't remember. You know something? Your girlfriend's right. She's hit the nail on the head. You're selfish.

YOUNG MAN

Hey, wait a minute. Just a minute ago we were having a great conversation about—

YOUNG WOMAN

Conversation. Is this what you call a conversation? I stand here and listen to you rattle on about your goat's milk and your girlfriend and getting hit on the head by a plate full of butter and what a hero you are because you actually take a couple of sheets down to the—

YOUNG MAN

Hey—

YOUNG WOMAN

What about me? *What about me?*

YOUNG MAN

What?

YOUNG WOMAN

Why don't *you* ask *me* about *me?* Me, me, me. Like maybe why I'm going down to L.A. and what I want out of life and whose sheets I'm washing down at the laundromat every Saturday morning—

YOUNG MAN

But you seemed . . . I thought—

YOUNG WOMAN

—I was enthralled with every golden word that—

YOUNG MAN

You know what I really thought? I thought, here's one woman who's a damned good listener. My girlfriend, on the other hand—

YOUNG WOMAN

Please. I don't want to hear about your girlfriend.

YOUNG MAN

Hey, I'm sorry. Listen, I really am.

YOUNG WOMAN

You should be. *You should be.*

YOUNG MAN

If I'd just stopped to think—

YOUNG WOMAN

Forget it.

YOUNG MAN

So tell me, what do you want to do? With your life, I mean.

YOUNG WOMAN

That's my business.

YOUNG MAN

But I really want to know.

YOUNG WOMAN

Too bad. You missed your chance.

YOUNG MAN

Couldn't you . . . give me another chance? I mean it. I can't stand it. I want to know. What do you want? Out of life?

YOUNG WOMAN

It won't work now.

YOUNG MAN

Oh, please!

YOUNG WOMAN

I want . . . I want to meet . . . someone. And it's hard. I ask questions. I draw people out, but—why can't someone, just once, draw *me* out?

YOUNG MAN

There are church groups.

YOUNG WOMAN

People always say that.

YOUNG MAN

Or bridge. Have you tried a bridge club?

YOUNG WOMAN

Be serious.

YOUNG MAN

Singles bars. People say they're shabby but—

YOUNG WOMAN

They *are* shabby.

YOUNG MAN

I know! A night course.

YOUNG WOMAN

I already told you—

YOUNG MAN

Or the art gallery. No, not a good idea, forget it.

YOUNG WOMAN

I thought maybe . . . an airport—

YOUNG MAN

An airport? Why an airport?

YOUNG WOMAN

I don't know. People who travel are, well, you know, they're sort of restless.

YOUNG MAN

Restless? Maybe. Could be.

YOUNG WOMAN

They're looking for . . . something.

YOUNG MAN

Maybe. You might be—

YOUNG WOMAN

Oh, sorry.

YOUNG MAN

Sorry?

YOUNG WOMAN

I knocked you. With my backpack. Again.

YOUNG MAN

That's a . . . that's a nice backpack. I really like that . . . stitching.

YOUNG WOMAN

I don't think this line has budged an inch.

YOUNG MAN

We'll get there eventually.

YOUNG WOMAN

I hope so.

YOUNG MAN

Why don't you . . . just to pass the time . . . why don't you . . . tell me about yourself? This course you were taking—
[They are overwhelmed by the noise of the airport. A WOMAN TELEPHONER *enters, goes to the phone booth and dials.]*

WOMAN TELEPHONER

[In affected French accent.] Allo? Is this Mrs. Harrow? Please may I speak with Mr. Harrow? It is a business affair, *oui? [Switches to regular voice.]* Josh! It's me. Ta da! I'm out at the airport. I know, I know, but I was hoping *you'd* answer, damn it. Anyway, I told her it was a business affair. Ha! Besides, I was curious, just a little bit curious. Well, just to see what her voice was like. No, I thought she sounded very . . . soft. Nice. Friendly, sort of. Sweet, in fact, damn it.

Josh, look, I'm just between planes kind of thing. Edmonton. Oh, the usual thing, we're setting up a new show, more grain elevators against the fading sun. It's a bottomless market, I'm happy to say. Anyway, what I want to know is, is there any chance you could get to Edmonton for a couple of days? I'm not going to be all that busy once the show's installed, and we could . . . What? I didn't think so. I guess this means you haven't told her yet. No, I know. Well, you did say that as soon as she got her root canal work done. You did say that. So how far along is she now? I see. Four more on the bottom. She didn't sound like she was in pain. No, I know it's serious. No, I'm not making light of it. Oh. Oh! Well, not exactly. What does that involve? Well, I can't help it, I never knew anyone who had a jaw realignment. Is she thinking about it, or . . . ? It's definite then. No, I can see that. But after they take the wires out—yes, it certainly does sound major. Uh-huh. No, you're right, you couldn't do that. I agree, only an out-and-out bastard would—no, I'm serious. I'm not being cynical. Teeth are teeth. We've got to hang on to our teeth. We've got to hang on to something in this rotten life.
[She hangs up and exits. A man, RICHARD, *and woman,* FRANNIE, *rush in from opposite sides, carrying luggage. They nearly collide.]*

RICHARD

Can you tell me which gate the plane for Toronto leaves from?

FRANNIE

Pardon?

RICHARD

For God's sake! Frannie!

FRANNIE

Christ, I don't believe this. You know something, Richard? You look like you've seen a ghost.

RICHARD

So do you. You look . . . stunned.

FRANNIE

It's just . . . I mean, this is the last place I expected to see you.

RICHARD

How long's it been? Eight years? Since the divorce, I mean.

FRANNIE

Let's see . . . it was 1981 when you went through that door—

RICHARD

[Wistful.] God, that long!

FRANNIE

[Nostalgic.] Yeah.

RICHARD

So how've you been? How you been doing?

FRANNIE

Not bad, not bad at all.

RICHARD

You're looking great. I mean it. Great.

FRANNIE

Really?

RICHARD

Really.

FRANNIE

So are you. Your hair—

RICHARD

Getting a little grey—

FRANNIE

It suits you. You know, it really does, really.

RICHARD

Well, well.

FRANNIE

[After a brief silence.] Well. So you're off to Toronto?

RICHARD

Just changing planes. I usually get the direct flight, but the goddamn air strike—

FRANNIE

[Deeply sympathetic.] I know.

RICHARD

You off to Toronto, too?

FRANNIE

The west coast.

RICHARD

The west coast?

FRANNIE

I live there now.

RICHARD

Well, what d'ya know. Lotus land. I heard you'd married again.

FRANNIE

I can't get over how terrific you look.

RICHARD

A lawyer or something like that. Someone I ran into, Reg, I think, told me you and some big shot lawyer were—

FRANNIE

Reg? You mean Reg Barnstable?

RICHARD

I run into Reg the odd time at the annual do.

FRANNIE

How is he anyway? Old Reg?

RICHARD

Not bad. Looking a little older but—

FRANNIE

—but who isn't?

RICHARD

And he told me you were seeing this guy, some lawyer—

FRANNIE

Now how would Reg Barnstable know a thing like that?

RICHARD

Well, you know Reg.

FRANNIE

Always had a nose for the latest dirt. Always poking his nose in—

RICHARD

Reg was saying it looked like wedding bells—you and this lawyer.

FRANNIE

Hmmm.

RICHARD

Well, for God's sake, Frannie, was it wedding bells? I mean, is it?

FRANNIE

It didn't work out.

RICHARD

Oh.

FRANNIE

Same old problem.

RICHARD

Oh?

FRANNIE

The old career me versus the old dependent me.

RICHARD

Oh, yeah.

FRANNIE

How about you? Still enjoying your . . . your . . . freedom? Or—?

RICHARD

Same old freedom!

FRANNIE

Do what you want—

RICHARD

—when you want—

FRANNIE

—with whomever you want—

RICHARD

Finding that great lotus land of the inner self.

FRANNIE

Right on.

RICHARD

What is lotus, anyway? I mean, what the hell is it?

FRANNIE

Hmmm. I'm not sure. Something Greek, anyway. Some kind of fruit maybe?

RICHARD

Something from mythology. We had it in school, I think.

FRANNIE

They're leaves. I just remembered. Lotus leaves.

RICHARD

Like spinach, you mean?

FRANNIE

No, they're from trees, I think. It's all coming back.

RICHARD

From trees? You sure?

FRANNIE

Just a min. I'll check.
[She sits down on her suitcase, rummages in her tote bag, pulls out a large dog-eared book and turns over the pages as RICHARD *listens.]*
Hmmm, "See jujube." *[Turns pages.]* "Any tree or shrub of the buckthorn family," hmmm. Richard? Are you listening?

RICHARD

All ears.

FRANNIE

You look like you're in some kind of trance. *[Snaps fingers.]* What's with it with you?

RICHARD

I was just thinking how you haven't changed a bit.

FRANNIE

Oh, I've changed. I'm a lotus-eater now, remember. So are you. I've . . . we've arrived.

RICHARD

But listen, you've still got your wonderful goddamn book. You still look up every goddamn thing.

FRANNIE

Well, of course, how else are you going to know anything?

RICHARD

I used to say, "Let's make love," and you'd pull out your book and you'd look it up in the index and you'd say, "Now, there are eight basic positions and twenty-six comfortable variations."

FRANNIE

Twenty-six? You sure? *[Turns pages.]* I think you're a little low there.

RICHARD

It was just an example.

FRANNIE

An example of what?

RICHARD

Of the way you were. Oh, you were lovely, you know.

FRANNIE

Do you know what you said to me once, Richard? It was the nicest thing you ever said to me.

RICHARD

What? Tell me.

FRANNIE

I don't think I want to now.

RICHARD

Why not? I said it, for God's sake. I have a right—

FRANNIE

It would spoil it, the memory. If I said it out loud. Especially in a . . . an airport.

RICHARD

But I must have said it out loud.

FRANNIE

There are some things you can only say once. Otherwise they get spoiled. You might turn around and say it to someone else.

RICHARD

Tell me. Please.
[FRANNIE *puts her mouth up to his ear; there is a sound of a plane in the background.*]

RICHARD

Can't hear you.

FRANNIE

I said—
[*She is drowned out by the sound of three people rushing by with suitcases.*]

RICHARD

Once more.

FRANNIE

I said, you said . . . you said, "Your body is like a bouquet of flowers."

RICHARD

I can't believe I said that. "Your body is like a bouquet of flowers."

FRANNIE

You said it all right. I can tell you exactly where and when it was if you like. *[Fishes in bag for another book.]* Here we go. My diary. Lake Louise. 1989. July second. Remember? We went for that long weekend.

RICHARD

Jesus, yes. That little cabin by the lake.

FRANNIE

Those crazy raccoons.
[They both laugh uproariously.]

RICHARD

And those goddamn cute squirrels. *[Laughs.]*

FRANNIE

[Choking with laughter.] And you fed them—*[laughs]* remember? You fed them . . . bread.
[They both explode with laughter.]

RICHARD

[Suddenly.] I loved the backs of your knees.

FRANNIE

Pardon?

RICHARD

The backs of your knees. I loved that particular part of your body, those little pink creases—

FRANNIE

Richard, for Pete's sake—

RICHARD

I used to nuzzle the backs of your knees. You'd be lying on the bed reading one of your goddamn books and I'd nuzzle and nuzzle and nuzzle and nuzzle—

FRANNIE

Really? I wonder why. There, I mean.

RICHARD

Because you had beautiful backs to your knees, that's why.

FRANNIE

[Turning and trying to look.] Did I really?

RICHARD

Yes. You did. And you probably still do. Some things don't change.

FRANNIE

[Tries again to see.] I can't quite—

RICHARD

Frannie, you know what I'd like?

FRANNIE

You'd like what?

RICHARD

Well, I haven't any right to ask this but—

FRANNIE

Go ahead.

RICHARD

I'd give a hell of a lot, Frannie, just to see the backs of your knees again.

FRANNIE

I thought you had a plane to catch.

RICHARD

I've got a couple of minutes. Look, Frannie, you could bend over and put your book back, and I could stoop down and pretend to tie my shoe at the same time—

FRANNIE

You sure this isn't a bit . . . perverted?

RICHARD

Frannie, oh Frannie. Just a quick look.

FRANNIE

Well, just a quick one. Are you ready?

RICHARD

One, two, three, go!
[In an orchestrated movement he stoops to tie his shoe; she bends over her bag. There is a drum roll, a clash of cymbals. She and he rise together, breathless.]
Oh, Frannie!
[A man, ONLOOKER, approaches from the side.]

ONLOOKER

Wait a minute. I've been watching you. Knees! Nuzzling!

FRANNIE

And who the hell are you?

ONLOOKER

I'm an onlooker. Just minding my business. Doing my job.

RICHARD

Seems to me you're minding our business.

FRANNIE

Butting in.

ONLOOKER

Onlookers have rights, too. Here's my card. "Onlookers, bystanders and passersby." And some of us have come out against drum rolls in public airports.

RICHARD

I can't be responsible for—

ONLOOKER

There are rules, you know, for estranged couples who meet accidentally—

FRANNIE

I happen to have my book of rules with me. *[Rummages in sack]* Now let me see—

RICHARD

Hey, wait a minute—

ONLOOKER

A calm handshake is usually recommended in cases—

FRANNIE

Hey, you're not just a random onlooker. I know who you are. You're—

RICHARD

Reg Barnstable!

FRANNIE

You old dirt-shoveller, you! *[Embraces him.]*

RICHARD

My favourite old rumour monger, how the hell are you?

[The three of them exit with arms around each other, talking inaudibly; lights go on, focusing on PILOT *and* FLIGHT ATTENDANT *in the fourth contretemps.]*

FLIGHT ATTENDANT

You sent for me.

PILOT

I did.

FLIGHT ATTENDANT

Well, here I am, sir.

PILOT

So I see.

FLIGHT ATTENDANT

Reporting for duty. Sir?

PILOT

You realize you have been assigned with me on the new north-west flight.

FLIGHT ATTENDANT

I do.

PILOT

You know my feelings about—

FLIGHT ATTENDANT

—women in the cockpit? Yes, I do, sir. I could apply for a transfer, sir.

PILOT

[Shifting tone.] How can you call me sir . . . after what we've meant to each other . . . that night at the Japanese rest—

FLIGHT ATTENDANT

I won't forget how you struggled . . . first with the sushi . . . then with the chopsticks . . . how hard you tried . . . persevering—

PILOT

It's not easy . . . not easy at all, for a man, a man like me . . . to change . . . to admit he might be wrong.

FLIGHT ATTENDANT

Are you saying what I think you're saying? What I hope you're saying?

PILOT

I'm not saying that . . . only that . . . times change, we all have to—
[They embrace; lights fade. A young man, CALLER, *approaches the phone booth and dials.]*

CALLER

Sherry Hutchuk, please. Sherry? Hey, it's great to hear your voice. Bet you can't guess who this is. No. No. Hey, wait a minute. Don't hang up. I'll give you a big hint. Quebec City. 1997. No, June. After the rock concert? Yeah. That's right. No, that was Arnie. I was the one with the CCM. Now you've got it. Yeah. Were we wiped! Yeah, well I remember part of it. Anyway, I'm on my way to Seattle. I gotta promise of a job out there, kind of important, and we had a stop here, so I pull out my book and there you are. Yeah, I'm out at the airport. No, I'm standing right here, no shit. Why should I lie?
[Lights go up on PILOT *and* FLIGHT ATTENDANT; *soap opera music.]*

PILOT

If only you'd told me. How you felt. I didn't . . . now I see what you—

FLIGHT ATTENDANT

I didn't want . . . to hurt you. I tried. You tried. We both tried. But . . .
[Lights fade; spotlight on the phone booth.]

CALLER

What d'ya mean, why? I don't have *anything* on my mind. The stewardess just said we could get off for twenty-five fast ones and stretch our legs and put in a call, so I thought, who do I know here? And then I thought of you and that terrific night in Kee-bec and—you've got to go right now? You mean this minute? Why can't you go to the dry cleaner's in twenty-five minutes? Oh. Well, if that's the way it is. Well, tell me quick then, how've you been? Oh. Oh? What d'ya know.
[Light fades and comes up on PILOT *and* FLIGHT ATTENDANT; *soap opera music.]*

PILOT

I understand.

FLIGHT ATTENDANT

No, I understand.

PILOT

We both understand. That's what's so—

FLIGHT ATTENDANT

Yes, yes, yes, yes, yes.
[Light snaps off and comes up on the phone booth.]

CALLER

Well. Well. Well, I guess I oughta say congrats. So when's the big day? Yeah? That right? Hey, you still there? Well, you said you had to go to the dry cleaner's so I thought . . . Listen, that night in Quebec City, I wasn't all that skunked, you know. I remember quite a lot, in fact. And I bet you do, too. Remember we were up there at the what-do-you-call-it, that place where you look down and see all the lights, and we got to talking and you told me about how your cat got killed and you started to cry and, Jesus, so did I almost, and yeah, yeah, well, I remember things like that. I really remem-ber that whole night. The stars and the moon and all that. That wet grass and those little, little bugs. I thought, this girl's special. I was hoping maybe, wishing you maybe, well, yeah, I know, you gotta go to the dry cleaner's, so well, all the best. *[Hangs up phone and an instant later kicks side of phone booth.]* Bitch!

[People cross and recross the stage with luggage. An elderly man, WESLEY, and an elderly woman, MYRA, are left standing by the luggage platform, which is revolving with MYRA's suitcase on it. WESLEY grabs for it, but misses.]

MYRA

That's mine, I believe.

WESLEY

Thought it might be.
[He grabs again, successfully.]

MYRA

You must be Wesley.

WESLEY

That's right. I am.

MYRA

Well, I'm Myra.

WESLEY

Pleased to meet you. *[Gesturing to the suitcase.]* Heavy.

MYRA

[Injured.] Heavy?

WESLEY

But not too heavy. You expect a suitcase to be heavy. This is almost . . . almost . . . light.

MYRA

You said you'd be wearing a fur-trimmed overcoat. That's how I knew you.

WESLEY

Well, it's not much of an overcoat. I shouldn't have worn it, but I said I would. The lining's getting worn and I only wore it because—

MYRA

It looks just fine to me. Serviceable. For the climate, I mean. It's a waste of money going along with the fashion every time some so-called designer down in New York City decides that now it's time for wide shoulders or narrow shoulders or—

WESLEY

That's what I think—

MYRA

So what if it's a little worn? If it's good quality to start with—and I can tell this is 100 percent wool—where are you going to find that these days? You get nothing but synthetics or blends, though I do say some of these blends are marvellous in their way. *[Pause.]* For wrinkles.

WESLEY

Yes, that's true. *[Pause.]* For wrinkles.

MYRA

A little altering can do wonders with a good basic overcoat with—

PA

Flight 756 for Detroit, Pittsburgh and Philadelphia now boarding.

MYRA

Wesley, I'm going to get right back on that plane and go back to New Brunswick.

WESLEY

But—

MYRA

I should never have come. My sister Ruth—I wrote you about her—she said it would never work out, two people with nothing in common.

WESLEY

But you just got here.

MYRA

We've just met and all we've talked about is your old overcoat. You'll think that's all I ever talk about. Just rattling on and on. That's not true. I don't usually go on this way. Now, I'm not going to say another word. I'm going to give you a chance to talk.

WESLEY

I'm not a great one for talking. I think that's why—

MYRA

—why you haven't met anyone—

WESLEY

—since my wife—

MYRA

—died.

WESLEY

Now, she was a talker.

MYRA

Not my husband. He was a quiet man. Kept to himself. But up here [*taps forehead*] there was plenty going on.

                              WESLEY

Oh.

                               MYRA

Only thing, I never knew what it was.

                              WESLEY

I guess I'm a little like that.

                               MYRA

Well, still waters—

                              WESLEY

—run deep.

                               MYRA

My mother used to say that. She was full of sayings. The stories she could
tell. Lots of people at home think I take after her.

                                PA

Last call for Detroit, Pittsburgh and Philadelphia.

                               MYRA

I shouldn't have come. This is . . . ridiculous. I see what Ruth meant when
she—

                              WESLEY

You're tired, all that distance . . .

                               MYRA

I didn't tell Ruth you paid for my ticket. She wouldn't have thought it was
right. It isn't right.

                              WESLEY

But I wanted—

MYRA

Now I'm really and truly not going to say one more word. I swear. I'm going to give you a chance to talk.
[A long pause.]

WESLEY

I don't know how to begin. What topic, I mean.

MYRA

[Through closed lips.] I'm not going to say another word.
[Very long pause.]

WESLEY

That's a pretty coat you're wearing.

MYRA

[Through closed lips.] Thank you.

WESLEY

I like that shade of . . . well, whatever it is . . . purple.

MYRA

[Through closed lips.] Burgundy.

WESLEY

What was that?

MYRA

[Through closed lips.] Burgundy. *[Opens mouth.]* Burgundy.

WESLEY

Oh.

MYRA

My favourite colour.
[Another long pause.]

WESLEY

It gets pretty cold here.
[Silence.]
You need a good warm coat like that . . . here.

MYRA

Go on. You're doing fine.

WESLEY

Take right now. Coldest winter since 1952. Said so in the paper the other night.

MYRA

Did it now? This is fascinating.

WESLEY

Of course you can't always believe the paper. Last fall they predicted a drought.

MYRA

And what happened? What happened, Wesley?

WESLEY

Rain.

MYRA

There, you see? You can't believe the papers. So there was rain, was there? How much rain?

WESLEY

Lots of rain. Of course, I don't mind the rain.

MYRA

I like to walk in the rain. Of course I take my umbrella and galoshes.

WESLEY

That's what caught my eye.

MYRA

How do you mean, Wesley? Caught your eye?

WESLEY

In the ad.

MYRA

Oh, that ad! I don't know what got into me.

WESLEY

It was the part where it said, "Likes long walks. And gardening."

MYRA

Ruth said I was out of my mind. She said some pervert would be writing back and answering that ad.

WESLEY

I almost didn't. *[Pause.]* Write, I mean.

MYRA

But one morning I was out walking. I do a mile and a half every day.

WESLEY

That's what struck me. A mile and a half. Now, I do three kilometres and that's just about, give or take a few yards, just about—

MYRA

I was going along this old road that leads out of town, pretty road, lots of elms, though the elms are pretty well gone—

WESLEY

It's starting here, too. The elms. It breaks your—

MYRA

—and I was going around this curve where the gas station is and the Bowie farm and then there's this straight stretch and I could see straight ahead for miles and miles, just straight ahead and . . . and there wasn't anything there.

WESLEY

It's like that here. You can see for miles and—

MYRA

Nothing at all. I don't know why, but it scared me to death. My teeth started to chatter, does that ever happen to you? It was just miles and miles and I could tell that if I walked along there, nothing was going to happen to me. I was just going to keep on walking, and then I got so hot and I started to . . . well . . . I started to cry, now isn't that the craziest thing you ever heard?

WESLEY

I like a good long walk.

MYRA

Well, I just decided right there on the spot that I'd put an ad in the *Rose Lovers' Quarterly*, even if it was a crazy thing to do and, like Ruth said, dangerous maybe, but I said to myself, now would a sex pervert be reading the *Rose Lovers' Quarterly*? Well, yes and no, I thought, you can never tell, but your letter came along—it was the only one, you know—and I knew right away that I didn't have to worry. But that's not true, I did worry. I worried all the way here—

WESLEY

It's only normal. To worry.

MYRA

And I've got the return ticket. It's good up till six months.

WESLEY

That'll be lots of time. To get acquainted, I mean. And you'll see my roses when they come out.

MYRA

That's right!

WESLEY

Lots of people in this climate give up on roses. It's getting them through the winter's the problem. I have these windbreaks, and of course, I cover everything in the fall. I use good quality canvas. Sometimes I lost a few, but—

MYRA

—but some of them get through!

WESLEY

They look dead at first. But little by little they come back.

MYRA

It's a challenge.

WESLEY

I forget who said it, but someone once said, "A Manitoba rose is a rose that knows no fear."

MYRA

Knows no fear! I like that.

WESLEY

I've got the spare room all spruced up. It's got a nice big closet. You'll like . . . the closet. My wife—

MYRA

Let's make a pact. Wesley. Do you like to be called Wesley or do you like Wes?

WESLEY

Wesley's fine with me. My wife always—

MYRA

Let's make a pact. Let's try not to talk too much about *them*.

WESLEY

Them? You mean—

MYRA

Them. You know. Your wife and—

WESLEY

—and your husband.

MYRA

I have this funny feeling that they're, you know—

WESLEY

—watching us. I know what you mean.

MYRA

Yes. Looking down at us and saying, aren't they the sillies!

WESLEY

And at their age! You should hear my son and his wife Darlene. They think I've gone senile. They wonder what the neighbours will think . . . about the spare room being all spruced up and all.

MYRA

Maybe we are senile. Have you thought of that?

WESLEY

Darlene says to me, "Well, I suppose you need the companionship."

MYRA

Everyone's always talkin' about companionship. Funny word that. Like companionship's all you're up to.

WESLEY

My wife—

MYRA

We weren't going to—

WESLEY

Just this once. My wife was . . . not very well . . . almost an invalid . . . for a long time. But . . . *[clears throat]* I'm in quite good health, excellent health.

MYRA

My husband, well, we were different. He wasn't all that, you know, demonstrative. But I was . . . always . . . demonstrative. That's the way I was made, I can't help it.

WESLEY

The spare room I've fixed up? If you don't feel comfortable there you could always . . . it does have a good closet, though.

MYRA

I don't have a lot of clothes. Just a few things, my walking shoes—

WESLEY

Good—

MYRA

And a few rose cuttings—

WESLEY

Cuttings!

MYRA

Just the hardier varieties, of course. And my garden tools. A person gets used to her own . . . trowel.

WESLEY

That's true. A person gets used to things.

MYRA

But a person can change. Adapt.

WESLEY

New growth.

MYRA

I like the way you put that, new growth. You're a very attractive man, Wesley. I'd say that snap you sent doesn't do you justice.

WESLEY

You're a little different than I thought, too. More filled out and happy looking.

MYRA

Shall we go? You sure that isn't too heavy?

WESLEY

Light as a feather. A feather!
[They exit. An ELDERLY MAN *and* ELDERLY WOMAN *are standing about halfway up the stairs. Lighting suggests their ethereal quality, and their voices have a degree of echo. They glide up the stairs together, in step, and stand facing the audience.]*

ELDERLY MAN

Did you hear that?

ELDERLY WOMAN

I certainly did.

ELDERLY MAN

Not too demonstrative, she says. Fine way for a woman to talk about her deceased spouse.

ELDERLY WOMAN

What about the part about the wife being an invalid?

ELDERLY MAN

I wondered about that.

ELDERLY WOMAN

Ever hear of an allergy to roses?

ELDERLY MAN

Never cared for roses myself. Too floppy.

ELDERLY WOMAN

Six months and she'll have her fill.

ELDERLY MAN

She'll talk his ears off, poor fellow.

ELDERLY WOMAN

He'll be dragging her to bulb shows and what not.

ELDERLY MAN

Tramping around the countryside.

ELDERLY WOMAN

Muddy boots.

ELDERLY MAN

What gets into folks?

ELDERLY WOMAN

Foolishness.

ELDERLY MAN

Well, shall we be getting on our way?

[They link arms and glide away. A MOTHER, *smartly dressed, enters holding two children by the hand,* BOY *and* GIRL, *who are adults dressed as children. She speaks in a loud stagey voice as though reading a script.]*

MOTHER

Well, children, isn't this nice! Daddy's coming home. His plane will be in in five minutes.

BOY AND GIRL

Yippee.

MOTHER

Now behave yourselves. And stop that, Sammy. You're getting your knees dirty. What will Daddy think?

BOY

[Mocking.] What will Daddy think?

MOTHER

[As though reading lines.] What *will* Daddy think?

BOY

Who cares what the old barf thinks?

MOTHER

Now don't be a Mr. Smarty-pants. Your Daddy's been on that plane all afternoon—

GIRL

He's always riding on planes, lucky suck.

MOTHER

I think he's coming now. Yes, there he is.

[FATHER *comes down the Arrivals stairs, pecks* MOTHER *on the cheek, pats* BOY *on the head, and twigs* GIRL*'s ear, then the four of them step back and appraise each other.*]

MOTHER

We never do it right, never. Other families can do it, but not us.

FATHER

What is it? Is it that we lack style? Panache?

BOY

We're boring.

GIRL

We're scared to rip loose.

MOTHER

[*Glances at watch.*] What do you say if . . . if we try it again?
[*The family resumes their former positions of waiting for* FATHER*'s arrival. This is not a "real" filming, but an extension of the characters' self-consciousness as they indulge in the self-conscious drama of an airport reunion.* DIRECTOR *and* ASSISTANT DIRECTOR *enter from the side dressed in white, carrying rope for partitions. They also carry white chairs, a white clapperboard, and a knitting bag.*]

DIRECTOR

Ready for the retake, everyone? Now look, guys, a little more . . . warmth?

ASSISTANT DIRECTOR

[*With clapperboard.*] One, two, three, roll.

MOTHER

[*Enthusiastically.*] Just five more minutes, kids.

GIRL

Whee! Daddy's going to be here in five minutes.

DIRECTOR

Wait a minute. I think what I'd like is to see you two kids jumping up and down.

BOY

What for?

DIRECTOR

Excitement. You're dying to see your old man. He's been away a whole week. And you, Mom, I want you carrying a knitting bag, okay? And can you loosen that coat a bit—great!

ASSISTANT DIRECTOR

[Giving MOTHER *a knitting bag; using clapperboard.]* One, two, three, roll 'em.

BOY

[Jumping up and down.] Five whole minutes, I can't wait.

GIRL

[Jumping and puffing.] I . . . can't . . . wait either.

MOTHER

[Waving bag.] There he is!
*[*FATHER *enters, descends, picks up* GIRL, *embraces* MOTHER *and chucks* BOY *under the chin.]*

DIRECTOR

Okay, hold everything. We still don't have it. Let's have some urgency. You, Dad, when you come down those stairs, I want you to give the crowd a . . . you know, a searching look. You're home, man, this is your own little nuclear unit. And I want one of you kids to duck under the rope when you see your old man coming.

[DIRECTOR *strings a rope across Arrivals and Departures stairs.*]

BOY

I will. I'll duck under the rope.

GIRL

What about me? I wanna—

ASSISTANT DIRECTOR

[*As though struck by creative thunder.*] What would happen, I wonder, if they both slipped under the rope?

DIRECTOR

I could go with that.

ASSISTANT DIRECTOR

Could be a nice touch. Kids released from maternal control for an instant, passion over reason kind of thing—

DIRECTOR

Okay, roll it. Oh, and you, Mama, let's see a look of longing on your face. Your mate's been gone for a whole week and—

MOTHER

How's that?

DIRECTOR

Let's get rid of the gloves, eh. Okay.

ASSISTANT DIRECTOR

One, two, three, action!

BOY

[*Jumping.*] Oh boy, oh boy, five more minutes!

                              GIRL

[Jumping.] Five minutes, four minutes, three minutes—

                             MOTHER

[Jumping.] A whole week!

                               BOY

There he is. *[Slips under the rope.]*

                              GIRL

Wait for me. *[Slips under the rope.]*

                             MOTHER

[Hitches up her dress and steps over the rope.] At last, darling.

                            DIRECTOR

Not bad. Night and day, in fact. One more take and we'll have it. I want
you to show me your pain this time. You, Pops, get a piece of rope around
that briefcase of yours . . . frayed rope. Now you've got it.

                        ASSISTANT DIRECTOR

Hey, what if we put the father in a wheelchair?

                            DIRECTOR

I dunno. It's a possibility . . . Hey! Crutches.

                        ASSISTANT DIRECTOR

I could go with crutches.

                            DIRECTOR

Listen, Pops, I want you to kiss the boy. It's okay, it goes nowadays. That's
the idea. Then you press the kids' heads to your belly—right, right, heads
to belly—and sort of shut your eyes and look upwards—terrific!

ASSISTANT DIRECTOR

Take your places, one, two, three.

BOY

[Half-crazed.] Five more minutes!

MOTHER

Mon Dieu, there he is, thank the dear Lord.

CHILDREN

Papa, Papa!

DIRECTOR

Okay, okay, focus on the kids, get the runny nose, good, great, go for it, show me what you're feeling, go for it.
*[*FATHER *enters, searches the crowd with a madman's eyes, runs and embraces his wildly heaving wife and hysterical children.]*

DIRECTOR

Hold it an extra second. Can you shudder just a bit more? God, it's fantastic, I love it, the moisture is—okay, break. *[To* ASSISTANT DIRECTOR.*]* What d'ya think?

ASSISTANT DIRECTOR

We've got it. Congrats, folks.
[He removes the rope.]

MOTHER

I knew we could do it.

PA

Ladies and gentlemen, will you kindly board.
[The six actors freeze. They listen to the announcement but don't know what to make of it. The announcement is repeated, growing more and more severe.]

Ladies and gentlemen, it is time to board. Now. This minute. Last call. Final call. Departure time has arrived and that means now!

[While PA *makes the announcement, five actors arrange themselves in the shape of an airplane; the two people in front simulate the sound of jets; the two people in the middle hold out arms to suggest wings and wing flaps; the last person forms the tail section. They go through the motions of takeoff. Overlapping voices form the sound of the motors.]*

VOICES

woe woe woe woe woe

man man man man man man man man

wo man wo man wo man wo man wo man

chow chow chow chow chow chow

ow ow ow ow ow ow ow ow

*[*FLIGHT ATTENDANT *stands to one side of the other actors, and as she speaks in sweet tones her arms follow the stylized movements that air personnel use while demonstrating safety procedures. She continues to do this throughout her speech, even though the gestures and words have nothing to connect them.]*

FLIGHT ATTENDANT

Ladies and gentlemen, *mesdames et messieurs*, we hope you have a pleasant flight today. Our flight attendants will soon be serving a light lunch followed by *gâteau cerise*—that's cherry cake—and a selection of drinks. Weather conditions are excellent, and below you, you can see vast fields of corn, wheat and other interesting grain crops. The clouds to your left are of the cumulus variety and typical of the region. You are invited to take photographs if you so wish. Aircraft personnel can assist you with manicures or small psychological crises. If you wish counselling, please put on your light and wait patiently and pleasantly. Or you may wish to join one of our in-flight clubs. We have stamp collecting in the forward section, crochet work in the rear and, conditions permitting, aerobic dancing in the aisle.

[She stops talking abruptly, as though a record has been switched off in her head, tiptoes to edge of the stage and looks down as though from a great height. Her tone becomes lyrical, a tone that is both a satire of cheap lyricism and a celebration of transcendence.]

Oh, look at that, just look at that. Did you ever . . . I can never get over it. I look down and suddenly this plane seems to turn transparent and I feel I'm made out of glass and I'm part of the sky and the clouds . . . and, oh my God, I look down and there it is, our own little green planet spinning and spinning and spinning with its own sweet crazy unsingable music and—

[She looks up dazed; rises; goes back to her official voice.]

Ladies and gentlemen, *mesdames et messieurs*, we are about to descend. Will you kindly lean to the left? Will the gentleman who is not leaning to the left please do so at this time? We ask that you remove your shoes for land-ing—we are about to land and require your co-operation in this matter. Lean left. Thank you. *Merci.* Left again. I see one of our lady passengers has not removed her designer boots at this time. May we ask for full co-opera-tion for a smooth and cheerful landing. A little to the left again. For addi-tional oxygen open mouth as wide as possible and please lean forward at this time and commence with foot action. Left, right, left, *mesdames et messieurs, gauche, gauche,* left for God's sake, left!

[Actors forming the plane shuffle-step offstage. A minor tinkling crash, more musical than otherwise—similar to the music box that ended Act One—is heard from the wings.]

We hope you have enjoyed your flight with us today, and I wish you all a pleasant evening. I wish you a splendid evening, a perfect evening. I wish you a night from which the clouds of pessimism have vanished and a qual-ity of rare moonlight that—

[Music; everyone sweeps in. PILOT *takes the* FLIGHT ATTENDANT*'s arm. Music swells, not quite a wedding march but a suggestion of one. The* PILOT *crowns the "bride" with ribbons and flowers suggesting reconciliation. They ascend the steps; others follow, hurling confetti. At the top of the stairs the bridal pair turn, face each other, salute and then embrace. They exit and others follow, throwing confetti and taking pictures. The airport* CLEANER *enters with a push broom, pauses at centre stage and addresses the audience. Lights dim.]*

CLEANER

[In sincere tones.] Very few people realize that in the busy life of a major air-port there are moments of silence. Generally it's about two or three in the morning. Like right now. Listen. The noise of the giant jets is stilled. Their

great silver bodies are at rest, the thunder of their engines silent. At this hour one senses a deep calm rising out of the absence of commerce and the petty distractions of human activity. For this brief interval:

The people of the sky are at peace;

Their frantic comings and goings have ceased

At this hour *[pause]* the airport *[pause]* sleeps.

[These last three lines should have the feeling of an epilogue, the rhyme stressed, a sense of winding down. The CLEANER *exits; the lights grow very dim. At the same instant, a tiny* FAIRY *appears spotlighted at the top of the Arrivals stairs. She is carrying a lighted wand. She dances lightly down the stairs in a dainty ballet step, pauses, surveys the dark and empty airport, spies the silver bag rotating on the luggage platform, takes it, then points her wand at the automatic doors, which open to the sound of tinkling music. She exits. The end.]*

ANNIVERSARY

Carol Shields & Dave Williamson

An earlier version of this play, entitled *Not Another Anniversary*, was first produced by Solar Stage, Toronto, and premiered October 28, 1986, with the following cast:

Marianne McIsaac: *Dianne*
Robbie O'Neill: *Tom*
Jennifer Allyson: *Shirley*
Robert Latimer: *Ben*
Andrew Lewarne: *Garth*

Director: Gene Tishauer
Set Design: Kathleen Climie
Costume Design: Julia Tribe
Lighting Design: Lesley Wilkinson
Stage Manager and Sound Design: Eric Nickerson

Anniversary, as published in this edition, premiered at the Gas Station Theatre, Winnipeg, on June 13, 1996, with the following cast:

Catherine Roberts: *Dianne*
Jason Broadfoot: *Tom*
Sharon Moore: *Shirley*
Dan Weber: *Ben*
Devin McCracken: *Garth*

Director: B. Pat Burns
Assistant Director: Kevin Longfield
Stage Manager: Sue Stone
Design Consultant: Andrea von Wichert
Technical Director: Todd Drader

Playwrights' Note

Despite the comical nature of the piece, a number of serious questions are put before the audience:

What does friendship mean and what are its obligations and loyalties? What does marriage involve, and can original marriage vows sustain renegotiation? When is a marriage or a friendship over? What is the nature of pretence and how damaging is it? And, finally, are we all, in some sense, pretenders?

Each of the five characters in this play behaves foolishly at times, but it is not the playwrights' intent to mock them or their enthusiasms. Tom's passion for the environment, Dianne's redemption through crafts and coffee, Ben's and Shirley's confusion over their private/public lives, Garth's attempt to mask his pain with irony—each of these characters deserves a presence on that narrow and difficult balancing beam of respect and humour.

Anniversary is particularly suitable for summer theatre and for dinner theatre. Its two acts can easily be rearranged into three acts, and a suggestion for this kind of alteration is made in the text.

It is taken for granted that geographical references will be changed to suit particular audiences.

We like to think this play will bring pleasure, laughter, recognition and perhaps even a little reflection.

Cast

DIANNE HART, a woman in her mid-thirties, casually but smartly dressed

GARTH, a young man in his late twenties

TOM HART, husband of Dianne, but currently separated and living on his own

SHIRLEY, a friend of the couple, in her early forties

BEN, Shirley's husband, also in his early forties

Setting

The two acts of the play are set in the Harts' middle-class living room. The usually tidy room is dishevelled as the play opens.

Act One

*At rise, the stage is arranged as a middle-class living-dining room, far from
luxurious, but containing a number of smart pieces. An eclectic mix indicates
a sure touch. On the left, visible, is a vestibule and the front door. To the
right is an archway to a hall and the bedrooms and, beside that, a door to the
kitchen.* GARTH *comes in through the archway on Rollerblades. He's wearing a
leather jacket, a skull-fitting wool toque and a too-long scarf. He finds the
wrapped bottle of champagne he hid earlier and goes out to the kitchen with
it surreptitiously.* DIANNE *appears, in casual-chic clothes, and begins to
straighten the room. She stops in front of the oil painting.*

DIANNE

Garth!

GARTH

[Appearing from the kitchen.] Want me to stay? Just say the word and I'll—

DIANNE

Would you give me a hand with this?

GARTH

[Helping her take the painting down.] Are you *sure* you don't want me to be
here? I could—

DIANNE

Thanks, but the last thing I want is for him to get the impression you're living here.

GARTH

But I . . . almost do . . . And I'd like . . . well, you know what I'd like.

DIANNE

I do know, Garth. We made a promise, remember? That we'd sit down and
talk about it tonight.

GARTH

I don't want to rush you.

DIANNE

I know you don't.

GARTH

It's just that—

DIANNE

It's nearly five, Garth. Maybe you'd better go.

GARTH

Are you sure?

DIANNE

Yes. And would you mind terribly going out the back door? He could be coming up the street right now.

GARTH

You know what I think, Di? I think you're protecting him. He does know I exist.

DIANNE

Look, this whole business is tough enough without having a third party present.

GARTH

I thought maybe I could be in another room, just in case he gets ugly.

DIANNE

[Smiling.] Tom? Ugly? He may get maudlin, but he's incapable of ugly. I really think . . . I think you'd better get going—

GARTH

Right. Good luck and all that. When should I come back?

DIANNE

I don't know. How long do these things take?

GARTH

Why don't I come back in an hour with some takeout? If the scene is getting heavy, well, I'll be here.

DIANNE

You're a dear. Are you okay on those blades?

GARTH

Road's pretty dry since the thaw. What would you like? Pizza? No, how about Chinese—

DIANNE

Surprise me—
[The doorbell rings.]

GARTH

Okay, I'm off. *[Skating toward the kitchen.]* About an hour, then. Back door or front?

DIANNE

Back. No, front—he's got to face up—no, better to use the back door.

GARTH

And tonight we'll talk—

DIANNE

Hurry!
*[*GARTH *exits. The instant he's gone,* DIANNE *opens the front door.]*
Tom. Come in.

TOM

[Entering.] Hi.

[He walks around the living room, looking around with a feeling of nostalgia. He's wearing an overcoat and scarf. DIANNE *closes the door and comes into the room, regarding him for an instant.]*

You took down the picture.

DIANNE

I want you to have it.

TOM

It belongs here.

DIANNE

I think Ben and Shirley would want you to have it.

TOM

My place is too small for a painting that size. I'd hit it every time I took off my coat.

DIANNE

Speaking of taking off your coat . . .

TOM

Oh—yes . . .

[He removes his coat and scarf and momentarily wonders what to do with them. DIANNE *takes them, brushing lint off the coat collar.]*

That was nice.

DIANNE

What?

[She hangs up his coat and scarf.]

TOM

What you did just then. Brushing off my coat collar. That was *nice*. I never used to notice . . . when you did . . . things like that. I never—

DIANNE

Maybe we'd better get started, Tom. We've got all the books and CDs—

TOM

Where's Tracy? And Troy—where are they?

DIANNE

Both over at Mother's. I thought it would be best if, you know, if they weren't here.

TOM

Won't they be bored? Troy said the last time they were there your mother tried to read them *Anne of Green Gables* when they wanted their Nintendo.

DIANNE

Anne of Green Gables may be just what they need right now.

TOM

You always had a soft spot for Anne. How come you never gave Tom Sawyer a chance?

DIANNE

Tom Sawyer capitulates to society. Anne transforms it.

TOM

Is that what you want to do with your shop?

DIANNE

I just want to . . . I don't know what I want to do.

TOM

Where's their stuff? This does not look like a place where kids live.

DIANNE

I put everything away. Less confusing—

TOM

What if I took some of their things over to my place, their board games or something, so they'd feel at home when they visited me?

DIANNE

I suppose, but you don't really have room for—

TOM

God, I miss those kids. You wouldn't believe how quiet my place is. I can hear the guy next door brushing his teeth.

DIANNE

[Smiling.] Maybe you could get him to floss instead.

TOM

Do they know I'm taking them skating tomorrow?

DIANNE

Of course they do. They're looking forward to it.

TOM

If I can find my skates.

DIANNE

They're probably here. Well. Where do you want to start?

TOM

Do you know what day it is?

DIANNE

Uh—yes, I do.

TOM

Doesn't that strike you as pretty ironic, dividing our so-called assets on our anniversary?

DIANNE

Tom, you picked the day, remember?

TOM

You're so busy all the time. I'm surprised you were able to get away from the shop on a Saturday afternoon.

DIANNE

Mrs. Connor is perfectly capable. Now, shouldn't we start?

TOM

It's crazy.

DIANNE

Crazy?

TOM

That twelve years ago today we walked down that aisle.

DIANNE

Let's begin, okay? Now, I want you to have the Neil Young tapes.

TOM

What do you mean? You love Neil Young.

DIANNE

I'll keep Carly Simon and Roberta Flack—

TOM

Neil Young belongs here. In this room. This is where—

DIANNE

The trouble with Neil Young is—well, I hate to say this, Tom—

TOM

What?

DIANNE

Well, Neil Young—he sort of whines.

TOM

Whines? I never noticed that. I just remember how you and I—

DIANNE

I thought you should have this chair, too.

TOM

I wouldn't say he whines, exactly. Expresses his feelings, his gut feelings, maybe, but I've never heard anyone say he—

DIANNE

[Wearily.] Look, Tom, we can't debate every single item. You're taking the chair, all right?

TOM

But the chair and the sofa are a match.

DIANNE

Chairs and sofas don't necessarily have to match anymore.

TOM

Oh?

DIANNE

Individual pieces are what people want now.

TOM

Just like us—we don't match anymore. We're individual pieces. Is that what you're saying?

DIANNE

[Sighing.] I thought you liked the chair.

TOM

I do.

DIANNE

Have you bought a new one?

TOM

Want to know what I've got? Come over sometime and have a look. I've got an apple box and a sleeping bag. My place is so empty, even the dripping tap echoes.

DIANNE

You wouldn't be whining, would you?

TOM

Me and . . . you know who.

DIANNE

Look, I really want you to have your favourite chair.

TOM

I'm not sure it's a good idea. When I sit in the chair, I'll think about the sofa and all the times we used to lie there in the dark and listen to Neil Young . . . whining . . . while we—

DIANNE

Then *leave* the chair. But I insist you take the ottoman.

TOM

Hey, Ben and Shirley gave us that ottoman. On our second wedding anniversary—

DIANNE

That's right, but look, it's falling to pieces. Look.
[She grabs the ottoman, stares at it and, with sudden deliberation, rips the cover violently.]

TOM

They brought it over as a surprise, remember?
[He, too, rips a piece off the cover.]

DIANNE

They were always full of surprises. *[She tears a side off the ottoman.]* Impromptu was their middle name.

TOM

Those were the days!
[He tears the other side off.]

DIANNE

Well, those days *[pulling a leg off viciously]* are over.

TOM

Old friends, old times. God, I hate to think they've just *[he rips off another leg]* vanished!

DIANNE

We'll never have *[she pulls off the third leg]* friends like that again.

TOM

At least we have our memories.
[He gives a karate chop to the remains of the ottoman.]

DIANNE

Here.
[She produces a green garbage bag and they throw the ottoman remains into it.]

TOM

Okay, now what?

DIANNE

Tom, please pick something.

TOM

Okay. I'll take the tiffany lamp.

DIANNE

Uh—no.

TOM

What do you mean, "no"?

DIANNE

You can't have the tiffany lamp.

TOM

You told me to pick something.

DIANNE

Anything but the tiffany lamp. My parents gave us that.

TOM

Okay, okay. Uhh—let's see. Right, I'll take the photo albums.

DIANNE

The albums? But—oh, all right.

TOM

Where are they, the albums—

DIANNE

In the closet, on the shelf over the coats.
[TOM *goes to the closet; he reaches up to the shelf.*]

TOM

Two . . . three . . . four albums—hey, is this what I think it is?
[*He pulls down a box and shows it to* DIANNE.]

DIANNE

The slides.

TOM

My God, I'd completely forgotten them. Does anyone take slides anymore?

DIANNE

It's all video cameras these days.

TOM

Do you know they have video cameras the size of your hand these days?

DIANNE

If you like that sort of thing.

TOM

I wish we had the kids on video.

DIANNE

Let's not get into that, okay?
[TOM *holds one of the slides up to the light.*]

TOM

Let's see . . . What's this? Where's the projector?

DIANNE

I don't know. Tom, nobody shows slides anymore.

TOM

Hey, it's the Yellowstone trip. What do you know.

DIANNE

[Looking over his shoulder and squinting at the slide.] Those crazy bears.

TOM

[Taking another slide from the box.] Hey, look, remember that little guy?

DIANNE

As if I could forget. He did somersaults.
[They both laugh.]

TOM

[Holding up another.] My God, our wedding.

DIANNE

There we are!

TOM

Look at old Ben!

DIANNE

Where's the one of Shirley in that hilarious dress?

TOM

I don't know, these are out of order . . .

DIANNE

The kids were looking at them the other day; they must've—

TOM

Then they must've had the projector.

DIANNE

It can't be far away. I'll find it tomorrow.

TOM

Those kids must really . . . run amok now.

DIANNE

Now?

TOM

Now that they don't have a father.

DIANNE

They do have a father. You aren't dead.

TOM

No firm guidance. No regular supervision.

DIANNE

They do have supervision. You know they do.

TOM

You still have that underemployed jack-of-no-trades babysitting them?

DIANNE

The store's giving him a lot more hours now. And the kids think he's a terrific sitter.

TOM

And you think he's terrific, too, I suppose.

DIANNE

He's company. He's someone to talk to. And he's a good listener. He's interested in how the shop's doing. He asks questions.

TOM

I'll bet.

DIANNE

Tom, this isn't getting us anywhere. Let's get to the important things. Now, if you don't mind, I really want to keep the copper fish-poacher.

TOM

Oh. I thought I'd like that.

DIANNE

You don't even like fish.

TOM

I've been trying to add seafood to my diet.

DIANNE

You hate shrimp!

TOM

I hate the fat ones with their eyes on the end of sticks. I've acquired a taste for the little ones.

DIANNE

You don't need a copper poacher for shell shrimp.

TOM

Let's put the poacher aside for now. What about the NordicTrack?

DIANNE

What about it? It's mine. You loathe exercising. You always said body worship was self-indulgent and time-wasting.

TOM

I said that when I lived in a house that I could roam around in. I need the NordicTrack now that I'm in an apartment.

DIANNE

Where would you put it?

TOM

It'll fill up the living room nicely.

DIANNE

I won't even discuss the NordicTrack until we decide on the silverware.

TOM

You take the knives and I'll take the forks.

DIANNE

Let's be sensible.

TOM

If we were sensible, we never would have—

DIANNE

You never would have.

TOM

It was only a couple of lousy afternoons! She meant nothing to me, you know that.

DIANNE

Tom, we officially did it three months ago. We signed the paper. There were witnesses.

TOM

We could've worked things out. All the things we used to like to do together —even shopping. How many guys actually enjoy watching their wives try on clothes and going to fetch the right size when—

DIANNE

Come on, Tom, say what we did.

TOM

I don't—

DIANNE

It'll help if you say it. Come on.

TOM

We . . .

DIANNE

That's it . . .

TOM

We . . .

DIANNE

Come on, you're doing fine.

TOM

We sep—

DIANNE

Yes? Yes?

TOM

Sep-ar—

DIANNE

You're almost there!

TOM

—ated.

DIANNE

All together now.

TOM

Sep-ar-a-ted.

DIANNE

That's terrific. Now, doesn't it feel good to—

TOM

No.

DIANNE

There's something about saying it out loud—

TOM

—that makes it—

DIANNE

—suddenly seem—

TOM

—true.

DIANNE

There.

TOM

"There"?

DIANNE

You've taken a big step. You've said it out loud. You've faced up to it. It's going to be easier now to get through all this stuff.

TOM

It's never going to be easy. Every CD is a memory, every coffee mug's a milestone—

DIANNE

Millstone, don't you mean? Ah, Tom, let's forget about dividing the stuff up and get Neighbourhood Services to—
[*The telephone rings. They freeze for a moment, looking at the phone and then at each other.*]

TOM

Wouldn't you think people would have the decency not to phone when we're . . . in the middle of an important ceremony.

DIANNE

We could let it ring.

TOM

It might be your . . . underemployed friend.

DIANNE

You take all the ashtrays. No one smokes around here.

TOM

No one smokes at my place.

DIANNE

I thought you might've started again. Now you're on your own—
[The phone continues to ring.]

TOM

You think, just because—hey, it could be your mother, couldn't it? Or
Tracy? Or Troy? One of them's fallen down her stairs—

DIANNE

Oh, you're right. *[She lifts the receiver.]* Hello? . . . It's who? . . . Ben! Ben
Forrester—my God, where are you? . . . I don't believe it . . . And Shirl,
too? . . . Great! . . . Well, thank you . . . Twelve years, that's right. Twelve
big ones . . . Tom? . . . No, he—I mean, *yes,* he's here, just a sec.
[She puts her hand over the receiver and hands it toward TOM.*]*
It's Ben and Shirl! They're in town at the Radisson and they want to come
over.

TOM

[In a loud whisper.] I can't talk to them now! I—

DIANNE

I've already said you're here. You've *got* to—

TOM

[Taking the phone.] Hello? . . . Ben, you old reprobate! What a surprise! . . .
We'd love to see you . . . You sure? . . . It's just a few minutes away and I'd
be glad to . . .
*[*DIANNE *gestures wildly, but he ignores her.]*
Hi, Shirl . . . Yes, we'll have the blueberry tea poured . . . Oh, port, now, is
it? . . . Of course . . . Right, see you in a few minutes. *[Hangs up, looking
pleased.]* They're getting a taxi.

DIANNE

Why didn't you tell them?

TOM

Don't we have any port?

DIANNE

We don't have any anything anymore. No joint possessions, that is. *We* aren't together. *We* are sep-ar-a-ted. Oh, Tom, why didn't you tell them?

TOM

[Pause.] They didn't ask.

DIANNE

But—

TOM

I thought you put it in the Christmas cards. You said you'd—

DIANNE

I never got around to the cards last Christmas.

TOM

Y'know, it was amazing—as soon as I heard their voices, I dropped straight through the time warp, back to the old days when the four of us—

DIANNE

Tom, I relied on you. I handed you the phone so that you'd have a chance to tell them.

TOM

And spoil their surprise?

DIANNE

You know it's going to be that much harder to tell them face to face.

TOM

[Shaking his head.] We don't . . . actually . . . *have* to tell them.

DIANNE

Tom—

TOM

We used to have the greatest times together, all of us. Remember Whitefish Lake?

DIANNE

I remember.

TOM

And that weekend in Montreal?

DIANNE

Montreal was a disaster.

TOM

Montreal was a challenge, but—

DIANNE

What's it been? Four years since we saw Ben and Shirl?

TOM

Three or four.

DIANNE

Three, four—we've changed. They've probably changed, too. In fact, I'm sure they've changed. For one thing, they're celebrities now.

TOM

So they're celebrities. They're still the same old Ben and Shirley to us. I could tell, just hearing their voices. Ben said when they remembered it was our anniversary, they just had to stop over. They're on a promotional tour, he said—

DIANNE

My God, I don't have a copy of their new book. Do you?

TOM

No, but I could run out and buy one.

DIANNE

There's no time now—

TOM

Why don't we say we lent it to your mother—

DIANNE

Mother would never—what about *your* mother?

TOM

My mother! Look, Dianne, for old time's sake, we can *pretend* we're still together. They'd never believe—

DIANNE

Oh, Tom, face it. Ever since you were elected president of the Endangered Species Society, you've lost . . . well . . . you've lost touch with reality. We can't pretend—

TOM

We can *try*. I'd rather do that than hurt them, our oldest friends.

DIANNE

That's one of the things that was wrong with our marriage—the trouble you had facing reality.

TOM

Oh, is that what was wrong? I've spent hours staring at my bare walls wondering just what—

DIANNE

Our compatibility, yours and mine, went the way of the buffalo and the long-tailed weasel.

TOM

Actually, there's still very real hope for the weasel—at the moment, it's merely threatened.

DIANNE

This is getting us nowhere.

TOM

So do we bop Ben and Shirl over the head with the truth as soon as they walk in, or do we have one last mellow evening for old time's sake?

DIANNE

I don't know about you, Tom, but I plan to greet them at the door with a resumé of the facts. We might even ask them to referee while we sort through the silver.

TOM

Hang on a minute. I just had a thought. What if Ben's developed a heart condition? Finding out we're sep—might just trigger an attack. Could we live with that?

DIANNE

I think we'd all feel a lot better.

TOM

And what about the Friendship Fund?

DIANNE

Oh! I'd forgotten about that—

TOM

Twelve years ago, wasn't it? All eight of us put in a thousand bucks each—

DIANNE

And there wasn't one of us who could afford it then.

TOM

But we invested in the name of what we all meant to each other. The good old Crazy Eights. We were going to get together and go on the cruise to end all cruises.

DIANNE

In 1996! We signed that ridiculous document—

TOM

Whoever loses touch or gets divorced forfeits their share.

DIANNE

Well, Gordie and Lou are divorced. Are they ever divorced!

TOM

And Genevieve left Whitney and ran off with her—was he her tennis coach?

DIANNE

Her personal trainer.

TOM

So it's come down to you and me and Shirley and Ben—

DIANNE

You're the official treasurer, so you can just hand the cheque over to them. Tonight's the ideal occasion—

TOM

We—you and I—aren't divorced exactly.

DIANNE

A technicality. *They* are still together, *they* aren't separated, ipso facto *they* get the money. Why not give it to them tonight?

TOM

One small problem. I don't have the money.

DIANNE

What?

TOM

Part of what I loaned you to set up the shop came out—

DIANNE

—out of the Friendship Fund!

TOM

I'm afraid so.

DIANNE

Tom, that's dishonest! Why didn't you tell me at the time?

TOM

I didn't. I couldn't. You wanted it so much, your own business. You said this town needed a coffee and crafts shop. And I wanted you to—

DIANNE

To what?

TOM

To have what you wanted. For once.

DIANNE

Oh, Tom—

TOM

And I knew you'd make a success of it.

DIANNE

Really. You really knew that? I didn't know you—

TOM

Are you—I don't want to pry—but are you in a position, *now*, to pay back the loan?

DIANNE

No. Not yet, not quite. Another good month or two—

TOM

So all we need is a little time. We'll explain everything, but, for tonight, why don't we play it by ear.

DIANNE

I guess . . . I guess we'll have to. But just for tonight. Good God, I'd better check the drink supply. What did you promise Shirley?

TOM

Port. But I'm sure she'll settle for vodka, or—
[DIANNE leaves the room, taking the garbage bag with her. TOM tries to re-hang the picture but it crashes to the floor.]
Damn! *[Calls out.]* Do we have any Scotch? Remember Ben and his Scotch?

DIANNE

[Calling from kitchen.] I'll check!

TOM

Maybe *I* should check, if I'm supposed to be still living here.
[He goes into the kitchen. For a couple of beats, there is no one onstage and no one speaks. Then there is a shriek from each of them offstage.]

DIANNE

[Off.] What are you doing in *there?*

TOM

[Off.] It's where we used to keep the booze—

DIANNE

[Off.] Well, I don't keep it there anymore. Please, if you don't mind, stay out of there.

TOM

[Off.] Sorry—

DIANNE

[Appearing.] That picture. We've got to hang it back up. Quick.

TOM

[Appearing.] I will, I will. You know, I can't get over how few traces of me there are around here.

DIANNE

You're right. We'd better—I think there's an old pair of slippers of yours that we could just sort of drop in some conspicuous place.

TOM

[Still musing.] You did a pretty good job of erasing me from the scene.

DIANNE

Tom, do you want to do this or not?

TOM

[Snapping out of it.] My clothes! Won't they notice none of my clothes are here?

DIANNE

We'll keep all the closet doors shut.

TOM

What if Ben wants to see my computer? My latest annual report design?

DIANNE

[Hurrying to and fro, closing doors.] We'll keep the den door closed. If he asks, your computer is out being fixed—or you've traded it in for more RAM and you haven't got the new one yet.

TOM

My workbench. Ben'll want to see my workbench.

DIANNE

But you haven't taken that yet. It's still here.

TOM

Right. My briefcase?

DIANNE

Uhh—you left it at the office.

TOM

Good Lord, the U-Haul out front! How do we explain that?

DIANNE

I don't know. *I don't know!*

TOM

We'll think of something.

DIANNE

It might be best, the minute they get here, to suggest we go out somewhere for dinner. It's a little early, but—

TOM

Good thinking.

DIANNE

Can we all fit in my Saturn?

TOM

I doubt it. We'll go in my—

DIANNE

U-Haul? We'll take a taxi.

TOM

The slippers! Better get the slippers. Oh, and you were going to show me where the Scotch is now.

DIANNE

Oh, yes.

TOM

Do we have single malt?

DIANNE

Do you know what single malt costs?

TOM

It's what Ben prefers.

DIANNE

Let's have a look—

[The bell rings. They freeze.]

Oh my God. I think you should be the one who answers it. I mean, would you? Please?

TOM

Do I look calm?

DIANNE

Mr. Rushmore.

TOM

Let's go together.

DIANNE

I don't know what to say. First, I mean.

TOM

Whatever comes naturally.

DIANNE

Should we go holding hands?

TOM

That sounds good—no, it might be too—try to remember the way it used to be when they dropped over and—
[The doorbell rings again, this time with a shave-and-a-haircut beat.]

DIANNE

Wait. I forget, do we kiss Ben and Shirley? Or not?

TOM

Yes. No. Yes. Oh hell, here we go.
[He goes to the door and makes an elaborate gesture of opening it.]

ALL

[Shouting together, overlapping.] Hello! Hi! How are you guys? Hey, look at you! *[Etc.]*

SHIRLEY

[Enters, carrying a parcel.] Where were you two? Up in the old boudoir, I'll bet, while we freeze our derrières on the doorstep. Goddamn it, come here, you. *[She grabs* TOM *and gives him an aggressive kiss.]*

BEN

[Embracing DIANNE *and patting her behind.]* How's my favourite little bimbo? Hey, hey—happy anniversary, for Chrissake.

SHIRLEY

[Still hanging on to TOM.*]* You look terrific. You *feel* terrific.
*[*TOM *starts to cough.]*

BEN

[Still holding DIANNE.*]* This is the greatest. This is tremendous.

SHIRLEY

Together again, the old gang . . . or at least half of the old gang.

BEN

It's so damned good to be here.
[He slaps TOM *on the back.]*

TOM

It's *[cough]* good to see *[cough]*—

SHIRLEY

Here, just a little anniversary present.

DIANNE

No! You shouldn't have. *[Unwrapping the gift.]* What can this be? I'll bet—

BEN

Three guesses.

DIANNE

It's . . . Tom, it's Ben and Shirley's new book! *Rooftops of the World.* Isn't it . . . lovely! And so . . . big!

SHIRLEY

The perfect coffee-table book—all it needs are legs.

DIANNE

[Reading.] "We travel from the glazed blue tiles of Japan to the shimmering red tiles of Spain, to the intricate straw and rope roofs of Peru, arriving finally at the dramatic roofs of Canada's Houses of Parliament, glistening under a patina of softest green." Good, some Canadian content.

TOM

[Reading.] "Roofs are human beings' crowning achievement, the means by which they protect themselves from the assaults of sun and rain, snow and hail. Whether it be corrugated tin or polished slate, the roof is a ubiquitous monument to civility, a concrete metaphor for our unique quest for containment . . ."

DIANNE

[Reading.] "Photographs by Ben Forrester, text by Shirley Forrester." Thank you—it's very . . . handsome.

BEN

[Grimacing.] Hey, what's the matter around here, did the bartender die?

TOM

Sorry, I was just about to ask you what you wanted to dr—

BEN

Okay, where is it? I get first dibs on the ottoman.

TOM

Let me take your coats—

SHIRLEY

[Giving her coat to TOM.*]* You know what Ben said just before we got here?
He said, "After all the travelling we've done these last few weeks, I can't wait
to get my feet up on Tom's old ottoman."

BEN

Where is it?
*[*TOM *looks at* DIANNE.*]*

TOM

It's . . .
*[Suggested break for a three act performance: The cast freezes; lights out. The
action resumes with* TOM *repeating "It's . . ."]*

DIANNE

Not here. Wouldn't you know it! It was getting . . . pretty tattered, and the
green corduroy—

BEN

[Taking off his coat.] Wasn't it blue?
[He tosses his coat over SHIRLEY*'s on* TOM*'s arm.]*

TOM

[Struggling with the coats as if they are a terrible burden.] Turquoise.

DIANNE

It was getting so worn, it was changing colour, so Tom said—

TOM

—I said, "We should get that ottoman recovered," and Dianne said—

DIANNE

—I said . . . I said, "Right you are," but Tom said—

TOM

—I said, "I don't know if I can get along without that great old ottoman for very long—"

DIANNE

Tom likes to come home every night—

TOM

—every night—

DIANNE

—and put his feet up on that good old ottoman, and there he is, the picture of—

TOM

—contentment.
*[*TOM *finally hangs up the coats.]*

DIANNE

And I said, "Well, look, face it, you're just going to have to do without it for a couple of weeks. We'll take it over to United Upholsterers, and—"

BEN

I *love* that ottoman.

SHIRLEY

He really does, you know. Well, you know he *must* love it, to mention the damned thing on the way here—

BEN

Hey, listen. *[He takes* TOM *and* DIANNE *by the hand.]* There's nothing like coming through that door and seeing the two of you. You're looking great, Dianne. And Tom here—same old Tom. Don't they look great, Shirl?

SHIRLEY

[Slipping an arm around TOM*'s waist.]* And *feel* great.

BEN

And this house. This room. God, even the pictures on the wall—hey! What happened to the picture? You have an earthquake here?

DIANNE

I—Tom—I took it down to dust it. It's amazing how dusty—

SHIRLEY

Wait. Wait a minute. These are your old pals, Ben and Shirl, remember? No need to be embarrassed around us. That painting of Ben's *is* a bit of a relic—

BEN

I don't know about that—it's from my pink and orange period—

SHIRLEY

I can understand why you haven't had it hanging lately. You didn't really have to rush it in here just because we were coming over.

TOM

We were not just putting it up—

BEN

No?

TOM

We were taking it *down*.

DIANNE

Yes—taking it down.

TOM

But not to dust. I've never quite liked it there.

DIANNE

Neither have I. The light—

SHIRLEY

Lighting's everything! Let's see. Ben . . . *[She and* BEN *hang the picture.]* No, it doesn't look so bad there.

DIANNE

Maybe you're right—

BEN

I'm flattered that you still have it in a place of honour, I really am— *[He gives* DIANNE *an exaggerated kiss on the cheek.]*

SHIRLEY

You know, when I walked in here and saw your stuff all over the room, I thought for an awful minute that you were moving.

DIANNE

Not exactly, but—

SHIRLEY

What a relief. You just about put a half nelson on my heart, do you know that? Sometimes, when Ben and I are in Venice or Singapore or God knows where, and I'm in some four-star hotel trying to get some sleep, I just shut my eyes and conjure up good old number 182 Eldrich Crescent, Winnipeg, Manitoba, and you two guys ensconced here—

BEN

All this travelling Shirl and I do, I suppose it sounds like a helluva good life, but it gets to you. Airports, hotels, publishers, interviews, talk shows. Moving all the time, and the goddamn technology! Always changing. Do you know this new book of ours is on CD-ROM? Then we hit this city—same old icy winds howling down the same old streets—

TOM

Actually, it's been quite mild—

DIANNE

You should've been here last week—

BEN

And the people always tell you you should've been here last week—I love it! And we come out here—the same old twin dormers and the blue shutters, and we come through that door and shazam! It's like hopping into a time machine. Jesus, this is a solace to the heart.

SHIRLEY

You know, kids, there's not a lot in my life I'm proud of—I mean, let's face it, people buy our books, but who the hell ever reads them? One thing I'm pretty proud of, though—that's bringing you two together.

BEN

The chemistry was right.

SHIRLEY

The chemistry was perfect.
[A sudden silence falls.]

TOM

Well. We all deserve a drink, don't we?

BEN

[With a croaky voice.] Christ, I'm *parched.*

TOM

Port for you, Shirl—

SHIRLEY

What the hell. Make it a martini. We're celebrating here.

TOM

Ben, Scotch on the rocks, right?

BEN

Single malt only, please.

TOM

I don't know if we—

DIANNE

We sure do. It's the vermouth for the martini I don't think we—

BEN

Hell, do you think Shirl wants you to ruin the gin?

SHIRLEY

Just an eyedropper of Ben's Scotch will do the trick—

TOM

In the gin?

SHIRLEY

Duh. No, in my eye.

DIANNE

What about you, Tom?

TOM

I'll have a rum.

DIANNE

You? Rum?

TOM

Just testing. I'd like a Caesar, but I'll—

DIANNE

No, you stay right here. I'll do the honours. Make yourself at home—everybody.
[She exits.]

BEN

You know, Tom, that bride of yours looks different, somehow.

TOM

She does?

SHIRLEY

Her hair's shorter, and I think she's put on a pound or two.

BEN

She's definitely changed. *[He snaps his fingers.]* You know what it is? She's got . . . sort of an air of confidence. Independence.

TOM

Well, you know, she has her own little business now. She got kind of tired of just being a—a—an unpaid domestic. Her words.

SHIRLEY

What kind of business?

TOM

A little shop.

BEN

When did this happen?

TOM

Oh, about six months or so ago.

BEN

Terrific! Just what Dianne always needed. What kind of—no, let me guess.
A bake shop! Specializing in fancy pastries, and you call it, you call it . . .
Lady Di's, right?

TOM

Well, no—

BEN

The Cake Walk?

TOM

No—

BEN

Hart's Tarts?

SHIRLEY

Sounds like a brothel.

TOM

Crafty Cappuccino.

BEN

What?

TOM

Crafty Cappuccino. A combination coffee-roasting house and craft shop.

BEN

Beautiful!

DIANNE

[Entering with a tray of drinks.] I think this should do it.
[She hands the drinks around.]

BEN

Tom's been telling us about your little venture. Congratulations.

DIANNE

Well, thank you—

BEN

Takes a lot of capital, starting a new business.

TOM

Well, Di managed—

DIANNE

I found a good backer.

SHIRLEY

[Raising her glass.] Here's to Looms and Lattes or whatever you call it—

BEN

And to your anniversary, for Chrissake.
[They all take good swigs of their drinks.]
Ahhh. Glenmorangie, am I right?

DIANNE

I—I think so.

BEN

You know what goes good with Glenmorangie? *[He reaches into his inside pocket and pulls out a large cigar.]* Especially purchased for this occasion in Monte Cristo's Cigar Lounge in Toronto. Hand-rolled on the thigh of a Cuban virgin . . .

TOM

I—I thought you'd given up smoking.

SHIRLEY

He doesn't inhale—or at least that's what he says.

DIANNE

Are you going to light up in here?

BEN

If you don't—

DIANNE

Tom's asthma—

TOM

My—?

BEN

I didn't know—

SHIRLEY

You never used to mind when I was a two-packs-a-day chick.

DIANNE

We were so happy when you quit—for your sake—

BEN

Mind if I—you know—just sort of chew it?

TOM

No, no. Ben, go ahead. Chew away.

SHIRLEY

[As BEN *unwraps the cigar.]* This shop of yours, Di. Is it all dried flowers and doorstops dressed as grandmothers—that sort of thing?

DIANNE

And coffee roasted right on the premises.

BEN

Pretty gutsy, getting a new business on its feet these days.

TOM

I wasn't so sure about it at first. I thought the two of us might team up—

DIANNE

But I didn't think it was a good idea to put all our eggs in one basket—

SHIRLEY

Or all your Christmas decorations on one tree—

BEN

Or all your beans in one roaster—

SHIRLEY

You know, Ben and I've worked together for a long time now, but it's not the best idea. No, I mean it, Ben, let me finish. Professional jealousy and all that. It stings sometimes. Ben's been in a big funk all week because—

BEN

Correction—a small funk. Bloody *Maclean's* thought my photographs—in the new book?—were "a touch baroque." Baroque!

SHIRLEY

They loved my text.

BEN

One chimney angle too many, they said. Bloody ignorant ignoramuses.

SHIRLEY

Take it from old Shirl here. You're smart to keep your careers separate. And I'll bet it keeps the old you-know-what alive in your—

DIANNE

Well—

SHIRLEY

When two people see each other all day, every day, the romance starts to get a *leetle* bit—I'll let you in on a secret.

DIANNE

Tell us.

TOM

What?

SHIRLEY

Well, sometimes, once in a while, Ben and I . . . dress up—

BEN

Shirl—

SHIRLEY

They'll get a kick out of this.

BEN

For the love of Pete.

SHIRLEY

Sometimes, when things get a little, you know, humdrum, well, Ben and I dress up and pretend we're—

BEN

—other people.

TOM

You do?

DIANNE

Go on.

SHIRLEY

Call it role-playing. I've got this Dolly Parton platinum wig and this clingy red sequined gown that I can hardly walk in, and Ben wears his tux and a bunch of rings and he's the showbiz impresario who's taking this flashy new torch singer out on the town.
[She stands and snake-hips across the room.]

BEN

Crazy broad.

SHIRLEY

And hey, this'll knock your eyebrows off—we've got this other routine where Ben gets into his blue tights and—

BEN

Is nothing sacred?

SHIRLEY

And picture this—a red cape, and me in my Lois Lane gear—

BEN

They get the idea, kiddo.

SHIRLEY

No, take it from Auntie Shirl, you're better off, Di, in your knick-knack and decaf store and Thomas in his graphics business—

BEN

[Clears his throat.] Still playing bridge?

DIANNE

Well, since Tom became president of the local chapter of the Endangered Species Society, we're both so incredibly busy—

TOM

I'm not that busy.

DIANNE

Four nights a week. You don't call that busy?

TOM

The fact is, we've had some close calls in this province. I guess you've heard about our problems with the burrowing owl—

SHIRLEY

Well, no, I can't say that I—

TOM

The problem is, it burrows, as you'd expect it to, but it burrows down in the ground, going after mice, and the mice are full of potent chemicals and—

BEN

So the mice are dead.

TOM

That's the curious thing. The chemicals don't hurt the mice, only the owls that eat the mice.

SHIRLEY

So, you're saying, one man's poison is—

BEN

—is sauce for the gander. Or something.

TOM

And then there's the piping plover—

DIANNE

Tom, I'm not sure Ben and Shirl want to discuss—

TOM

The problem with the piping plover is habitat. These birds are victims of our changing world. Suddenly there aren't enough nesting places for them.

SHIRLEY

Hey, it's a big country. I'm sure if your piping—?

TOM

—plovers.

SHIRLEY

I'm sure if they really wanted to . . . *nest [rolling her eyes]* . . . well, they'd find a way.

TOM

You'd think so, but nesting isn't that easy for highly specialized species. Conditions have to be just right. They lay their eggs on beaches, you see, so they've got to be out in the open, and yet not *too* out in the open or their predators—

BEN

These seem like pretty damn fussy birds to me. Most of us can't afford to be that choosy, we *nest* where we have to nest—

SHIRLEY

Make the best of things—like, what kind of choice do *we* get anyway? And believe me, there are plenty of predators out there to make things messy. Maybe I should tell you about—

BEN

Skip it, Shirl. Not tonight. We're here to celebrate old times. Wasn't it you, Tom, who got the Crazy Eights going?

TOM

I think it was you and Shirl—

SHIRLEY

That was a damned long time ago.

BEN

You know, Shirl and I've been married so long, we're on our second bottle of Tabasco sauce.

SHIRLEY

Hell of a lot of water under the bridge, all right.

BEN

Speaking of water under the bridge, any of you remember how we spent your first wedding anniversary?

DIANNE

Here we go!

SHIRLEY

Wasn't that the year we went to Whitefish Lake, all eight of us? Thomas here talked Ben and you and me into taking out a canoe when not one of us had a clue—

TOM

You talked *us* into it—

SHIRLEY

You came on as if you were the expert! You'd been a counsellor at Camp Stevens—

TOM

I had not! I was never—

SHIRLEY

You were the first one in the canoe.

DIANNE

He was in the back—

BEN

—giving directions—

DIANNE

—yelling, "J-stroke, J-stroke!"

TOM

No, I was in the front—

BEN

Yeah, I think you're right. You should've been in the back, but . . . I was in the back. I was here, right?
[He gets down on the floor to demonstrate.]

DIANNE

[Also getting down.] I was here and, Shirl, you were there.
[She indicates the space between herself and BEN.]

SHIRLEY

No, no, I was here, in front of you.
[She gets down.]

DIANNE

Okay—yes. *[Pushing herself back closer to* BEN.*]* Yes, this is how we were.

SHIRLEY

[Grabbing TOM*'s hand and pulling him down.]* You were here, Tomcat, right in front of old pal Shirley.

TOM

Like this?

SHIRLEY

[Wrapping her legs around TOM.*]* Yeah, that's better—

TOM

Hey, this is a boat, not a bobsled.

BEN

So there we were, and someone—was it me or you, Tom?—said, "Look out for the goddamn pier!"

SHIRLEY

It was Di. I remember her yelling like it was yesterday. Only, it was more like "Holy mackerel, what's *that?*"

DIANNE

We were heading straight for that concrete pillar—

SHIRLEY

And we were all paddling like mad and the damned canoe wouldn't—

BEN

And Tom kept yelling, "J-stroke!"

TOM

I don't think it was me—

BEN

And o-o-over we went!
[They all tumble onto the floor.]

SHIRLEY

And the water was like ice—

DIANNE

And Shirl, you were hanging on to Tom's jacket and—

TOM

—dragging me down—

SHIRLEY

—screaming like mad and Di was—

DIANNE

—screaming at everybody to hang on to the boat and Ben was—

BEN

—yelling at Tom, and Tom was yelling—

TOM

I wasn't yelling. I was under the water.

DIANNE

And I said—

SHIRLEY

You said, "My brand new wristwatch, one day old."

BEN

How did we get out?

DIANNE

Wasn't it—

TOM

Gordie and Lou. In that old rowboat.

SHIRLEY

Gordie and Lou to the rescue! Of course.

DIANNE

They wrapped us in blankets—

BEN

—and gave us some hot drinks and we all got high as kites—

SHIRLEY

I guess you heard about Gordie and Lou.

DIANNE

We heard.

SHIRLEY

He actually married that Cathi. With an *i*.

BEN

Genevieve and Whitney, too.

TOM

We know.

BEN

Ran off with her fencing instructor.

SHIRLEY

Those who live by the sword, die by the sword, if you know what I mean.

DIANNE

I thought he was her personal trainer—

TOM

Can I get up now?

SHIRLEY

Not till you say the magic words.

TOM

Another martini?

SHIRLEY

Mind reader.
[She untangles herself and gets up.]

TOM

[Getting up.] Another Scotch, Ben?

BEN

[As he and DIANNE get up.] I won't say no.

DIANNE

[To TOM.] You sure you can find—

TOM

Certainly.
[He exits to the kitchen.]

SHIRLEY

I don't want to seem too personal, Di, but what's bugging old John Thomas?

DIANNE

Why, nothing—

BEN

He sort of seems not quite the same somehow.

SHIRLEY

The first thing I thought when I walked in here was, Tom's looking pale.

DIANNE

Pale?

BEN

I wouldn't have said pale, Shirl. I thought he looked a bit flushed.

DIANNE

Flushed?

SHIRLEY

Well, under the flush, he looks . . . pale. Like he's been under a strain sort-of-thing.

DIANNE

The Endangered Species Society does keep him—right now, he's worried about the small white lady's slipper—

SHIRLEY

Screw the small white lady's slipper! I look into those beautiful brown eyes and I see a man in turmoil.

BEN

If something's bothering Tom, he can tell us. I mean, what are old friends for? *[Silence.]* I think that's a good question. I'm going to try it again. Here goes: What are old friends for? *[Silence.]* Let me ask the wallpaper: What are old friends for?

SHIRLEY

I'm not just some ship passing in the night, for God's sake. Tom and I, we went under the water together, remember? The two of us.

DIANNE

I think . . . with the two of you arriving out of the blue like this . . . well, he was just *surprised*.

SHIRLEY

Hey, hey, hey, that doesn't sound like the Tom and Di that I used to know. The Tom and Di that I used to know loved surprises.

TOM

[Entering, holding a champagne bottle aloft.] Surprise! Look what I found in the fridge. Champagne. Dianne, you actually—

DIANNE

But I didn't—

TOM

[To DIANNE.*]* That was nice. That was very nice. Our anniversary! I can't tell you how nice—I mean, that *says* something.

DIANNE

No, it *doesn't*.

TOM

Just a second—I'll get the drinks.
[He exits, leaving the champagne on the dining room table.]

SHIRLEY

That was so sweet of you, Di.

DIANNE

I didn't—

BEN

It means a lot to Tom. He's beaming!

TOM

[Returning with the drinks.] I never expected—what a surprise!

SHIRLEY

We were just talking about surprises. Remember those last-minute potlucks? Half an hour's notice and Di would have one of her famous pastas whipped up.

BEN

And a bottle of wine and we'd be launched for the night. Good old Crazy Eights. We had some good times.

SHIRLEY

[After a long pull of her martini.] Is something bugging you, Tom?

TOM

Not now, that's for sure. I mean, right now, I feel—

BEN

Before, when we first arrived. Shirl noticed something different. You know Shirl, she's got an instinct for these things.

SHIRLEY

A sort of sixth sense. I can sniff things out. Come on, Tom, you can level with us. Did you have something else planned for tonight, you and Di?

DIANNE

No, it isn't that—

BEN

A cozy dinner. Followed by—

TOM

No, nothing like that—

SHIRLEY

Well, what is it, then? Tom, take the four of us. If one of the four notices that another of the four is acting sort of distant or different or . . . vulnerable . . . in some way, shouldn't the first of the four mention it to the second of the four?

TOM

Well, sure—

SHIRLEY

Then what's bugging you, Tom?

TOM

[Looking at DIANNE.*]* The fact is, there's something I should've told you—

DIANNE

Tom—

TOM

This may not be what you want to hear, but—

SHIRLEY

Spill it all out, kid. We're all friends here, remember?

DIANNE

Tom, you don't have to—

TOM

It's just that . . .

SHIRLEY

You can do it!

TOM

This may come as something of a surprise . . .

SHIRLEY

Yes? Yes?

TOM

Dianne and I . . . Dianne and I . . .

BEN

[Jubilant.] Hey, hey, hey! I think I can guess.

SHIRLEY

Jesus H. Christ, so can I!

BEN

Why didn't you tell us the minute we walked in?

DIANNE

Well, we—

BEN

Didn't I tell you Dianne was looking different? I noticed!

SHIRLEY

A few pounds, I said.

TOM

We never expected it would happen to us. Other people, yes, but we were
the last—

DIANNE

We should've told you right away, but—

SHIRLEY

I just hope you'll keep working, Di. It'd be a shame to give that up—

TOM

Wait, what is it we're—

SHIRLEY

Di, lots of women your age—

DIANNE

I know, I'm not that old—

BEN

I say congratulations!
[BEN *shakes* TOM's *hand.*]

TOM

You do?

SHIRLEY

And I say, the more the merrier!
[SHIRLEY *kisses* DIANNE *on the cheek.*]

BEN

Let's get that champagne opened and we'll propose a toast to the new little—
[*The doorbell rings.*]

TOM

I'll get it.
[*He goes to the door.*]

SHIRLEY

Who could! that be? More people to wish you well?

GARTH

[Entering on Rollerblades and carrying a short stack of white takeout boxes.]
Hey, gang! Anyone like some sushi?
[End of Act One.]

Act Two

At rise, the five people are exactly where we left them at the end of Act One.
DIANNE, BEN *and* SHIRLEY *are seated in the living room.* TOM *has just answered the door and is holding it open.* GARTH *is inside, holding up the boxes for all to see.*

DIANNE

[Leaping to her feet.] Garth! Sushi! What an angel of mercy! We were just saying how famished we are.

TOM

We were?

BEN

[Rising.] I don't believe I've—

DIANNE

[Turning to the others.] Out of the winter and the night comes our very own rescue dog.

GARTH

Dog?

DIANNE

Ben, Shirley. I'd like you to meet Garth Morton. Garth, this is Ben and Shirley Forrester . . . and of course you know Tom.

GARTH

[Confused but ready to follow DIANNE*'s lead.]* Hey, Ben!
[He balances the boxes on one arm so that he can shake BEN*'s hand.]*

BEN

Great timing, Garth.

TOM

Yeah, great.

GARTH

Tom. Hey, Shirley!

SHIRLEY

[Getting up and moving toward GARTH.*]* Well, hel-lo, Garth.
[She shakes his hand.]
So, this is the surprise you were saving for Di, Tom.

BEN

I'll bet half an hour from now somebody's going to arrive with a cake.

SHIRLEY

So—you live in the neighbourhood, Garth?

GARTH

No, but—

BEN

Great neighbourhood. Quiet. Settled. You involved in the Endangered Species Society?

SHIRLEY

You look like a rare specimen to me—but definitely not a burrowing owl.

GARTH

I'm—

DIANNE

[Flurried, hostessy, speaking with great deliberation.] Garth is a friend. Garth, Ben and Shirley introduced Tom and me way back when and today, *which is our wedding anniversary*—bet you didn't know that—they decided to surprise us—

SHIRLEY

Hey, don't forget to tell him I was your matron of honour. Gorgeous wedding, Garth. You should've been there. Of course, you would've been about twelve years old.

DIANNE

Here, let me take those.
[She takes the boxes from GARTH.*]*
Do you think there's enough?

GARTH

I *didn't* know it was your anniversary—

DIANNE

Well—Tom and I don't make a big thing out of anniversaries . . . anymore.

TOM

Oh? I wouldn't say that. *[Holding the bottle of champagne aloft.]* Champagne in the fridge—now that says something. That says a lot.

GARTH

The champagne in the . . . that's—

DIANNE

Tom, you open the bottle while Shirley and I put out the sushi.
[She moves to the dining table and sets the boxes down.]
I'll get the plates.
[She goes to the kitchen and brings them out while SHIRLEY *is opening the boxes.]*

SHIRLEY

Ahh—let's see . . . there's the eel . . . oh good, the satanically hot wasabi sauce . . . pickled ginger . . . nori maki . . . sashimi . . . Here, Tom, try a California roll.

TOM

[Working at the cork.] Uh—no, thanks.

DIANNE

You love fish. Especially the endangered ones.
*[*TOM *pops the cork.]*

TOM

Ahhh.

DIANNE

And small shrimp, well-steamed.
*[*DIANNE *hands out glasses, and* TOM *pours as* BEN *speaks.]*

BEN

You know, Garth, I was the best man, so it's only fitting that I propose the toast. Everybody got some poison? A little more there, Tom boy. Okay. To Dianne and Tom Hart on the occasion of their twelfth wedding anniversary—Shirl, what's the gift for twelve?

SHIRLEY

Silk, isn't it?

BEN

May the future shimmer like a fine silk gown—

SHIRLEY

You're veering toward the baroque again, Ben boy.

BEN

And to our friendship.

DIANNE, TIM, SHIRLEY AND BEN

To our friendship. *[Etc.]*

SHIRLEY

Garth, you too. Don't be shy.

GARTH

To friendship.

SHIRLEY

To Gordie and Lou—damn them, anyway—

BEN

To Genevieve and Whitney, you scoundrels, wherever the hell you are.

SHIRLEY

And here's to nesting.

BEN

One more toast. And this one, ladies and gentlemen, I mean from the heart. Shirl and I rejoice with you in the good—the *marvellous*—news, and I want to propose a toast—are you ready, everyone?—a toast to the new addition.

SHIRLEY

I'll drink to that.
[Puzzled, GARTH *drinks along with the others.* TOM *and* DIANNE *stand with their glasses untouched, staring.]*

GARTH

I think I missed that last bit. The new . . .?

BEN

Addition.

DIANNE

It's nothing, Garth.

TOM

Private joke.

GARTH

Addition? You mean you're going to go ahead and enlarge the bathroom the way we—

BEN

Not that kind of addition, my friend—

SHIRLEY

Oh God, I hope we haven't boobed. Old blabbergums here.

BEN

How was I supposed to—you said Garth was a friend, so naturally I assumed—

DIANNE

[To change the subject.] I'm starving! *[Putting some sushi on a plate.]* Let's dig in, shall we? Shirl, have this—

SHIRLEY

Wait, Di. Now that the cat's out of the bag, how far along are you?

DIANNE

I—

GARTH

"How far along are you?"

DIANNE

Tom—here, try this—with a little pickled ginger—

GARTH

Dianne, what did Mrs. Forrester mean when she said—

SHIRLEY

Mrs. Forrester? Look, Garth, I'm Shirl to the world so I'm Shirl to you, all right? We were just drinking a toast—and by the way, I could use a top-me-up—a toast to the new little one.

GARTH

The new little one.

TOM

Ben, some more Scotch?

BEN

Damn right. Best thing to chase down the champagne.

GARTH

This is an in-joke, right?

DIANNE

[Desperately.] Shirl needs another martini, too. And we could use some napkins. Come on, Tom, you and I can—
[DIANNE and TOM exit to the kitchen.]

GARTH

I have to sit down.
[He drops into an armchair and lifts his feet as if to put them onto something; he looks around, and then sets his feet on the floor.]

SHIRLEY

They sent it to the upholsterers.

BEN

I loved that ottoman.

GARTH

Me too. When did they send it?

BEN

Last week, I think Di said.

GARTH

I swear it was here—

SHIRLEY

Don't you ever take those Rollerblades off?

GARTH

Sorry—
[He begins to take them off.]

BEN

It's not just the ottoman—I'm pretty crazy about this painting, too.
[He picks up the picture.]

SHIRLEY

I'll let you in on another secret, Garth. Ben painted that. We gave it to Tom
and Dianne for a wedding present.

GARTH

It's impossible.

BEN

Hey, listen! I used to knock off some not-bad landscapes—

GARTH

I mean, it's impossible that Dianne is pregnant.
[The Rollerblades are now off, revealing loud coloured socks.]

SHIRLEY

The mysteries of human biology do unfold in strange but inevitable ways.

GARTH

She would've told me.

BEN

Forgive me, Garth, but are you a *very* close friend?

GARTH

Very, very.

SHIRLEY

You see, we are very, very, very, *very* close old, old, old friends, so it was only natural that they told us.

BEN

But it took them a while before they worked up to it. We aren't based here anymore, so we don't see each other as often as we used to. Well, Shirl had to sort of bang Tom on the head and drag it out of him.

SHIRLEY

I could tell the minute I walked in here that something was in the air—I've got these deep intuitions—so I just hammered away. I mean, what the hell are friends for?

BEN

Damned good question.

GARTH

Impossible—

SHIRLEY

Let me level with you, Garth. Are you married?

GARTH

No. I mean, I was once, but—

SHIRLEY

When women reach a certain age and they've had their heir and a spare, they're not exactly jumping for joy when they find out they're going to get in to the diaper business again.

BEN

It takes a certain amount of adjustment—

SHIRLEY

—and supportive friends.

BEN

Friends like you, Garth, can really help by showing how pleased they are to hear the good news.

SHIRLEY

Do you have kids? You and your ex?

GARTH

No, we made a decision not to—

BEN

Like Shirl and me here.

SHIRLEY

Well, that decision was made for us—

BEN

More or less. But let's not get into—

SHIRLEY

Just one of the many, *many* adjustments in a long relationship.
[DIANNE *and* TOM *come back in, carrying drinks and napkins and a tossed salad.*]
Garth was just telling us about *his* marriage.

DIANNE

Oh?

BEN

How long were you married?

GARTH

Two years. Long enough to—

SHIRLEY

Two years! I'll bet you hardly had time to unpack the china and sort out the socks.

GARTH

Long enough to know we were headed in different directions.

BEN

How so?

GARTH

[Tearing at a piece of fish.] She liked polyester sheets and I liked cotton. I liked porridge and she liked muesli. I bought a Jeep and she traded it in on a Volvo.

SHIRLEY

You mean you split up over consumer preferences?

GARTH

We knew our relationship was over. And we had the guts to make a clean break of it.

SHIRLEY

You know who a breakup hurts the most?

TOM AND GARTH

[Coincidentally in unison.] Who?

SHIRLEY

The couple's friends.

DIANNE

Ben, you haven't had any Shirley. I mean *sushi*.

SHIRLEY

Yep, it's the friends who suffer. Look, suppose Ben and I decided to split up. Admit it—you'd both be heartbroken about it. It wouldn't feel right. We wouldn't be a foursome anymore.

BEN

Just like we're not an eightsome anymore.

SHIRLEY

[Silence.] Okay, I guess I *do* want an answer. If Ben and I were to call it quits, how much would you, our old friends, mind?

GARTH

I'd say, go for it!

BEN

Would anyone mind if I lit up this cigar?

DIANNE

Go ahead. Just go ahead.
[He does.]

SHIRLEY

Every time Ben has to face the truth, he lights up a cigar. It's his way of . . . burrowing.

GARTH

Personally, I think marriage can be a form of slavery if you hang in there just because you made a promise in front of a few friends in some frothing adolescent moment—

BEN

I don't think Shirley and I—*[he puffs on his cigar]* went into our marriage in a state of frothing—

SHIRLEY

In fact, a bit of froth might've livened things up a bit.

TOM

Hey, wait, you aren't really—

DIANNE

You aren't saying—I mean, this is a hypothetical situation you're setting up here.

SHIRLEY

What if . . . what if I were to say that Ben's been offered a teaching job in California—

BEN

A regular salary, not so much running around—

GARTH

I'd say, go for it!

SHIRLEY

And what if I were to say there's a novel in me just crying to be born and the only place it can be properly nurtured is in the B.C. interior—

DIANNE

Shirl, this is crazy. I'm not going to listen to this kind of talk—Ben, tell us she's not serious.

BEN

[Putting out the cigar rather vigorously.] Well, now, just a damned minute here.

TOM

Superman and Lois Lane! Come on, you're still the wild and crazy pair—

BEN

I know, I know—hey, look, sometimes we pretend we're about to split up, that we're headed for separate lives—

SHIRLEY

And the best part of the game is the last part, or at least it used to be. The kiss-and-make-up part. Is anything sweeter than that?

DIANNE

It's all a game, then. You're just—

TOM

—toying with—

GARTH

It doesn't sound like a game to me. It sounds like the end. Full stop. Thirty. Curtain.

DIANNE

Oh, be quiet, Garth.

TOM

No one throws away fourteen years.

BEN

Fifteen and a half.

SHIRLEY

They do, Tom. Oh, they do. And maybe that's where we're at.

DIANNE

Counselling! Have you tried marriage counselling?

TOM

If you make a real effort to stand back and see where you failed—

DIANNE

Sometimes you have to negotiate a new contract because—

TOM

—because people change. Nobody stands still. We say things are over—

DIANNE

You know, I never did explain why I got into the coffee and crafts business. As a matter of fact, no one's actually asked me.

BEN

I was just about to ask you that, Di. How did you get into the coffee and crafts business?

DIANNE

Well, I thought to myself, Something's missing in my life, so what should I do? Then I asked myself, What are the things I love? Well, I love coffee, good coffee, the smell of good coffee. And I love to be around things, beautiful things that people make with their own hands.

SHIRLEY

Pot holders, pots—

BEN

—those wire candle-holder thingamajigs—

DIANNE

Yes, yes. Some of it's art and some of it isn't, but it's still something people put together carefully. And more and more I've been thinking—I've had a lot of time to think lately—and it seems to me that's what love and friendship are. They're these handmade *things*. It's this *stuff*. You have to pat it into shape, you have to tend to it, pay attention to it. You can have the mass-produced kind, but who wants it?

SHIRLEY

Not me.

DIANNE

Like, maybe you and Ben feel your marriage has turned into a piece of dried wood—

TOM

—but you scratch the surface—

DIANNE

—and you find there's something alive—

TOM

—and breathing inside, which you'd almost forgotten.

GARTH

Or you scratch a living relationship and find it's dead inside.

DIANNE

Oh, who asked *you?*

BEN

Know what Shirl did in the cab on the way over here? Rode in the front with the cabby and told him he had a nice meter.

TOM

Well, maybe you have to listen to what the other person is saying—

DIANNE

Just what I was going to say.

TOM

You have to *really* listen, not just to the words. You have to say, "What does this person want?"

DIANNE

People can become more flexible if—

TOM

—if they think it's going to be worth it—

DIANNE

—and quite often it is worth it—

TOM

—if you just hang in there long enough—

GARTH

Speaking from experience, I've never looked back. The way I see it, life's a card game. And you have to do a certain amount of discarding.

DIANNE

[Raising her voice.] Two years! Garth, two years is a long weekend!

SHIRLEY

Why are you yelling?

DIANNE

I . . . I don't know.

BEN

I think I do.

SHIRLEY

Because old friends don't want to be levelled with. They say they do, but they don't. Shake old friends up and they start feeling insecure.

GARTH

True. I mean, suppose the situation were reversed. Suppose—

DIANNE

Garth—

GARTH

Just suppose that Dianne and Tom here—

BEN

Our old friends, the friends of our youth. Garth, do you know what Shirley and I gave each other? What Tom and Di gave each other? Our young hearts. Our young bodies. You can't do that again; you only get to do that once.

GARTH

But what *if* Tom and Dianne split up and you'd just found out about it. As old friends, how would you react?

SHIRLEY

I could handle it. I think. But I'd feel kinda bad about the baby.

DIANNE

For God's sake, there is no—

SHIRLEY

Then I'd probably act like most people. I'd be damned mad at them because we wouldn't be a foursome anymore.

GARTH

Maybe you'd envy them for being able to handle a purely natural development in a mature and honest way.

SHIRLEY

Maybe, but either way, I'd probably never see them again. Or want to see them.

DIANNE

Oh, Shirl—

SHIRLEY

And given my current shaky circumstances, I might even make a play for Tom. Because I always did—

GARTH

Aha!

BEN

Christ!

SHIRLEY

Oh, you're all getting so bloody uptight! Mind if I help myself to another martini?

DIANNE

I'll get it.

SHIRLEY

Let me.

DIANNE

You'll need the new bottle of gin—down in the cupboard, under the sink.
[SHIRLEY exits.]
Ben, this is just a passing phase of Shirl's, isn't it?

BEN

Sorry, little bimbo. I'm afraid it's more than that. Forgive us for dumping on your anniversary.

TOM

Maybe . . . maybe . . . after a few months apart you'll decide you really . . . that sometimes happens—

GARTH

I wouldn't give you odds. I've got a theory. When you unravel a sweater, you can't ever knit it together again. All you get is a scarf.

TOM

I'd rather have a scarf than nothing.

DIANNE

No. Nobody should settle for a scarf. I mean that, Tom.

TOM

Take the case of the small white lady's slipper—

DIANNE

Tom, is this really the time to—

TOM

There's something frightening about the small white lady's slipper. It's beautiful—that's part of the problem—so people pick it. But once you pick it, it won't seed again in that spot, it doesn't re-establish itself easily like other plants. It's as though it loses a sense of trust . . .

BEN

What exactly is your point, Tom?

TOM

I . . . don't . . . know.
[SHIRLEY *enters with a green garbage bag and dumps it upside down on the floor.*]

SHIRLEY

Look what I found.

GARTH

Hey, that looks like—

DIANNE

It was falling apart. We're having it renovated—

TOM

In actual fact, the ottoman is no more. It has been . . . dispatched.

DIANNE

De-acquisitioned.

TOM

It's toast.

SHIRLEY

Why didn't you tell us?

DIANNE

We didn't want—

TOM

We didn't want to hurt Ben's feelings. We know how much he liked it.

GARTH

It looked okay this morning.

SHIRLEY

Just happened to be skating by this morning, Garth?

DIANNE

How about a singsong? A game of charades? Books. Five words.

BEN

You Can't Go Home Again.

SHIRLEY

How Green Is My Valley. [*Sadly.*] *How Green Was My Valley.*

TOM

Wait. I think it's time we got a few things out in the air.

GARTH

Now you're talking! One thing I've learned—

DIANNE

One thing! You've only learned *one* thing?

GARTH

I'm just at the beginning of the journey—

SHIRLEY

Journey? Life's a bus stop, not a journey.

GARTH

I do my best thinking on buses. I look around at all those sad faces, those eyes and noses and mouths and teeth, and I ask myself, what do they want?

SHIRLEY

And?

GARTH

They want . . . some . . . one.

TOM

[To BEN.*]* We're old friends, right?

BEN

Right.

TOM

Well, I'm not sure what old friends are for.

BEN

Exactly the question I was asking earlier, but nobody—

SHIRLEY

Old friends are people you can level with.

BEN

Old friends are an endangered species. Like old marriages.

TOM

There's a difference between endangered and threatened, remember. Two separate categories.

BEN

You've got to be able to tell an old friend you threw out his favourite piece of furniture.

SHIRLEY

Ben and I tried to share something with you here tonight. We said to each other that our oldest friends had to be the first to know—

DIANNE

But we haven't seen you in—what is it?—four years?

SHIRLEY

There was a time when you would've offered us a bed. We get pretty damn sick of hotels, let me tell you—

TOM

Do you know something? If you're both such good old friends, tell me this How come neither of you has asked one question about the kids?

SHIRLEY

The kids! How are they, Timmy and that cute little Tory! The little rascals!

BEN

Bless their hearts. *[To* SHIRLEY.*]* It's Terry and Todd.

DIANNE, TOM AND GARTH

[In unison.] Tracy and Troy!

SHIRLEY

Well, for crying in the sink, neither of you has asked about my mother.

DIANNE

Your mother! How is she? I always adored your—

SHIRLEY

Dead.

TOM

My God, Shirl, I'm really sorry—you should've let us know.

SHIRLEY

You're probably all sitting here wondering, what did she die of and did she suffer and when was it and—

DIANNE

What did she die of?

TOM

Did she suffer?

GARTH

When was it?

SHIRLEY

[Weeping.] Two years ago, in White Rock. She was run down by a truck loaded with dried apricots.

BEN

Take it easy, Shirl. Don't go and get all worked up—

DIANNE

Why didn't you write us, Shirl?

SHIRLEY

When was the last time *you* wrote *us?*

DIANNE

At Christmas, I always try—

BEN

We got your card.

SHIRLEY

A *year ago* last Christmas.

BEN

Was it a year ago?

SHIRLEY

Yup. "Best wishes, Tom and Di." Real newsy.

TOM

Di's been pretty busy with the business. Christmas is a peak time in crafts, you know—

SHIRLEY

Haven't you ever heard of the Internet?

DIANNE

I—we haven't got your e-mail address—

SHIRLEY

You could've faxed us!

DIANNE

Tom told you—we're both busy—

SHIRLEY

You know how busy *we* are, and I mean *busy*-busy, but we always find time to send a proper Christmas message. I believe we sent yours by snail mail.

TOM

A proper Christmas message!

DIANNE

Do you mean that photocopied newsletter? That recital of triumphs and trips—

TOM

"Ben's picked up his third Stanbury Award and—"

DIANNE

"Shirl's latest plaything is silver and scarlet with mag wheels—"

TOM

"Two weeks in Palm Springs—"

DIANNE

"Then off to Mount Fuji in March—"

GARTH

My ex-wife? She sends out six-page, single-spaced typewritten Christmas letters—they're a sort of chronicle of all the different places she's been laid in the past year.

SHIRLEY

Clear Lake? Grand Beach? Lac du Bonnet?

GARTH

No, the kitchen table, the hammock, the stairs—

SHIRLEY

A joke, right?

GARTH

No, she—

SHIRLEY

Right?

GARTH

Right.

SHIRLEY

So why d'you want to make a joke out of your own . . . your own—

GARTH

My own failure? I don't know. You tell me.

BEN

Because you haven't faced up to it yet. That's my guess.

DIANNE

That's not true. Garth told me he's—

SHIRLEY

What does your ex really put in her Christmas letters?

GARTH

She doesn't send Christmas letters. She's not organized enough for Christmas letters. She's a mess since the divorce. So am I. As you may have noticed.

DIANNE

I thought you said you were healing. You told me—

SHIRLEY

You want to put this behind you, Garth. Accept your grief. Heal.

GARTH

You know, I wonder what makes people feel they have the right to counsel others. Does a little light go on, letting you know you're old enough and smart enough now to dispense the soothing syrup of wisdom to those of us who sit at the children's table?

DIANNE

Shirley only meant—

GARTH

Shirley doesn't know one damn thing about my grief.

SHIRLEY

I'd be happy to listen.

GARTH

And I don't want Shirley to know about my grief. My grief belongs to me and my ex. I just met you a few minutes ago, Shirley, and you want my grief. Well, it's *mine*, and it's . . . it's sacred.

DIANNE

We just thought you'd feel better—

GARTH

I don't tell you everything I feel, Dianne. I can't. And you know something? You haven't really asked. Maybe you've noticed that *I'm* the one who asks *you* questions. You never ask me anything.

DIANNE

You're a great listener, I've told you that—

GARTH

You never ask me about love. Did I love my ex? What is love anyway? What's it for?

BEN

Good question, Garth, good question. I was wondering what friendship was for, but love is even more . . . uh—

DIANNE

I don't think anyone knows what love is for.

GARTH

It keeps us from crying in the dark, that's what it's for.

SHIRLEY

Two people can cry in the dark—

BEN

They can cry right in each other's goddamn faces—

GARTH

That's what I mean. That's what I'm telling you, but no one listens to a man on Rollerblades.

DIANNE

I didn't know, Garth. I mean, you never expressed—

GARTH

Love. Friendship. It's awful—half the time it's hell—but at the same time it's full of noise, and we need that noise. It keeps us—

TOM

—out of danger.

SHIRLEY

Safe. Or pretending to be safe.

DIANNE

But . . . should we go on pretending forever?

BEN

At least we call you guys when we're in town.

DIANNE

And we appreciate it—

BEN

So why didn't you call us last year when you were in Vancouver?

DIANNE

I wasn't—

TOM

How—

SHIRLEY

July, wasn't it? Cy Hendrickson swears he saw you at the airport.

TOM

I was just passing through. Just going to a design conference in San Francisco.

SHIRLEY

And you didn't have a quarter for the phone, right?

BEN

We would've come to the airport to see you.

TOM

You were probably in Singapore.

BEN

Well, if we weren't in Singapore, we would've come out to see you.

SHIRLEY

Anyhoo, we arrive in town and we come over to see you, and what happens? Tom goes into his stranger act, and then we hear about a baby that may or may not be on the way, and then you've got this visiting jock who seems to have moved in—

TOM

My workbench. My lathe. You haven't asked me anything about my lathe.

DIANNE

Tom, you haven't used your lathe in ten years.

SHIRLEY

Then there's *The Edible Woman.*

TOM

What's she got to do with this?

SHIRLEY

Margaret Atwood's *The Edible Woman.*

TOM

I—

SHIRLEY

You borrowed it from me, remember? You were going to return it just as soon as—

TOM

I'll mail it to you. I can't put my hands on it right this minute, but I'll mail it—

BEN

You probably haven't even read our book on fences.

SHIRLEY

Fences of the World. [Looking around.] I don't see it anywhere.

DIANNE

I'm sure we had a copy, didn't we, Tom?

TOM

No.

BEN

No?

DIANNE

No, we didn't. Have a copy. No, we never bought a copy.

SHIRLEY

Okay, okay, so you never bought a copy. Is that going to affect our sales figures?

DIANNE

While we're being honest, I have to tell you—

TOM

Don't, Di—

GARTH

Go for it, Dianne!

DIANNE

It's about that cigar. You asked if I minded if you smoked a cigar.
[Shouting.] I mind! I really mind! And it gives Tom hives.

BEN

Sorry. Well, I don't know if you know this, but I've had a very serious oper-
ation. Major surgery.

DIANNE

It was in your newsletter.

TOM

I was out of work for three months last winter when the firm laid off a
bunch of us.

SHIRLEY

Tough. I've got fibroids. Ever had fibroids?

GARTH

Coffee, anyone?

SHIRLEY

What?

GARTH

I thought I might make some coffee if you—

SHIRLEY

You certainly do make yourself at home here, don't you?

DIANNE

Garth and I are neighbours in the shopping mall. He works in the sporting goods store next door—

SHIRLEY

And he's also the resident caterer. Tell me, Garth, are you the resident anything else?

BEN

Hey, hey, let's all kiss and make up and stop being so New Age honest—

TOM

It might be more honest to kiss and say good night.

GARTH

If you really wanted to be honest, you'd explain—

DIANNE

No, we wouldn't, Garth.

TOM

Maybe we should . . . admit it's over.

GARTH

Go for it, Tom.

DIANNE

Wait a minute. There's always room to, you know . . . negotiate? Nothing's over.

GARTH

I'm with Tom on this one. Time to admit it's over.

BEN

What's over?

SHIRLEY

I think Tom's trying to say, in his usual convoluted way, that this foursome is over. This friendship.

BEN

Maybe it's over, Tom, but you can't take away our canoeing weekend.

TOM

We'll always have Whitefish Lake, okay, but I don't think it's a crime to admit that we're not the people we were—

DIANNE

I don't want to be the people we were.

TOM

Let's call it a night, folks. Let's call it a day.
[There is a long, long, long silence, penetrated by throat-clearing, body-shifting, etc.]

SHIRLEY

Maybe I will have a little coffee.

DIANNE

Will you make the coffee . . . Garth?

GARTH

Is Tom finished? I thought . . . well, I thought he might want to make clear—

TOM

I'm finished . . . except to say . . . there's nothing wrong with acknowledging that something is over. It's just that no one ever wants to say the last rites.

BEN

We tried to tell you that our marriage was over and you couldn't accept it—

TOM

How could we? You and Shirl come here together tonight. In all likelihood, you'll go back to the hotel together. I don't want to be unduly suspicious, but that's pretty perverse behaviour for a couple who've—

DIANNE

Tom's got this sixth sense—

GARTH

Speaking of couples who've—

DIANNE

The coffee!
[Everyone freezes for a moment. GARTH *exits.]*

SHIRLEY

Here we are, the craziest four in the Crazy Eights. Shit. *[With real sadness.]* To think we invested hard-earned cash in our friendship.

BEN

Jesus, that's right. How's the interest mounting, bimbo? Bet we've got ourselves a bundle.

DIANNE

Ben, please do me a favour and drop the "bimbo." When you call me a bimbo, *[shouting]* I feel like a bimbo!

BEN

Sorry, little b—sorry, Di.

SHIRLEY

I guess the money is all yours now.

DIANNE

How do you figure—

SHIRLEY

The Crazy Eights are kaput and so are the Forresters, so the money goes to the last intact couple.

TOM

But you and Ben—

SHIRLEY

It's yours, okay? Accept.

TOM

But it isn't ours—

BEN

Look, donate it to the Endangered Species Society, if you like. Seems fitting, somehow.

TOM

But—

SHIRLEY

Listen. While the young stud's out of the room, do you mind telling us what he's *doing* here?

DIANNE

Garth's . . . been very supportive . . . while I've been getting the business on its feet. He even does a bit of babysitting—

BEN

Do I detect a little menagerie a troys?

SHIRLEY

You know what I think?

BEN

Isn't that what we've been hearing all night—Shirley's chaos theories?

SHIRLEY

I think . . . Garth is a little more than a friend. Maybe everybody isn't all uptight about our friendship, our imploded friendship—maybe they're just not sure whose baby this is.

DIANNE

Listen to me for a change. There is no baby!

BEN

No baby?

GARTH

[Entering with mugs, spoons, etc.] What did she say?

SHIRLEY

She isn't pregnant.

GARTH

Didn't I tell you?

SHIRLEY

How do we know for sure?

DIANNE

Because it's the truth. Someone has to tell the truth.

SHIRLEY

I've had enough truth for one night. Some people think truth is the only form of honesty.

GARTH

Huh?

SHIRLEY

In a minute I might start talking about the time Tom and I—

BEN

[Getting their coats.] Come on, Lois Lane, we'll take a rain check on the coffee. Time we left.

TOM

I'll drive you to your hotel. If you don't mind riding in a U-Haul.

DIANNE

Maybe Garth would drive them.

GARTH

Me?

SHIRLEY

A U-Haul?

TOM

It's a long story—

BEN

So, you're a big mover these days. *[Laughs falsely.]*

SHIRLEY

[Slipping into her coat.] Get a move on, Superman.

DIANNE

Listen. Let's not let the fact that this friendship is over prevent us from . . . keeping in touch. Don't take us off your mailing list.

BEN

See you on the information highway.

TOM

I'd like . . . I'd like to give the two of you something. *[He picks up the painting.]* You gave it to us when we were old friends. Now it should be yours. *[He gives it to* BEN.*]*

BEN

But—oh hell, thanks. If you're sure.

SHIRLEY

It's been . . . rotten.
[She starts to shake hands with DIANNE, *then suddenly embraces her.]*

DIANNE

[Taking BEN *into the embrace.]* So long, you old . . . darling.

BEN

Take care, my little b—usinesswoman.

TOM

[Embracing BEN.*]* Keep those books rolling off the presses.

BEN

[Gesturing to an empty spot in the room.] Our next title: "The Ottoman Empire."

SHIRLEY

[As the four of them laugh and hug each other.] Christ, this is getting cozy. Time to go. Come on, lover. You too, Monsieur Chauffeur.
[She snake-dances out the door, followed by BEN.*]*

GARTH

About the U-Haul?

DIANNE

Why don't you keep it tonight?
*[*TOM *gives her the keys and she gives them to* GARTH.*]*
It's been an exhausting evening.

GARTH

But . . . we were going to talk—

DIANNE

Tomorrow. I promise.

GARTH

[Taking in the sight of DIANNE *and* TOM.*]* Okay. Okay, I guess. Tomorrow.
[He puts on his outer garments, realizes he's still shoeless.]
Oh. My Rollerblades.

DIANNE

You can't drive the U-Haul in Rollerblades.

GARTH

What can I—
*[*DIANNE *rummages in the coat closet and comes up with* TOM*'s slippers.]*

DIANNE

These will do.

GARTH

Are you—
[He begins to protest, decides not to, and steps into the slippers.]
Bye, then.
*[He exits, and we hear a muffled sound of voices, shrieks of laughter. Brief
silence.* DIANNE *returns to the closet.]*

DIANNE

Look what was on the floor under the slippers.

[She picks a box up off the closet floor and takes a slide projector out of it.]

TOM

It's not that late. Still want to sort through some of this stuff?

DIANNE

There's no hurry.

TOM

Mind if I . . .?

[He gestures toward the projector.]

DIANNE

No, go ahead.

[She hands it to TOM. *He sets up the projector and* DIANNE *smiles, watching him as she sinks back on the sofa. With the appearance of the first slide on the wall, a Neil Young song quietly begins. Slides show scenes of him, then her, then the two of them dancing.* TOM *manipulates the changes of slide at first. He silently asks her to dance as the slides change slowly and automatically. She hesitates, then grins, shakes her head, stands up and moves into his arms as the music comes up and the lights go down. The End.]*

FASHION, POWER, GUILT
AND THE CHARITY OF FAMILIES

CAROL SHIELDS & CATHERINE SHIELDS

Playwrights' Note

In our revised script, we have enlarged and altered the role of Character Five. We see her as one who beckons to the audience, inviting their participation and explaining the action of the play, nudging the developing idea of family along and keeping it on track. She is narrator and chairwoman, instructor and interpreter. Her tone is one of amiability, knowing and wise but without the least suggestion of irony. She is unhurried; she recognizes that the concept of family is difficult, but that the effort of explication is worthy.

Cast

FATHER, in his early forties (the same actor portrays MAN ONE in Act One)

MOTHER, in her early forties or late thirties (the same actor portrays WOMAN in Act One)

SALLY, teenage daughter, about sixteen

MICHAEL, young son, about twelve

CHARACTER FIVE, a woman, mature, with a winning manner (CHARACTER FIVE also plays HOST, MAN TWO, REAL ESTATE AGENT, CONSULTANT, POET, NEWSPAPER CARRIER and REPORTER)

Setting

The very front of the stage forms the exterior of the house. In fact, there are no real house walls. We are able to look directly into the living-dining room and kitchen with its table and chairs and see a set of stairs that leads up to two loft bedrooms belonging to the children of the family. In the girl's room there is a suspended French window, which remains shut until near the end of the play.

Act One

Scene I

The stage is a dark and vacant house. It is obvious that the house has been unoccupied and unheated for some time. HOST *enters. She wears a graceful suit and carries a portable stereo. It is on and set to loud applause. She walks with confidence through the kitchen and flicks on a light. She sets the stereo on the kitchen table and turns to beam at the audience. She pauses and turns the stereo off.*

HOST

Today is another wonderful day. Hello! I am Character Five. *[She turns and addresses one member of the audience.]* The keys are in your right coat pocket. *[She looks at a different audience member.]* Would you say that you are lonely? *[She now addresses all with intelligence and grace.]* Now, I am going to tell you everything. Perhaps the best place to start is with the theme of our play: loneliness versus family structure. The nuclear family, as you know, is a very recent North American invention. Product of corporate think tanks; engineered and refined by Chrysler and IBM, for profit. The marketing was ingenious. Happiness was set as the goal. Who could resist? It's so . . . good for you! Naturally we went for it. We positively ran to provide children a perch at the breakfast bar of the model home. So here is our jumping off point for this piece of theatre: model family, model home.

We'll do some role-playing tonight. See a few dramatic examples . . . Of course there'll be some song and dance. And there will be time for a Q & A session at the end. What we hope is that we will get some answers about the nuclear family. Most importantly, is it working?

Now, let us begin. It just so happens that I will be participating in our first vignette. Here we go.

*[*HOST *presses applause button, which gradually fades and is replaced by shushing and a couple of coughs and low murmurs as the canned audience prepares for the theatre to begin.* HOST *picks up the stereo, turns off the lights and walks out the front of the house. She sets the stereo down away from the*

action, smooths her suit and prepares to become MAN TWO. *In character now,*
he *stands to the side.* MAN ONE *walks through the front door of the house and*
enters the darkened house. He fumbles for the light switch and looks chilled.
He sits down at the kitchen table and begins writing a letter.]

MAN ONE

Dear Sir or Madam, I have a complaint that I wish to draw to your attention. Your . . . immediate attention. Despite the rising economy . . . despite
the network of . . . social programs . . . despite the free library lectures . . .
despite the postal service second to none . . . despite the availability of high
quality television programming . . . and here I'd like to congratulate you,
dear sir or madam . . . despite your unquestionable good will . . . I find
myself . . . I find myself . . . extremely . . . lonely. L-o-n-e-l-y. *[He looks out*
at the audience.] I never can remember how to spell that word. Lonely.
Without an *e*? Or with an *e*. Hmmm, with, I think.
[He exits, just as WOMAN *enters, wearing a trench coat. She sits at the table*
to write a letter.]

WOMAN

To . . . whom . . . it . . . may . . . concern. My friends inform me that I do
not have a complaining nature. The earth . . . and the fullness thereof . . .
is perfectly evident to me, and if that earth were to be divided between the
privileged and the underprivileged, I would count myself among the former. Nevertheless, I feel I was set up to be disappointed. Lonely.
[She glides away, just as MICHAEL *and* SALLY *enter and write letters.]*

MICHAEL

Thanks . . . a lot . . . for all the good stuff I've got. Like . . .

SALLY

. . . having a house, lots of . . .

MICHAEL

. . . food, clothes . . .

SALLY AND MICHAEL

TV.

MICHAEL

I sure do have a lot of . . .

SALLY AND MICHAEL

Fun.

MICHAEL

Makes me feel bad that I still want . . .

SALLY

I want to feel . . .

MICHAEL

I'm lonely.

SALLY

Alone.

*[*MICHAEL *and* SALLY *exit, as* MAN ONE *and* WOMAN *enter, talking. They are dressed identically, and each carries a briefcase.* MAN ONE *has a laptop computer. From this point, the scene moves very quickly.]*

WOMAN

[With a stack of printouts in her hand.] Hundreds of e-mails. Even letters! *[Waves envelopes.]* More every day. They're lonely, they say. They need!

MAN ONE

It's just the current must-have. I put it down to unrealistic expectations. Every man is an island onto himself—and every woman and child, too, of course. That was settled long ago.

WOMAN

But it is our mandate to examine current . . .

MAN ONE

Our mandate? To deal with human loneliness?
*[*MAN TWO *enters wearing the identical outfit. He, too, is carrying a laptop.]*

WOMAN

[Checking her watch.] We've been waiting for you. This meeting was called for three o'clock.

MAN TWO

Sorry. I've been sorting these e-mails. We've got to do something.

WOMAN

Exactly what I've been saying. But apparently it's unconstitutional to—

MAN TWO

Units. The solution is units! That's what I've come up with. That's my concept.

MAN ONE

[Turns on the laptop.] Units? Units.

MAN TWO

Social units. I've done a spreadsheet of the complaints and petitions and sorted them by common elements. I've plotted the results, and you can see a strong curve of ascending desperation, which intersects with the line of basic human need. Factoring in other variables such as geography and age, the answer is clear: small social units. Or cells, if you like.

MAN ONE

Unworkable.

MAN TWO

We could start with units of two. One male, one female. What do you think?

WOMAN

This makes sense biologically but—

MAN ONE

But will it stand up in the courts?

WOMAN

Is it enforceable?

MAN TWO

We'll keep it optional, but once the social and economic model demonstrates its viability—

MAN ONE

I suppose it could catch on. If—

MAN TWO

One male, one female per unit, but with legislation allowing for *[holds up a finger, for emphasis]* group . . . growth.

WOMAN

God, I love it. Group growth.

MAN ONE

The symmetry! It's almost, well, sort of nuclear. But can we market it?

WOMAN

Female. Male. We could call it fe-male-ie. Fe-mal-ie. How about Family!

MAN ONE

Brilliant. Fami-ly singular. Famil-ies plural. Let's go with it.

ALL

[In unison.] Families.

[Lights dim. MAN TWO *stands at attention. He is being interviewed by two* REPORTERS *with oversized microphones. They are part of an enormous press event. Lights come on blindingly.]*

MAN TWO

[To audience in a beaming, smoothy way.] Everyone will have equal opportunity to apply for family grants monies.

WOMAN

Mr. Minister. Within these so-called families, what about duplication of labour?

MAN TWO

Good question, Sharon. As part of today's announcements we will be holding a public draw to provide a fair answer to the very question of labour apportionment. Shall we begin?
*[*MAN TWO *extends his hat to* WOMAN *and* MAN ONE.*]*

MAN TWO

The rules have been explained. You *[to* WOMAN*]* will draw on the side of female labour, and you *[to* MAN ONE*]* for the male component.

MAN ONE

[Reaching into the hat, his eyes shut. He pulls out a paper and reads.] Hunting. *[Smiles.]* Hunting!

MAN TWO

[Inputting into his laptop.] Males, hunting. *[Nods at* WOMAN.*]* Your turn.

WOMAN

[Drawing out a paper and reading.] Gathering? What's that supposed to— What exactly am I supposed to gather?

MAN TWO

Ready for round two?

MAN ONE

[Drawing again and reading.] Protection of unit. Does that mean full responsibility? That seems rather—

MAN TWO

[Inputting responses.] Male. Protection of unit.

WOMAN

[Drawing again and reading.] Child-bearing. Hey, wait a minute—

MAN TWO

Let's move right along here.

MAN ONE

Provisioning and maintenance of shelter. Navigation of the high seas. I can't even swim—

WOMAN

Child-rearing?
*[*MAN ONE *draws another paper, reads, crumples it and puts it back.]*

MAN TWO

[Retrieves paper and reads it out loud.] Swineherding, sheep shearing, animal husbandry.

WOMAN

[Carefully stirring the papers before extracting one.] Cleaning. Sweeping. Scrubbing!
[She puts her head on the table.]

MAN ONE

Exploration. Discovery.

WOMAN

Hospitality. Tending fires.

MAN ONE

Jurisprudence. Execution.

WOMAN

Care of the sick. Mourning the dead.

MAN ONE

Invention.

WOMAN

Application.

MAN ONE

Mores.

WOMAN

Manners.

MAN ONE

Expansion of territories.

WOMAN

Spinning, weaving. Now wait a minute—

MAN ONE

Investing of wealth.

WOMAN

Consumer activities.

MAN ONE

Creation of ritual.

WOMAN

Perpetration of ritual.

MAN ONE

Education, politics.

WOMAN

Morality. And—I do not believe this—peace!

MAN TWO

[Shakes the hat upside down; only one piece of paper falls out. He reads it.] All other duties to be shared and negotiated. And now—are we ready?
[He pulls two paper doll–style wedding costumes from the briefcase and puts them on the other two. MAN ONE *and* WOMAN *rise; there is a burst of wedding music. They join hands.]*

MAN ONE

Till death us do part.
[They exit, arm in arm, in time to the music.]

MAN TWO

[Speaking to the audience.] We believe that the new family system is strengthened by a public act of commitment, a tangible example that the public can grasp and pattern itself on and—
[From offstage, voices can be heard calling on the minister. He smiles broadly and ducks out of the bright lights. He walks over to the portable stereo and changes himself back into the HOST, *while the questions continue to be heard.]*

VOICE OFFSTAGE

Hey—what about gay people! Can they apply for the family model grant?

VOICE OFFSTAGE

I live with my mom. We're together. We could use that family money!
[The HOST *presses the applause button, and the offstage voices and questions fade away. The* HOST *turns off the stereo and walks out toward the audience, smiling.]*

HOST

The invented family. This is theatre—we'll try it on. Test it out. Thousands have actually done the real thing; followed the rules. Isn't it more sensible to run a model? Put it on stage? We gain distance, perspective. *[HOST slips off her lovely jacket and puts on a very structured blazer to play the role of* REAL ESTATE AGENT. *She walks back toward the front door of the house.]* Just slipping into my real estate agent role here. I'm going to take you now to the house we've constructed for our model family. Imagine this is one of many that are running at the same time.

*[*REAL ESTATE AGENT *shakes some keys from her purse and unlocks the door. She quickly punches in some numbers to deactivate the alarm. She walks about as she speaks, opening doors, rolling up shades and gesturing broadly.]*

REAL ESTATE AGENT

An excellent property. Quiet neighbourhood, gracious tree-lined street, solid foundation. Now, in my professional opinion, this house should suit our trial-balloon family of four. Your mother and father, your son and daughter. Your patriarchal set-up. Mother and father both employed, for the moment, but keeping their fingers crossed about the future. Health reasonable. Debts manageable. Family members morally accountable. What we are seeing here is a fairly accurate, but improbable and randomly unaccountable statistical model.

*[*REAL ESTATE AGENT *steps into the kitchen, flicks the light switch.* MOTHER *is frozen in front of the stove, oven door half open. The* REAL ESTATE AGENT *ignores her.]*

The kitchen, ladies and gentlemen, *la cuisine.* Recently renovated. Notice hooks for outerwear. His, hers, his, hers. And let's see, we have . . . *[opens fridge, which gives off a blue sci-fi light, and a deep sigh is heard; the sound ceases when she closes the door. She turns to address the audience.]* An important piece of family mythology has it that all serious issues are raised and resolved in the food preparation area. We don't yet know what these family issues will be, of course—we can only speculate.

[She walks into the living room and turns on a light; lights go off automatically in the kitchen area. FATHER *is frozen into position, seated on an ottoman, hunched over his newspaper.]*

A living room. Here our putative family of four finds ease and a sense of their own microcosmic community. It is here that family ceremonies are performed, though we don't yet know what these ceremonies will consist of. Here our family will connect. Or disconnect. Connections appear in the manual—but we'll see.

[Lights go out, and then come up as strong sunlight through SALLY*'s upstairs bedroom.]*

Scene II

SALLY, *dressed in jeans, is frozen, leaning in front of a mirror, examining her skin.*

REAL ESTATE AGENT

Now, here before you is a fairly typical child's or teenager's bedroom. Bed *[pats the bed]* room. A place of privacy for individual family members and yet! Yet never far from the resonating pulse of the family unit. Within these protective walls many a family crisis is aired, or *[pause]* not aired—notice how bright this room is? Marvellous French window. Southern exposure. Lets in light but—*[consults her clipboard]* it seems it has been sealed shut by owner. *[Tests the window.]* Not to be opened, it says here. Not ever.

[The light through the window snaps off with a loud click and comes up on MICHAEL*'s room.* MICHAEL *is frozen into a headstand position.]*

Now we have the second child's room. *Child,* according to legislation, means anyone from one week to twelve or eighteen years—the term is flexible. We are all, in a sense, children, the inhabitants of children's rooms. Here we can hide. Here we can perform strange acts and rituals—the unrevealed mysteries of human lives in these rumpled corners. And yet, there are palpable certainties, too—the bed, the curtains, the sense of confinement, which will sometimes swallow up our family members but offer . . . a blessed asylum. The committee has thought of everything. *[With a flourish.]* The House!

[Lights go on one by one all over the house; all darken for a second, then come up brightly so that all the rooms are revealed.]

A visible and, in my opinion, a highly charged metaphor for the family as we idealize it.
[Music begins to play.]

FATHER

[From the living room, putting down the paper, he stands and addresses the audience.] Metaphor? The word *family* means people in a house together. Look it up in a dictionary. And a house is something definable, specific. If you lived somewhere else you'd be someone else. A house, an apartment, a dwelling, a shelter of some kind—why, it's much, much more than a metaphor. What I mean is, real estate is real, not a flimsy stage setting. It's—

MOTHER

[From the kitchen.] A roof is a roof is a roof, as the saying goes.

FATHER

Think about it. *[Singing.]*
    We commence,
    All of us, with a place of res-i-dence.

MOTHER

I absolutely agree. *[Singing.]*
    A family must give
    Thought to where they live.
[The song takes on a rockabilly rhythm.]

ALL

    Walls and floors, ceilings and doors,
    A window to let in air.
    A family needs a base, a place,
    A family needs a so-o-omewhere,
    A house is more.

FATHER

A family must give consideration
To a place of habitation.

ALL

A base, a place,
A so-o-o-mewhere,
A house is more.

MICHAEL

[Speaking.] Hey, no one likes to get tied down, that's for sure, but I guess in the final analysis a family needs—

SALLY

[Speaking.] —an address.

ALL

[Singing.]
Somewhere to live, somewhere to be,
Somewhere to be—
A fam-i-ly.

MOTHER

[Speaking.] You know, the way I think of it . . . a family unit doesn't make a whole lot of sense without a—

MICHAEL

[Speaking.] —a picket fence?

SALLY

Forget your picket fence, this is 1995. *[Half speaking, half singing.]* If the family unit is going to survive . . .

ALL

[Singing.]
It needs definition,
It needs absolute space . . .

MICHAEL

[Speaking.] A fireplace?

FATHER

[Speaking.] Strictly optional. I'd say no. Now a furnace is more to the point, or one of these *[singing]* new solar-powered heat exchangers—

ALL

[Singing.]
Walls and floors, ceilings and doors,
A window to let in air.
A family needs a base, a place,
A family needs a so-o-o-mewhere.

MICHAEL

[Speaking.] There are homeless people, you know. Let's not forget—

SALLY

[Speaking.] About that window, I hate to keep coming down on this topic, this issue, but wouldn't it be nice, I mean wouldn't it be sort of, you know, a good idea, Mom? Dad? If we could . . . really, you know, like open this window now and then?

MOTHER

Shhhhh. That's enough.

FATHER

Not up for discussion.

MOTHER

We never open that window.

FATHER

Never.

[They all fall silent for a beat or two and then start to sing again.]

ALL

A house is more

Than a metaphor.

A house encloses, comforts, keeps you warm

From virtual reality storms.

A house is more . . .

[MICHAEL and SALLY move to lie on their beds, while MOTHER and FATHER settle together on the sofa.]

A bed, a place to put your head,

A place, a base,

A so-o-o-mewhere.

A house is more.

[The house darkens.]

Scene III

Morning light comes up slowly on MICHAEL's bedroom.

MICHAEL

[Standing, he puts on a baseball cap and speaks to the audience.] Hello there. I'm the son. You can call me, uhhh, Michael.

MOTHER

[Calling.] Michael.

FATHER

[Calling sharply.] Michael!

SALLY

[Exasperated.] Michael.

MICHAEL

Okay, so I'm Michael, the youngest in the family, the only boy. Am I spoiled? Yeah, maybe a little.

MOTHER, FATHER AND SALLY

[Overlapping.] A little!

MICHAEL

I'm the adventurous type—but the kind that doesn't do or say anything yet. I'm moody, like that guy . . .

SALLY

James Dean.

MICHAEL

What more can I tell you? Interests? Well, once I made one of those model airplanes. Another time I started a rock collection, but that only lasted one day.

MOTHER AND FATHER

[Overlapping.] One afternoon.

MICHAEL

The fact is, I've still got a night light in my room.

SALLY

Yeah, Mickey Mouse.

MICHAEL

I'm not quite a person yet. I'm still getting, you know, ready.
[Lights fade and come back up in SALLY'S *room.]*

SALLY

Hi. I'm the daughter. Self-centred teenager sulking in her teenage-y room.
Which is . . . I mean, look at it . . . a . . .

MOTHER

A disgusting mess.

SALLY

But a mess that is more or less tolerated, for the moment, anyway. That's
how the family—

MOTHER, FATHER AND MICHAEL

[In unison.] —is handling it!

SALLY

My name is *[pause]* Sally?

MICHAEL

Sally!

MOTHER

Sally?

FATHER

[Calling.] Sal-ly!

SALLY

Yeah, Sally. I don't like to talk about myself all that much—never, in fact—
but if someone came out and asked me to describe myself, I'd say that there
are, well, hundreds and hundreds of deep, deep layers to my personality.
Good layers and we-ei-rd layers.

MOTHER

Uh-huh.

SALLY

And one thing more you should know about me. I cry . . . at least once every day.
[The lights fade in SALLY's *bedroom and come up in the kitchen, where* FATHER *is opening the fridge door, poking his finger into it and then licking his finger.]*

FATHER

Good evening. I'm the father. And husband. I earn money and try to be humane and agreeable and not—*[he spies a neighbour out the window and calls out.]* Clark! I'll bring the drill bits over this afternoon *[returns his attention back to audience]*—and not come on, you know, too heavy, too . . .

MOTHER

Patriarchal.

FATHER

Like I've got power in our unit, but we all pretend I don't. I also have a real name, Brian.

MOTHER

[Calling.] Brian.

MICHAEL AND SALLY

[Slightly mocking.] Brian.

FATHER

But it's strictly arbitrary. How did I become a husband and father? It was just something that happened to me, and I . . . I welcomed it. It struck me across the eyes one day, the person I could be, husband, father, and ever since, I've been walking around, sort of . . . sort of blinking.
[The lights fade in the kitchen and go up in the living room, where MOTHER *is turning off the TV.]*

MOTHER

I'm the mother. Called . . .

SALLY

Mum.

MICHAEL

Mummy.

FATHER

Honey, sweetheart.

MOTHER

Et cetera, et cetera. My real name is Jane.

SALLY

Brian's wife.

MOTHER

Slightly out-of-shape mother of two fairly typical offspring. Sally and Michael, their names are. I try to keep things functioning around here. And I try very, very hard to keep things light. That's spelled l-i-t-e. A tough job, but I've learned to do it. I've learned to keep my sorrow dark and secret, to keep it from . . . spreading. Sorrow can find its way into every room . . . every corner, if you let it. I hum under my breath quite a lot and whistle little tunes . . .
[MICHAEL *whistles under her words.*]
and make cooing sounds and say, "Uh-huh," when someone tells me something really, really awful.

SALLY

Uh-huh.

MOTHER

That kind of thing. Now, what I thought I would do is take you through an average day in this household, okay?
[*Lights go off.*]

Scene IV

Music. This scene is played very quickly, like a sped-up movie, and is announced by an overhead electric title or by an actor carrying a sign across the stage that says, A Typical Day. There is the sound of ticking clocks and then the sound of alarm clocks going off and clock radios turning on upstairs. Simultaneously, MOTHER *watches TV while* FATHER *moves to the kitchen, banging pans, singing loudly. Four different sound systems fight against each other while each family member prepares for the day:* SALLY *and* MICHAEL *put on sweaters, brush their hair;* FATHER *sets cereal bowls on the table;* MOTHER *stares continually at the TV screen until she rises, runs to the kitchen and rings the dinner gong. The noise from the sound systems stop at the same instant all over the house. They all mime peering into a nearby mirror for a minute, examining and preparing their faces, and then rush to the kitchen table.*

FATHER

I have so terribly much to do today, so many concerns, I hardly know where to begin. There's an appointment at nine sharp and already I'm running late—

MOTHER

[Simultaneously with FATHER*'s speech.]* I should have looked over my notes. Am I going to be late for my meeting? Am I going to get the car started? I'm running late—

SALLY

My hair, it looks like hell, my face has broken out again. I like this sweater though, it makes me look just like Isabella Rossellini in that picture of—

MICHAEL

[Spoken simultaneously with SALLY*'s speech.]* Math test, math test, my head hurts, I hate morning, I love Shredded Wheat, math test, 50 percent at least, she's taken all the milk, what's the point of—

[They all abruptly fall silent, eat away with their spoons, then start speaking in overlapping speeches again.]

FATHER

Do they appreciate all they have?

MOTHER

[Overlapping with FATHER.*]* Does anyone ever say thank you?

SALLY

Doesn't anyone ever look at me, really look at me?

MICHAEL

[Overlapping with SALLY.*]* Does anyone say, "Good luck on your stupid math test"?
[They fall silent again, while the clock ticks and a microwave dings. Everyone rises in one synchronized motion, grabs their books, bags and coats from hooks. Each pauses an instant to look in a mirror, pats their hair in a synchronized motion and then leaves. A clock ticks quickly; the lights darken outside; lamps go on inside. A door opens, the family rushes in one by one, and hangs their coats on hooks; Michael's coat immediately falls off the hook.]

FATHER

What a day, not a minute to myself, just hope there's time to read the paper tonight.

MOTHER

[Simultaneously with FATHER's *speech.]* Too much salt, not enough sugar, overcooked, forgot to pick up milk, all that work I brought home—

SALLY

I got three compliments on my sweater, one was from a boy, I can't eat that, I'm allergic to that.

MICHAEL

[Simultaneously with SALLY's *speech.]* Hey, it was a breeze, I whizzed through, almost got the last problem finished even . . .

[They fall silent. Sound of ticking clock. FATHER *rushes to the living room to turn on the TV,* MOTHER *clears the plates from the table, and the children go upstairs and lie on their beds. Lights go down all over the house while the sound of the ticking clock resounds and there is one final microwave ding. A long sorrowful sound of dog barking is heard in the distance until complete silence. The sign, either shown on the screen overhead or carried by* CHARAC-TER FIVE, *says,* End of a Typical Day.*]*

Scene V

The sound of birds chirping. Lights come up on MICHAEL's *bedroom, where he is standing on his head.* MOTHER *enters.*

MOTHER

Oh, there you are, Michael. Well! Happy birthday, love.
*[*MICHAEL *grunts.]*
My Michael's growing up. Before you know it, you'll—

MICHAEL

Uh-huh.

MOTHER

Now, Michael, I have a question. I need your co-operation. I've been look-ing all over the house for your jean jacket.

MICHAEL

[Remaining on his head.] It's under the bed.

MOTHER

Where?

MICHAEL

Under the bed. I think. *[Stands upright.]*

MOTHER

Good. *[Crooning.]* Now Michael, listen to me, the time has come. I hope you don't mind, but I'm going to wash your jacket today. *[Angrily.]* And I'm going to—*[sweetly]* are you listening? *[Angrily.]* I'm going to iron it, too.

MICHAEL

I like it dirty. I like it wrinkled. But thanks for the offer.

MOTHER

You can't go to Grandma and Grandpa's tonight with a dirty jacket. I mean, I don't personally care about that kind of thing. As a bona fide survivor of the sixties, I'm not uptight in that way. I respect difference and allow for variant behaviours. It's a fact that grooming and cleanliness are more relaxed these days than they ever were *[suddenly loud and angry]* in your grandmother's day, but *[softening]* when people get older they tend to make judgments—

MICHAEL

No.

MOTHER

[Confidingly.] Michael, I want to tell you something about *[angrily]* your grandmother. *[Softly.]* Are you listening? When your grandmother was a young girl, eighteen, nineteen, from a very poor family, incredibly poor, you would not believe how poor that family was, well, she got a scholarship to go to teacher's training college, and can you guess how many dresses she had to her name?

MICHAEL

[Guessing.] One?

MOTHER

Two. Just two dresses. Her whole wardrobe. Imagine. Every night she'd wash one of her dresses, and that night she'd have to get the other one all neat and ironed and mended for the next day. Looking fresh and attractive was extremely important to her. And to her parents before her. To present a neat appearance. That meant something. Appearance is more than, you know, just appearances. It says a whole lot about the inner you. And about the home you come from. The values of that home. What they represent. That's how she felt. She did that for two years. Now what I'm saying—

MICHAEL

No, Mom.

MOTHER

[Angrily shouting.] I'm saying that my mother, your grandmother, has this unholy, relentless fixation on what people are going to think. *[Sweetly, speaking softly.]* She does not see the point of grime and grunge, Michael. She would never understand in a million years how a person could *[suddenly angry again]* take a pair of scissors and actually cut holes in a perfectly good jean jacket—

MICHAEL

It just wore like that—

MOTHER

Uh-huh. Anyway, all I want is to make your jacket a little more presentable *[suddenly angry]* for Grandma. *[Softening.]* A little soap and water, and I'll cut off some of those loose threads around the sleeves—

MICHAEL

[Pleading.] Just one more week. I'll put it in the wash next week.

MOTHER

Is that a promise?

MICHAEL

Maybe.

MOTHER

Sorry, what was that you said?

*[*MICHAEL *grunts.* MOTHER *leaves.* FATHER *enters.]*

FATHER

Oh, there you are. Just wanted a word or two with you, son.

MICHAEL

[Still standing on his head.] Yeah?

FATHER

Happy birthday.

MICHAEL

Thanks.

FATHER

You know, son, I've never been one to put all that much importance on physical appearances, that is, on exterior considerations—

MICHAEL

Here we go . . .

FATHER

Michael, look, you know I don't care about superficial—

MICHAEL

Uh-huh, I know. *[Returns to headstand position.]*

FATHER

But that . . . jacket you've been wearing lately. It's just a little on the . . . scruffy side, know what I mean?

MICHAEL

I like it.

FATHER

You wouldn't want people to think—I mean, we're going to Grandma and Grandpa's for dinner tonight. Grandma's probably made you a special cake, one of her three-layer *[angry]* nightmares, *[softening]* and she might look at you and think—

MICHAEL

I like it, I like it. I really do like it.

FATHER

It's Saturday, son, the whole day's free. Hey, how about we go down to the mall this morning, the two of us—it's your birthday after all—and see if we can find something a bit more—

MICHAEL

Next year, okay? *[Stands upright again.]* Next time around.

FATHER

But don't you care if *[angry]* Grandma—

MICHAEL

No. No, no, no. I care, but I don't care . . . enough.

FATHER

Mind if I tell you a story?

MICHAEL

Go ahead.

FATHER

Well, when I was a boy, hmmmmmm, there was another boy in our class and he had very, very strict parents. Every day after school—well, can you just guess what they made him do every day after school?

MICHAEL

[Pause.] No.

FATHER

They made that young boy, twelve, thirteen years of age, go straight home and polish his shoes.

MICHAEL

Every day, huh.

FATHER

Amazing, isn't it? These days we'd call it abuse. The rest of us would be playing baseball or larking around or goofing off or whatever, and this kid would be on his way home to polish his shoes. Well, I guess we thought that was pretty terrible at the time, having to do that every single day, but do you know what?

MICHAEL

What?

FATHER

Today, that little boy is president of United Insurance Corporation of Canada. And chairman of the Board of Trade. There isn't a person on Bay Street who doesn't know and respect his name. His picture very often appears in the business pages of *The Globe and Mail*! And so, Michael, I think you can understand now what I'm saying.

MICHAEL

[After a long pause.] Well . . . you didn't shine your shoes every day and you've done okay. Haven't you?

FATHER

But compared to—?

MICHAEL

Yeah, what?

FATHER

This person I'm telling you about.

MICHAEL

This big shot insurance guy?

FATHER

He didn't get where he got because of destiny. He got there because of rig-
orous training, because of character development. He couldn't miss. He
became the person he was. This motivated, focused human being. That's
what we do—we are what we were. Remember that, son. We are what we
were. That's how I—

MICHAEL

Why are you trying to scare me?

FATHER

I'm just saying that it's here, it's now, that things happen. It's in your home,
your family, the formative years, that you find your, your . . .

MICHAEL

[Desperately.] My what?

FATHER

[Faltering.] Your identity, sort of. Who you are.

MICHAEL

Now you're really scaring me.

FATHER

So, well, maybe now you see what I'm talking about. About this jacket of yours—

MICHAEL

Wait a minute, wait a minute. You just about had me for a minute there, all that stuff about the guy shining his shoes, you just about had a hammerlock on my brain. You got me all twisted up, but no. No. I do . . . not . . . want . . . a new jacket.

FATHER

[Exits, shaking his head and muttering.] I was only trying. This man's picture, I mean, he's in *[in an awed tone] The Globe and Mail,* frequently. Think about it, son, you could—
*[*MICHAEL *resumes standing on his head.* SALLY *enters.]*

SALLY

Hey Michael, I've got a favour to ask you.

MICHAEL

[Still on his head.] Yeah?

SALLY

You know your jean jacket?

MICHAEL

Yeah.

SALLY

Can I borrow it?

MICHAEL

I thought you hated my jean jacket. You said I looked like a scuzz.

SALLY

I just said that.

MICHAEL

[Pause.] Why?

SALLY

I don't know. I was . . . jealous. I mean, that jacket of yours is a really neat piece of clothing. It makes you look . . . revolutionary and . . . attractive.

MICHAEL

[Pause.] You don't think Grandma's going to—?

SALLY

Look, I really need to borrow it today. Your jacket. For something special.

MICHAEL

Like what?

SALLY

A secret, sort of. But, don't worry, it's a good secret.

MICHAEL

Good for who?

SALLY

You'll see.

MICHAEL

You better not get it ripped off.

SALLY

[Scooping up the jacket and exiting.] I'll take good care of it, trust me.
[Lights dim.]

Scene VI

Lights come up on the family in the living room. MOTHER, FATHER *and* SALLY *are singing.*

MOTHER, FATHER AND SALLY

Happy birthday dear Michael,
Happy birthday to you.

SALLY

[Handing MICHAEL *a box.]* Open mine first.
*[*MICHAEL *tears open the box and pulls out his jean jacket, which has been embroidered all over and trimmed with gold braid.]*

MICHAEL

Is this my—?

SALLY

I worked all day on it. Hours and hours. Kelly helped me and Patty and Tracy. And Laurie and Tiffany.

MICHAEL

My jean jacket! You took it and you—

SALLY

We got the idea from this article we read in the paper? The leisure section? Everyone in New York is like starting to wear retro jackets just like this. And even Toronto. Here, try it on.

MICHAEL

[Slips it on slowly.] I wouldn't be seen dead—

MOTHER

At least the dirt won't show as much.

SALLY

This gold ribbon stuff on the shoulders? That was Tiffany's idea.

MICHAEL

[Looking interested.] Tiffany? Really?

FATHER

We're going to be late for Grandma's—

SALLY

Well, birthday brother, didn't I say I had a great surprise for you!

MICHAEL

I trusted you.

MOTHER

[In a singsong voice.] I think you're forgetting something, Michael.

MICHAEL

What?

FATHER

Don't you have something to say to your sister, Michael?

MICHAEL

[Turns and regards himself in the mirror.] Thanks. *[Turns again, pleased with his image, posing.]* Thanks . . . a lot.
[He wears the jacket for the rest of the play. "Happy Birthday to You" music fades out as the lights go down.]

Scene VII

The lights come up on the lower level of the house. MOTHER *is staring at a cookbook,* MICHAEL *is sprawled on the floor,* SALLY *is doing homework at the kitchen table and* FATHER *is standing at the open fridge door, snacking. Outside the front door stands the* HOST. *She is wearing her lovely jacket, and addresses the audience. The family is unaware of her presence.*

HOST

Hello again! I think you can see that our family experiment is coming along. A few ups. A few downs. We knew that would happen, of course. You can't put four people, two genders and two age groups under one roof and expect insta-bond. We've agreed that professional assistance up front will save years down the road. I think it's time to introduce you to the Fret and Worry Management consultant.

*[*HOST *slips out of her jacket and puts on a smock or lab coat, becoming the* CONSULTANT. *This character's goodness shines through. She knocks and enters the house.* SALLY *gets up to answer the door.]*

SALLY

Oh, it's you. Oh! I didn't know—I mean, we forgot you were coming today.

CONSULTANT

It's the third Thursday of the month. *[*CONSULTANT *speaks without irony.]* Our scheduled date.

FATHER

[Calling out to SALLY.*]* Who is it, Sally?

SALLY

It's the Fret and Worry consultant.

FATHER

Oh, of course, of course, come right in, let me take your coat.

CONSULTANT

It is our regular day. But please don't become worried, and certainly not fretful, about forgetting our appointment. It is important, however, that we document ongoing stresses so that we can work together on . . .

FATHER

Oh, yes, yes. Sally, if you'll just move your books—*[He seats the* CONSULTANT *down at the table.]* You did say, last time, that the kitchen table was a good place for our . . . our meetings?

CONSULTANT

There's nothing like getting your elbows together on a kitchen table. I'm a minute and a half late, I'm afraid. But nothing to fret over . . .

MICHAEL

[Whispering to MOTHER.*]* Wasn't she just here? I'm halfway through the scramble.

MOTHER

[Whispering back.] A month ago. Oh dear, I was just about to start dinner. I'd better go first.
*[*MOTHER *joins the* CONSULTANT *at the kitchen table.* FATHER, MICHAEL *and* SALLY *mime making the dinner as the two talk at the table. They move in slow motion, in a non-distracting manner. They do not react to what is being said.]*

MOTHER

[Clearing her throat.] Always first, it seems I always have to go first. Well . . . on a part-time basis I worry about my teenage daughter, who's always crying in her bedroom. She thinks I don't know, but it's like I'm cursed with X-ray vision, I can tell when she's crying. I worry about my son, too, who stands on his head a lot. That's something I've noticed, but so far I haven't said anything. I've got this sixth sense about everyone in this house, *[angrily]* everyone except me. *[Softening.]* How can that be? It's a mystery, and the mystery keeps getting deeper *[angry]* and deeper. *[Softer.]* I worry—this is

an on-and-off worry—about Brian. I try to buy only healthy things, but he somehow finds *[angry]* all the bad stuff. *[Softer.]* Also he blinks a lot. All the time. I worry because I spend so much time being nonchalant, *[self-mocking]* humming, singing, murmuring my motherly murmurs, keeping things light-hearted and casual, keeping trouble away. Nonchalance—it used to be a kind of girlish hobby with me, ha—*[angry]* but now it's like a full-time job. Sometimes I look up and I seem to see someone like me, but not exactly like me, standing with her arms spread out, trying to hold it— everything—all together. I hold the whole house together, *[angry]* the whole universe. Everyone expects me to be nonchalant, it's my only talent. I don't dare stop humming. *[Softening.]* I also worry about the window, how I can't stop thinking about it. I'm at a place in my life where I'm sick of my inner thoughts *[angry]* and my outer thoughts. And something elsesometimes, late at night when everyone's asleep, *[angrily]* except for me that is, *[softening]* I hear this dog barking. Most of the neighbours around here are pretty good about their dogs, keeping them quiet, I mean. But there's this one, I don't know who he belongs to, maybe no one. A stray dog. He'll start barking and he'll keep it up. Like he wants something, or someone, and whatever it is, he wants it just terribly.

CONSULTANT

We'll move on now, thank you.

*[*MICHAEL *exchanges places with* MOTHER. MOTHER *takes over his dinner preparation duties.]*

MICHAEL

Well, I dunno, there's the usual worry, the same old one I mentioned last time. *[Laughs nervously.]* That I'm a little—ha!—crazy? You know? Insane? But I'm getting used to that one. It feels almost like normal now. But I've got this weird feeling . . . that something's not quite right in this house, y'know? Something's not . . . here. It's not finished, there's like a hole in the roof or something. The problem is I notice things that other people don't notice. It's like my eyes and ears are too sharp for my own good. Here's a for instance: I can hear my sister, Sally, crying at night. Only, I couldn't possibly hear something like that, could I? Not when my mom's got the TV turned up full blast and my dad's rattling things in the kitchen. And when he rattles things, he rattles things hard. Like he'd like to kill all that stuff we've got in the cupboards. The plates and cups, the knives and forks, the pans, the pots, the oven door, you name it, he's rattling everything to death! He's like this terrible rock band that can't stop playing, like someone's put a magic spell on it, turned the key all the way, it's just going to go on playing forever and ever, and so loud it's covering up all the good healthy sounds. *[Pause.]* Like, like the snowplow going by at night. *Dchchewvvv.* *[Lingers over this.]* *Dchchewvvv.* Clearing away the snow while the rest of the world is sleeping, he's like a hero, y'know. I love that sound. And then there's this dog I hear barking sometimes at night. I really like lying in bed and listening to that dog. It's like he's barking just for me. If I could bark, I'd bark just like that. A big, loud, wild bark that says—it says everything. Like it doesn't leave one single thing out, it's the greatest. But the funny thing is, when I hear it, it makes me sort of want to cry.

[MICHAEL exchanges places with SALLY, who comes to sit at the table.]

SALLY

I worry because I have this hideous affliction. I'm forced to do this impersonation all the time of this vacuous person who worries about like zits and boyfriends and how my hair looks, and the truth is I'm worried about God and peace and humankind and the future of women in the national workforce. I'm falling behind, too. My brain, I mean. Like, I've learned the solar system ten times already. The first time in grade three, then there was grade six with Mr. Neilson; he did the rotation of the earth and sun with a flashlight and an orange. God, it was like beautiful—half the orange turning dark, half of it lit up golden-like. For about two seconds there, I actually understood the whole concept of the cosmos, you know? Every year we do it again. I keep learning it and forgetting, learning and forgetting, and how am I going to be able to live in the world if I can't remember what goes around what, and how long it takes to—

CONSULTANT

[Writing in her notebook.] Just a minute now, please. Is this particular concern a worry or a fret, would you say?

SALLY

That's the problem right there. I've got like zero perspective. Mountain, molehill, it's all the same, and it's all sliding by me, like a television show. I'll grab hold of a brand new worry, I'll get all worked up, and I'll start to cry, and then it goes by, zoooooom, like it doesn't even care if I'm fretting and worrying about it. Like this week, right now, I've got this huge, gigantic worry about the end of the world coming? The end of the world, and then y'know, I go down to the mall and see these people shuffling out of the garden centre with those tray things of marigolds that they're actually going to take home and plant in their poor, stupid, doomed gardens, for God's sake. I worry because I can't decide what my opinions are; if I'm going to like grow up and be one of those women eating salads in cafeterias or if I'm going to get fat and go out to the library a lot and wear Rockports that don't go with my outfits, but I don't care about that one little bit because they feel so nice and comfy on my feet. You probably won't believe this, but inside my brain I've got all these lovely, graceful ideas folded up, beautiful thoughts, unselfish thoughts, thoughtful thoughts, but when I open my mouth . . . out comes this, this . . . garbage. I'm like a poison pasta machine, I'm spewing out black, oily streams of . . . worry. And at night, you know, I dream about this dog that's barking? It's just a bark, your regular neighbourhood dog bark, but this particular dog is, like, *[pause]* talking? Oh my God, it's awful what he's saying. He's saying *[whispering in a tiny voice]* help me, help me.

[SALLY exchanges places with FATHER.]

FATHER

This house, these walls, these rooms. Maybe people aren't meant to live like this, in separate cubicles with doors between them that open and shut. Now if Sally and Michael and Jane and I moved to a nice, big, friendly *[long pause]* cave, maybe I wouldn't worry and fret so much about being . . . lonely. Not that I'm lonely at this precise moment. I'm just getting ready to be lonely. I'm steeling myself, you might say. I'm in a sort of holding pattern at the moment. The kids are growing up, my daughter cries her eyes out, my son stands on his head, so what can I do? I see loneliness in the future; I see disappointments ahead. I feel we're on the verge of something.

Sometimes I feel like I'm a squatter in this family, watching and waiting for "it" to happen. Whatever "it" is. Y'know, what I'd really like to be is one of those men with a twinkle in his eye. I've practised in the mirror a lot, but all I can do is . . . blink. At my time of life, I should be delving into the higher truths, the nature of the universe, good versus evil, but it's hard to concentrate. My neckties are all mixed up, the wide ones and the narrow ones, the plains and the patterns, the stripes and the . . . My golf clubs, my fishing tackle, everything's jumbled together. Something's been misplaced, something important, but I can't seem to concentrate on what it is. Forgetting is what I worry about, not remembering. Forgetting is what hurts. Also my wife. You know how most people turn the sound off on the TV and just leave the picture? Well, she does just the opposite. She turns the sound up as loud as it'll go and she sits there, just staring into that little grey screen like she's looking for something that's lost and gone forever. Something that can't be replaced. Part of her body. Or part of us. Another thing, real estate values are dropping, the neighbourhood's going to hell, stray cats and dogs running all over the place. There's this one dog that keeps everyone awake, howling and barking. I keep meaning to phone the police or the dog catchers or whatever, but the days go by and I . . . forget.
[The microwave dings, the CONSULTANT *stands up, puts her notes in her bag and pulls out a small parcel, which she places in the middle of the table.]*

CONSULTANT

Now here's your coping kit for this month. Or no—*[she replaces the parcel and pulls out an identical one]* that's for another family. Here's yours. Keep the frets in check and remember to update your worry charts, but don't be overly concerned about . . . about anything. I'll see you in thirty-one days. *[The* CONSULTANT *exits. The family turns from their dinner preparations, each holding a cooking utensil.]*

FATHER

[Clearing his throat and speaking.] Well, that's over for another month. And now it's time—
[This next song is a gospel, Jesus-at-the-river song. Beautiful and sincere.]

MOTHER

[Singing, holding note.]
    It's time.

MICHAEL

[Singing, holding note.]
    It's time.

SALLY

[Singing.]
    It's ti-i-me!
[They set the table rhythmically as though they are part of a moving train, one behind the other, as they sing. Occasionally hanging on to the table and swaying in unison.]

ALL

[Singing.]
    Time to climb on
    The worry-worry train,
    All alone on the worry-worry train,
    All abooooarddd.
    All alone on the worry-worry train.

MOTHER

    Why can't we talk to each other?
    Why can't we share concern?

FATHER

    Mother, father, sister, brother,
    Our troubles simmer and burn,
    Our sorrows darken and die.

ALL

    And life goes by.
    It's time, it's time, it's time,

It's time to hurry,
Time to hurry,
Gotta hurry up for
The worry-worry train.

SALLY

All these thoughts that weigh me down,
All the things I keep inside.

MICHAEL AND SALLY

All the troubles we've got stored
Could be lighter if we only shared.

ALL

Allllll abooooard!
Time to climb on
The worry-worry train,
All alone on the worry-worry train.
Track one, track two, track three, track four,
It's time, it's time, it's time.
Hurry up for the worry-worry train,
All alone on the worry-worry train.

MOTHER AND FATHER

If you confessed, and you confessed,
And he confessed and she confessed,
Then less would be more
And more would be less.
Everyboooody, everyboooody,
Hurry, hurry,
All aboard for the worry express.

ALL

North, south, east, west,
We're each alone on

The worry-worry train.
All abooooardd.

SALLY

All the stuff that makes us blue.

MICHAEL

Bottled up like crazy glue.

MOTHER AND FATHER

Down to the station,
Down to the station.
What became of communication?

ALL

It's time, it's time, it's time,
Time for the worry-worry train,
All alone on the worry-worry train.

MOTHER AND FATHER

All the cares that go unshared
Keep us separate.

MICHAEL

Keep us scared.

SALLY

I'm scared.

MOTHER

And I'm scared.

ALL

Everyone's scared
On the worry-worry train.

Solitude is fuel for grief
And grief is food for solitude.
Secrecy contaminates.

FATHER

Liberates?

MOTHER

Exaggerates.

ALL

Grief and frenzy and despair,
All they need is a little air.
A little air and a little time,
It's time, it's time, it's time, it's time,
All alone on the worry-worry train.

[Part of the song is repeated as a lullaby, as the family withdraws for the night. MICHAEL *and* SALLY *go to their beds;* MOTHER *and* FATHER *disappear into their bedroom. Darkness and silence falls over the house. The long, lonely bark of a dog can be heard. Then* MICHAEL *sits up in bed, turns on a flashlight and goes downstairs through the kitchen, and opens the door to let a dog in.* SALLY *has also turned on a light; she descends, stoops and pats the imaginary dog. Then* MOTHER *and* FATHER *arrive in the kitchen, observing the scene.* MOTHER *opens the fridge to get out some milk and pours it into a bowl for the dog.* FATHER *rummages in a cupboard for Cheerios and puts a few on the floor for the dog. The family gathers around, making it clear that the dog has been welcomed. The lights fade. End of Act One]*

Act Two

Scene I

A dark stage with the set completely blacked out. An immense face, belonging to the POET, *is projected on the floor. Loud hip-hop music plays under the monotone, but ultra-hip, voice of the* POET. *His voice is like a beat poet's underwater with run-on sentences that rise rather than fall at the ends. He speaks slowly and very clearly. Everything is very loud and pulsing.*

POET
[Emphasizing italicized words and syllables.] To-*day* I *pressed* my eyes into a *mirror.* I could see *bet*-ter, *clear*-er.
*[*FATHER *comes down "runway," posing and turning.]*

Here's our *father.* Righteous *function* man. Shoulders *expand through cloth.* Ready to *listen*—he's made *room.* He's done his time in the *rethink tank.* Authentic jeans have more give. He can *stand* or sit. A witness to *form.*
*[*MOTHER *comes down runway, posing and turning.]*

Mother *forms* her *seams,* finishing things *off*—but not all at once. She can *layer,* taking up more room. Air fills the new spaces. She howls at the *moon.* She's got *moon* clothes from the *Eaton's third floor.* She can *slow* her rush *forward* and her silhouette gives *nothing* away. *Secret fashion dance* moves *unnoticed. Language* is *discreet;* her *meaning* is her *own.*
*[*SALLY *comes down runway, posing and turning.]*

Girrrl, she's *here.* She's *checked in. Trans-avant-garde* screened on her chest. *Imprint* structure. She's *retro-fitted.* Her *industrial* constructions show *through*—*each line* a *connector.* She can *spell kinetic.*
*[*MICHAEL *comes down runway, posing and turning.]*

He's holding *on-line.* His *fabric* is in *questions; expressionist alternatives surface.* His parameters *expand at will. Humour* him. He looks for *patterns;* he *gets* hard-edge *abstraction.* And *now,* *[breaking mood slightly]* now we eat.

[The face of the POET *on the floor disappears. Lights pick up the family on their way to the kitchen.* MOTHER *is already there.]*

MICHAEL

Pot roast and gravy. And mashed potatoes.

SALLY

Cherry cobbler. With real whipped cream.

FATHER

Homemade, too.

SALLY

Homemade and from scratch, or I'll eat my cotton gym socks.

FATHER

[Leaning back.] Now that's what I call one great family meal.

MICHAEL

Yeah. How come?

FATHER

But just look at the time, everyone. That special rerun of *Road to Avonlea* comes on in three and a half minutes.

MOTHER

Not so fast, Brian. Have you forgotten . . .

FATHER

But *Anne of—*

MOTHER

[Patiently explaining.] It's time . . . it's time for the whole family to sit down together and play a board game.

SALLY

A what?

MOTHER

A board game. You know, Monopoly, Chinese checkers, Clue, and so on and so forth. All happy families play board games.

MICHAEL

Only happy families play board games.

ALL

[After a pause.] And so they did!

SALLY

Maybe we could sing around the piano instead. "Down by the Old Mill Stream," "My Grandfather's Clock"—

FATHER

Charades anyone? I'll go first . . . Or we could talk in the living room and tune into—

MOTHER

I really appreciate all the input each and every one of you is putting in—let me make that perfectly clear. Your commitment thing, Michael, Sally, Brian, to family fashion values touches me where it counts—right here, it really does. But ask not what your family can do for you, ask what you can do along with your family, and so tonight, tonight is Scrabble night.

FATHER

[Introducing farcical nature of scene.] Right you are. I was kidding about *Road to Avon*—

MICHAEL

[Running up to the table, breathless.] Here it is! Here's the Scrabble board. Here, let me open it. There! Now, here's the score pad and a freshly-sharpened

pencil. Here's the box of Scrabble tiles, which I've already shaken thoroughly. And here's the timer and, just in case, you never know, the dictionary. I'm pretty sure, as least I sure hope, that I've assembled everything we need tonight. Mom, Dad, Sally, we're ready to begin!

FATHER

Why don't you go first, Sally?

SALLY

Oh, no, I think Mom should go first.

FATHER

Great idea, Sally.

MOTHER

Are you sure—all of you—that you really want me to lead off?

FATHER, MICHAEL AND SALLY

Yes, yes.

MICHAEL

Sounds to me, Mom, like we've got a 100 percent consensus going here.

MOTHER

Well, hmmm, let's see now. How about—I suppose I could put down—it only uses up three of these little letters—but I might as well. I don't want to hold up the game for the rest of you. [She puts down the letters.]

FATHER

Why, that's absolutely terrific.

MOTHER

F - U - N. Fun. It's not much, but it—

SALLY

Good thinking, Mom. You're really on the ball when it comes to strategy.

FATHER

And resourcefulness.

MICHAEL

And that gives you—wow, six whole points. No! Double points for going first.

SALLY

Your turn, Dad. I hope you can do as well as Mom just did.

FATHER

Well, maybe I could . . . Yes, I think I can, if it's all right with the rest of you. I don't want to take an unfair advantage, but I could add on to Mom's word—*C-T-I-O-N*.

MICHAEL

Fun-ction. Function. Hey, Dad, you're hot tonight!

SALLY

You're really working together, the two of you, that's what I think. Like a team kind of thing? You know?

MOTHER

And just look, everyone, two double-letter scores. Sixteen whole points.

FATHER

And now, Sally, it's your turn to show us what you can do.

SALLY

I'll just never be able to compete with you two, Mom and Dad, but hey, there is one thing I could do maybe, I could sort of take these two letters

I've got on my rack, this little *A* and this little *L*, and just sort of . . . you know . . . add them on?

MOTHER

Function-al! Functional. That shows quick thinking, Sally. Ingenuity and innovation, and everyone knows that that's the key to Scrabble success.

FATHER

And not only that, it seems as though—yes, look everyone—Sally's *L* has landed on the—

MICHAEL

The triple word score!

FATHER

Forty-five points. Be sure you write down Sally's score, Michael.

MICHAEL

I've already got it down, right after Sally's name, forty-five points. Congratulations are in order.

FATHER

I'll second that.

SALLY

Wow. Thanks, Michael, Dad.

FATHER

Okay, Michael. Now let's see where your tactical skills are going to take you tonight.

MICHAEL

I don't know, Mom, Dad, Sally. I just don't see any possibilities here for me at all. I'm afraid I'm going to have to pass.

MOTHER

Come on, Michael. Don't give up. I just know, with a little bit of persistence and effort, you can do it.

MICHAEL

Thanks a lot, Mom, for the encouragement. But, you see, I've got this *Y* on my rack. I was hoping for a couple of vowels but—

SALLY

Y's are the absolute worst. Except for *Z*'s. That's too bad, Michael, getting stuck with a *Y*.

FATHER

It's not your fault, son. Getting a *Y* could happen to anyone.

MICHAEL

Of course, maybe I could . . . I don't know, but I could—

MOTHER

Go ahead, Michael. Don't hold back. Do what you have to do.

MICHAEL

Well I could take this *D* I've got and this *Y*, and stick this *S* in—

SALLY

And?

MICHAEL

And put all three letters in front of functional, and I'd get—

MOTHER

Dys-functional.

MOTHER, FATHER AND SALLY

Dysfunctional? *[They roll their eyes.]*

SALLY

[Sarcastically.] What is it? Four o'clock? Oprah's on!!

MICHAEL

It's a real word.

SALLY

[Sarcastically.] Maybe we should dialogue about this new word.

MICHAEL

The *Y*'s worth twelve points on its own, plus three points for *D* and *S*, plus fifteen points for the rest—

MOTHER

Look me in the eye, Michael. I want the truth. Where, and from whom, did you pick up this . . . dys-functional.

FATHER

Those no-good friends he's always hanging around with. I told you—

SALLY

A bunch of dickheads.

FATHER

Sally!

SALLY

[Overlapping with FATHER.*]* You could be watching *Anne of Avon*—

MOTHER

I'm disappointed in all of you. What kind of family is this! I thought when we got the Scrabble board out tonight, after pot roast and mashed potatoes, after homemade cherry cobbler and real whipped cream, that we were going to have a little . . . fun.

FATHER

Exactly what I thought. Some family fun.

SALLY

So, Michael, why do you always have to go and spoil our fun?

MICHAEL

[Pause.] What is fun anyway? I mean, what is it? *[He pronounces the word* fun *in different ways, like a word in a foreign language.]* Fun. Fun. Fun? Fun . . . *[sings]* fuuuun, fuuuunnnnn.

SALLY

[Joining in song, running up and down scale.]
    Fun, fun, fun, fun, fun, fun . . .

FATHER

[Singing in Pachelbel's "Canon"–mode, not ironically or exaggerated, but with beautiful phrasing and voices overlapping at some points.]
    Fun, functional, fun, functional, I say fun-fun-function—

MOTHER

[Singing along.]
    More or less functional,
    Occasionally functional,
    Monday-to-Friday functional,
    Fun, fun, fun-functional

ALL

Functional family, functional family,
That's us!

FATHER

We agree . . .

MOTHER

Most of the time.

SALLY

Some of the time.

MICHAEL

Occasional-ly.

ALL

We're functional, fun, fun-functional,
Hitting on functional, that's our style.
Coming up functional, once in a while.
Once in a while, that's our style.
Fun, fun, functional,
That's us.

MICHAEL

Dys, dys, dys . . .

SALLY

[Overlapping.]
    . . . dys, dys, dys.

MOTHER

[Overlapping.]
    . . . hiisssssssss.

FATHER

[Overlapping.]
    What's this, what's this?
    What's this you're telling me? What's this?

MOTHER, SALLY AND MICHAEL

Dysfunctional,

Dys, dys, dys-functional,
That's us.

FATHER

[Sung as recitative.] What do you mean dysfunctional? Haven't I provided for this intact family? Put my paycheque straight into the family bank account? And another thing—

MOTHER, SALLY AND MICHAEL

Dys, dys, dys-functional,
That's us!

FATHER

The real struggle is seeing how functional this family really is—

MOTHER, SALLY AND MICHAEL

Dysfunctional, dys, dys, dys-functional—

MOTHER

Who is it that puts a hot meal on this very intact table
Every single night?
And with moderate good cheer, too.
Why, as a functioning mother, I've been just about . . . perfect.
But, but, maybe, maybe that's not enough.
Maybe I've failed somehow, yes, yes, that's it.

FATHER, SALLY AND MICHAEL

Dys, dys, dys-functional
Dys, dys, dys-functional.

SALLY

[Speaking.] I mean, look at it this way: *[Singing.]* I could be a helluva lot worse than I am. It's not like I'm into . . . shoplifting.

MOTHER, FATHER AND MICHAEL

Dysfunctional, dysfunctional,
Dys, dys, dys-functional,
That's us.

MICHAEL

[Recitative.] Look at me, hey. Just take a good look at me. I stand on my head and keep quiet and go along. What d'ya want anyway from a kid like me? Sometimes the only thing in the world I want is to get away from this family. And sometimes I can't seem to be here . . . enough, you know? Anyway, I'm not old enough to be dysfunctional—

MOTHER, FATHER AND SALLY

[Overlapping with MICHAEL.*]*

Dys, dys, dys-functional,
That's us.

FATHER

[Holding the last note.]

Like it's not as though we're into booze . . .

MOTHER

[Holding the last note.]

Physical or psychological abuse . . .

SALLY

[Holding the last note.]

Still, there are, if you look closely, certain clues . . .

MICHAEL

[Holding the last note.]

I'm only a kid, I'm too young to lose . . .

ALL

We're dysfunctional, dys, dys, dys-functional,
We've got, we've got—

FATHER

What've we got?

MOTHER

Sing it out, sing it out—

ALL

[Dancing]
     We've got it,
     We've reeeee-ally got it,
     We've absolutely, poooositively got it,
     Might as well admit it, we've got it, let's hear it, we've got it,
     Have we e-ver got it,
     We've got the dysfunctional,
     Dys, dys, dys-functional b-lues.
     Yeah!
     The dysfunctional blues.
[They strike a pose at the end; the stage darkens. The only sound is a dog barking. They continue to speak to each other in the darkness.]

MICHAEL

'Night, Sally.

SALLY

'Night Michael. Good night, Mom.

MOTHER

'Night children. Good night, dear.

FATHER

'Night, honey. Good night children.

[A clock ticks as the darkness continues for a moment. MICHAEL *turns on a flashlight, directs it around the room, then gets up and knocks on* SALLY'*s door.* SALLY *turns on her bedside lamp and sits up.]*

SALLY

Who's that?

MICHAEL

Me. Michael.

SALLY

What d'ya want? I'm sleeping.

MICHAEL

Can I come in?

SALLY

No. *[Sighing.]* Family, the real f-word!

MICHAEL

[He enters.] Just for a sec.

SALLY

I'm in bed.

MICHAEL

[Sits on her bed.] I know.

SALLY

You're mucking up my Laura Ashley duvet cover—

MICHAEL

I'll be careful.

SALLY

You better be. What do you want anyway?

MICHAEL

I want to ask you something. It's . . . important.
[MICHAEL *and* SALLY *freeze as the light dims slightly. The light comes up in the kitchen.* FATHER, *in his dressing gown, opens the refrigerator and pokes around. He takes out a piece of cake and begins to eat it.* MOTHER, *also wearing a dressing gown, enters.*]

MOTHER

Can't sleep?

FATHER

You too?

MOTHER

Upset stomach?

FATHER

You want a sandwich?

MOTHER

You really hungry?

FATHER

Are you?

MOTHER

Or is it something else on your mind?

FATHER

I'm always eating, aren't I? Thinking too much.

MOTHER

So am I, I guess. And another thing, I hear that dog barking again at night.

FATHER

Sometimes two or three of them.

MOTHER

Those dogs, they're always going to be there, aren't they?

FATHER

[Pause.] Yes. The same old thing.
[They embrace each other and freeze as the lights dim and come up again in SALLY*'s room.]*

SALLY

So what's so important you have to come barging into my private space in the middle of the night when I'm sound asleep?

MICHAEL

Were you really asleep?

SALLY

[Pause.] I was . . . almost.

MICHAEL

[Conversationally.] Hey, I haven't been in your room for a long time. Not in the middle of the night like this, kind of thing. So who's the guy? The picture on the wall?

SALLY

No one. *[Relenting.]* Elvis. That's his name, he can't help it. His parents liked the name.

MICHAEL

Is he the—no, he's not. He's the ice-skating guy.

SALLY

Look, you're supposed to be sleeping. That's what people do at night.

MICHAEL

Mom and Dad aren't sleeping. I can hear them down in the kitchen.

SALLY

Well, they have their separate . . . eating disorders to deal with.

MICHAEL

They do? Both of them?

SALLY

[Mimicking FATHER'*s voice.]* Hey, let's make some popcorn. *[Mimicking* MOTHER'*s voice.]* Okay, sweetie pie, eating's better than thinking, let's get those kernels dancing.

MICHAEL AND SALLY

[In unison.] And so they did!
[They freeze; lights dim and come up again on the kitchen.]

MOTHER

Sometimes I think that if I can avert my attention from *it*, if I look not quite *at* it, there's a chance we'll all get by—

FATHER

And we'll stop thinking about *it*.

MOTHER

It's not so much that I'm thinking about it. It's not as organized as that. I'm just feeling it. It's pushing, pushing into me. And I still dream . . . about it . . . every . . . night.

FATHER

The window.

MOTHER

It comes back. I can't help it. I see the window standing there. Wide open. Do you? See it in your mind, I mean. I've never asked you before. But do you? Dream about it?

FATHER

It's worse in the daytime. I'll be at work, and all of a sudden something will remind me. I hear that sound. And then—

MOTHER

And then?

FATHER

Then I hear . . . everything going quiet. It presses . . . down.

MOTHER

I know.

FATHER

And it goes on and on.
[They freeze; lights dim and come up on SALLY'S *bedroom.]*

SALLY

You better believe it, he's up every night around this time. In the fridge, cake, ice cream, muffins, leftover salad, everything. His real life goes on inside that fridge, you know. Now Mom, she's probably making herself a sandwich. Basically, she's a more disciplined person than he is.

MICHAEL

So, how do you know all this?

SALLY

Someone has to keep track of things around here.

MICHAEL

I remember once, when I was little, I was scared there was an extraterrestrial in my room. Behind the door.

SALLY

Hey, it's late.

MICHAEL

I didn't want to wake up Mom and Dad about . . . about the extraterrestrial . . . you know? . . . Being there? So do you remember what I did?

SALLY

You shot him with your ray gun.

MICHAEL

I came in here. In your room. I woke you up. This was a long time ago. You really were asleep, I think, but you woke up. You let me . . . get into your bed.

SALLY

What is this! An investigation into family incest? Give me a break.
[They freeze; lights dim and come up on the kitchen.]

MOTHER

Sometimes, sometimes I think you're right.

FATHER

About what?

MOTHER

About Michael and Sally. That we ought to tell them. You know. Everything.

FATHER

We've been over and over this.

MOTHER

It's just that I have this feeling, the way they look at me sometimes, that they suspect . . . something. Something missing.

FATHER

It might be better for us all. If we did tell them, I mean.

MOTHER

I make up my mind that I'm going to do it. And then the next minute I think, they're just . . . they're just children. If I can't bear it, how can they? And another thing—*[She stops herself.]*

FATHER

[Prompting.] Another thing?

MOTHER

I'm afraid, if we tell them, they'd never trust me again. Never trust us. Why would . . . anyone . . . trust us? I don't even trust us. *[Pause.]* Do you trust me?

FATHER

[After a long pause.] Do you trust me?
[They freeze; lights dim and come up on SALLY's *bedroom.]*

MICHAEL

What is incest exactly? What's it mean?

SALLY

Never mind. Forget about it.

MICHAEL

That other time? With the extraterrestrial behind my door? You let me get under the covers. You told me there wasn't anyone there, just a bunch of shadows. And then do you remember what you did?

SALLY

Look, I don't remember any of this. You're crazy, you know that?

MICHAEL

You showed me this warm place on the wall next to your bed. You put my hand on it. I think it's where the hot water pipe goes through. That's what you told me anyway.

SALLY

Hey, I remember that place. It's *[she gropes behind the picture of Elvis]* still here. Underneath Elvis.

MICHAEL

You told me how you always put your hand on that spot when you were scared at night. Remember, you used to be scared of the window . . .

SALLY

It's just a window. For God's sake—

MICHAEL

And then you'd touch that warm spot on the wall and it . . .

SALLY

It made the bad things go away. *[Gently.]* Yeah. It's still here. Can you feel it?

MICHAEL

[Putting his hand on the wall next to hers.] Yeah.

SALLY

So you said, when you came in here, you said you had something important to ask me.

MICHAEL

You know, I've been trying to kind of figure out how you get to be a person. You know? Like I'm waiting all the time for my life to start.

SALLY

[Explaining.] Michael, listen, you're already doing it; it's talking and sleeping and putting on your pyjamas. This is it!

MICHAEL

Do you ever think, what I mean is, do you think that maybe there's something wrong?

SALLY

Wrong with what?

MICHAEL

Why don't we do things like other families? Hug, and kiss on both cheeks. And those feast days . . . all that Folklorama stuff.

SALLY

Well, we have boiled eggs and root beer floats on Friday nights. And we always go to the sugar bush every April.

MICHAEL

I guess. But the way we are . . . My friend Arnie? . . . At his place, they just leave their bikes in the front hall. Just leaning there against the wallpaper.

SALLY

At Sue's? Everyone reads at the table. No one talks much, and they don't play Scrabble ever. And no one goes to work even.

MICHAEL

But our house—*[his voice breaks]* is it always going to be like . . . this?

SALLY

[After a long pause.] Here, Michael, why don't you put your hand here again. On the wall. Next to mine.

[They freeze with their hands on the wall; lights dim. In the kitchen, MOTHER *and* FATHER *sit on their ends of the table. They then swing their legs around to front so that they are facing the audience, side by side.]*

MOTHER

You didn't answer my question. Do you trust me?

FATHER

I don't know about trust. I don't know what it means.
*[*MOTHER *and* FATHER *freeze. Light comes up on* CHARACTER FIVE *alone at a podium to the side. She is detached from the scene.]*

CHARACTER FIVE

Sometimes there are no words. The family relies on gestures. Displays of tenderness.
*[*MOTHER *and* FATHER *are kissing.]*

CHARACTER FIVE

A solution can be found through silence or through an embrace.

MOTHER

I trust you.

FATHER

I trust you, too.

CHARACTER FIVE

Sometimes a decision is arrived at through a change in the weather, or perhaps saying something that isn't, strictly speaking, true.

MOTHER

We trust each other. Yes. We do.
[Blackout.]

Scene II

The sound of birds singing as the darkness yields to the brilliance of a sunny morning. MOTHER *is upstairs polishing a window;* MICHAEL *is at the kitchen table eating cereal;* SALLY *is in the kitchen ironing a shirt; and* FATHER *is at front stage, bending over with hedge clippers. The birdsong grows louder while the family does a stretch and yawn. A* NEWSPAPER CARRIER (CHARACTER FIVE) *approaches* FATHER *quickly, breathing hard, and hands over the paper.*

NEWSPAPER CARRIER

[Tripping over the curb.] Hey, I'm kinda late this morning, sorry 'bout that.

FATHER

Not to worry, not to worry.

NEWSPAPER CARRIER

[Panting.] What happened was I slept in.

FATHER

[Happily.] Well, it's Saturday morning. Why not sleep in? That's what Saturdays are for.

NEWSPAPER CARRIER

Some people on my route, maybe I'd better not say who, but their name begins with *B*, and they drive a big Buick, well, they get real bent out of shape when . . .

FATHER

[Looks up from his paper and pretends to see a neighbour. He calls out.] Hey, it's Bill and Betty Bentley! See you at the barbecue, Bill and Betty!

NEWSPAPER CARRIER

[Calling in the same direction.] I left it in the screen door, Mr. Bentley.

FATHER

Well, speaking personally, I can always wait for the paper. Just take a look. Murder. Epidemics. The education system. The economy. Bombings. Governmental trial balloons. But along comes a morning like this, flowers coming up out of the ground, out of nowhere, the grass so bright and green and tender, and you say to yourself, who would believe we live in a troubled, misbegotten world.

NEWSPAPER CARRIER

[Gesturing to the hedge.] Hey, are you trying to cut that thing crooked? Like a modern art statement or something?
[MICHAEL enters and FATHER hands over the coloured comics automatically. MICHAEL kneels down to read.]

FATHER

[Clipping.] What I'm saying is it's harder and harder to fall asleep at night, thinking of all the things wrong in the world.

NEWSPAPER CARRIER

Yeah, you guys sure messed things up.

FATHER

And then, this happens.

NEWSPAPER CARRIER

What happens?

FATHER

Look around. A fresh, crisp, brand new morning. The sun comes up. There's just the right velocity of breeze blowing through. And everyone, the whole family, awake and ready to—

NEWSPAPER CARRIER

I think there's something in the paper about a storm coming up.

FATHER

And you know the best part? It's Saturday. There's something special about Saturday. It's like we can put everything on hold, you know? And just look around. *[Seeing another neighbour, he calls out.]* Hey, Mrs. Sweeney, you were right about those numbers. Thanks! *[To the* NEWSPAPER CARRIER.*]* Just see the way the sunlight falls and rolls on that bush over there. A little miracle, yes it is. And take a deep breath. Go ahead, inhale. Now, doesn't that smell like a Saturday smell?

*[*NEWSPAPER CARRIER *breathes deeply;* MICHAEL, *pained, sniffs the air, too.]*

On Saturday morning you forget your nightmares. You look around—*[he looks upstairs at* MOTHER *in the window, and then at* SALLY *in the kitchen and* MICHAEL *next to him]* and well, Saturdays save us somehow. They hold back the world for a little while. Saturday makes you feel you're in one of those old musicals, and everyone all of a sudden bursts into song.

[The following song has an exaggerated forties big musical feel. MOTHER *and* SALLY *sing from their spots in the house while* FATHER *and* MICHAEL *sing from the front of the stage.]*

SALLY

[Singing as she irons.]

Saturday has a special
Wha'd'ya call it?
Kind of feel.
Like getting, I don't know,
A free five-course gourmet meal.

FATHER

Right on, Sally. And not only that.

[Sings.]

Saturday has a special, it's hard to describe . . .
Look! I mean, Saturdays give you a break, let you off the hook.
If you know what I mean.

ALL

[Singing.]

There's something about a Saturday,
Something gentle, something kind,
You can take your time on a Saturday,
And let the day unwind.
Oh, there's nothing so winning
As a Saturday morning.
There's nothing so warming
As a Saturday morning.
[Lights dim slightly, and a very faint roll of thunder is heard.]

SALLY

Saturday irons the wrinkles out . . .

MOTHER

Saturday shines bright . . .

FATHER

Saturday is an all-day day . . .

FATHER AND MICHAEL

And then there's Saturday night. *[They give a high-five sign, as the faint sound of the* Hockey Night in Canada *theme can be heard in the background.]*

NEWSPAPER CARRIER

Saturday tastes like peppermint.

ALL

It's filled with Saturday ways,
Saturday's like a birthday present
Ev-ery se-ven days . . .
[A flash of light suggests the onset of a storm.]

NEWSPAPER CARRIER

[To MICHAEL, *looking up at the house.]* You know something? Your mother's going to wear a hole right through that window.

[Lightning, thunder and the sound of raindrops as the NEWSPAPER CARRIER *hurries offstage.* MICHAEL *and* FATHER *run into the kitchen as the interior house lights go out.]*

MICHAEL

Hey, the power's gone off. It's like—like nighttime.

SALLY

The iron. I have to wear this shirt tomorrow.

FATHER

And I was going to watch the golf tournament on TV.

MOTHER

[Coming into the kitchen with a candle, she carries a photo album under her arm.] Here!

MICHAEL

What's that?

MOTHER

A photo album. I thought, since it's raining outside, we might as well sit down and look through . . .

SALLY

[Sarcastically.] My, my, what a cozy idea.

MOTHER

Please, children, sit down. I want to show you some of these old photos.

MICHAEL

Not those old photos again.

SALLY

We've seen them before. A million times. *[She crumples to the floor in total defeat.]*

MOTHER

Not these photos. You've never seen these.

FATHER

Honey, are you sure you want to—?

MOTHER

[Her voice shaky but firm.] Yes. Yes.

MOTHER

Now here I am, your mother, when I was, let's see now, about eighteen. You see, even prototypical nuclear families like us have their specific histories.

MICHAEL

Hey, black and white pictures. This was way, way back, right?

SALLY

What's that thing you're wearing, Mom? It looks like a, like a rug.

MOTHER

It's a poncho. Red and pink, if I remember right. With purple fringe.

MICHAEL

And who's that?

MOTHER

That's your father.

SALLY

Dad?

MICHAEL

Why's he . . . why's he wearing . . . beads . . . around his neck? And that vest. Fringe! Cool. Do you still have that? I could . . .

FATHER

No. It's gone.

MICHAEL

Aw! It's retro.

MOTHER

Now here we are at our wedding. You've seen some of these before—

SALLY

Neat dress. For that time, I mean.

MOTHER

And look, this is what I . . . wanted to show you. What I want you to—
your father and and me and—*[Her voice breaks.]*

SALLY

Is that me? Hey, was I ever cute, just the sweetest little—hey, you look really happy, both of you, holding me up like that in that little sack thing. Like
a magazine.

MICHAEL

Is that really you?

SALLY

[Sentimentally.] Yeah! What a doll face.

MOTHER

No.

SALLY

No what?

MOTHER

It isn't you.

SALLY

It's Michael?

MOTHER

It's your sister. *[After a long pause.]* Your older sister.

MICHAEL

Older sister.

SALLY

What—?

FATHER

She was . . . beautiful, the most beautiful little thing, perfect. Little fingers, toes. Right from the beginning, these strong little legs kicking away. We couldn't believe—

MOTHER

We could not believe how lucky we were. She'd be asleep in her crib, and we'd tiptoe in and just stand there, just looking at her. We'd sort of pat her from across the room.

SALLY

What is this? What are you guys talking about? Who is this baby?

MOTHER

[Trying to be chatty.] There she is on her first birthday. I made this terrible cake, in the shape of a teddy bear, vanilla and chocolate icing. It fell com-ple-te-ly to pieces when I tried to cut it, but, just look at her smile, she didn't care one little bit—

MICHAEL

I don't get it. I don't get what you're talking about. Who is this baby?

SALLY

What are you doing?

FATHER

Well, your mother's trying to explain—

MOTHER

She was . . . she was your sister, before you two were even born or thought
of, and she—
[Interior lights come back on suddenly, and MOTHER *slams the photo album
shut.]*

FATHER

The power's back on.

MOTHER

[She leaps up, reprieved, but desperate.] Yes.

SALLY

Wait a minute. I want to hear—

MOTHER

[Moving away.] Never mind. It doesn't matter—

FATHER

You can't just—

MOTHER

Just forget I ever said anything. About anything.
[She tries to run into the living room, but MICHAEL *stands in her way.]*

MICHAEL

[Crying.] I don't like this. This feels crazy.

MOTHER

Let me by, Michael.

MICHAEL

Not until you tell us what you're talking about.
[MOTHER tries to leave again, but FATHER stands in her way.]

FATHER

Look, I know it's hard, but we've started and we have to go through with it—
[MOTHER tries to flee through the front of the stage, but SALLY stops her.]

SALLY

[Numbly, dazed.] A baby sister. There was a little baby sister? Our sister! And she was older than me? Is this our family?
[MOTHER looks about desperately for a way to escape. She turns suddenly, opens the refrigerator door and enters it, shutting the door behind her. There is another flash of lightning and clap of thunder, and the lights turn off again.]

Scene III

MOTHER

[In the darkness, she speaks from SALLY's bedroom.] No! No, no, no, no, no. *[The lights come back on. MICHAEL, SALLY and FATHER stand frozen in the kitchen. MOTHER stands upstairs by the French window, which is now opened.]* She was sound asleep, her afternoon nap. Oh, she was such an active little thing, she really needed that afternoon nap. She'd just go down without a word. Everyone said, "What an angel!" Oh my.

FATHER

Then, something must have woken her up. A car going by, honking. Or else it was me. It was a Saturday, like today. I was cutting the grass, you see. At the far end of the yard. It could be she heard the sound of the mower; we had one of those old gasoline—

MOTHER

She got out of her crib. Climbed out. She'd never done that before.

FATHER

Never.

MOTHER

We had no idea she was capable of—

FATHER

She always had such strong little legs, right from the beginning she had these strong little—

MOTHER

The side was down, the side of the crib. She must have wanted to see what the noise was. She was always so curious. About everything that went on around her—

FATHER

So she came over to where the window was—

MOTHER

[Proudly.] She took her first steps at eleven months! Everyone said how—

FATHER

The window, it was . . . open.

MOTHER

[Touching the window.] Opened.

FATHER

It was such a bright day. A hot day. Exceptional. It could have been the sunlight and her a little dizzy—

MOTHER

And of course she'd just woken up—

FATHER

I looked up and saw her up there, just this flash, her face, her little wisp of hair, she was swaying sort of—

MOTHER

She waved, remember, that's what you said afterwards. She saw you out at the far end of the yard and she—
*[*BABY CARRIER (CHARACTER FIVE) *quietly enters carrying a rolled up blanket, pausing to listen.]*

FATHER

She waved, yes, she waved to me, her little arm, hi Daddy, and then—

MOTHER

She must have lost her balance, she'd only been walking a few weeks—

FATHER

And she . . . she started to fall—
*[*BABY CARRIER *drops the blanket in a heap on the floor and then exits.]*

FATHER

[Rushing to the blanket, kneeling.] My God, my God, my God. *[Looking up.]* What's happened? No, no, no—baby, baby.

MOTHER

[Appearing by FATHER, *kneeling with him by the blanket.]* Sweetheart, sweetie. Move your arms, say something, cry. Cry, oh please cry, say something.

FATHER

How did she—?

MOTHER

I don't know. I went into her room and her crib was empty, and then I saw the window was open and I—

FATHER

[Accusingly, he shouts.] You left the side of her crib down. I've told you a hundred times not to—

MOTHER

[Hitting FATHER.*]* The window. You left the window open, you knew there wasn't a screen on that window and you left it wide open—

FATHER

She never could have got out of the crib if the side hadn't been—

MOTHER

You killed her. *[Cradling the blanket.]* The window. A second storey window, my baby, my baby, and you left it open and she just—

FATHER

It was such a hot day, she had to have some air, how could she breathe? I thought—

MOTHER

[She hits him again.] You killed her, you went and let it happen. You did it, you let it happen.
*[*MICHAEL *and* SALLY *approach and the parents step aside.* MICHAEL *and* SALLY *stoop down, and then* SALLY *takes the blanket and rocks it in her arms like a baby.* MOTHER *and* FATHER *stand close by, side by side, but without touching.]*

SALLY

There now, there, there now, hey, oh hey, what a beautiful little thing you are.

MICHAEL

Hey now, hey now. I always, I always liked . . . babies.

SALLY

Shhh, now don't cry, it's over now. It's okay. Shhhh.

MICHAEL

[Stroking the blanket.] Don't be scared. That was pretty scary all right, but it's all over now.
[He turns and, seeing his parents, reaches for their hands. SALLY *turns and sees them, too. They draw* MOTHER *and* FATHER *together until the parents are standing behind the children.* MICHAEL *continues talking to the blanket but also to all of them.]*
It's okay, it's okay, we've got you safe. We've got you now.
*[*FATHER *and* MICHAEL *step out of the group as* SALLY *and* MOTHER *begin singing a ballad.]*

SALLY

Mother, mother,
Why don't you hand me your troubles.
I've got a basket
To carry them in.

MOTHER

Daughter, daughter,
Won't you please hand me your basket.
I've had my sorrows
And heavy they've been.

MOTHER AND SALLY

These words, now spoken,
They'll lighten our burden.

SALLY

You take one handle . . .

MOTHER

And I'll take the other.
Daughter, daughter,
I know your hands are willing.
But burdens this grievous
Are not for the young.

SALLY

Mother, mother,
Give me more than your gladness.
I can share your smiles
And carry your sadness.
Mother, mother.

MOTHER AND SALLY

These words now spoken,
They'll lighten our burden.

MOTHER

I feel my heart
Rising up from within.

[The lights dim to near darkness. The last part of this scene is performed in silence. The only sound is a flash camera. A flashbulb goes poof, *briefly illuminating* SALLY *holding the baby blanket.* MOTHER, FATHER *and* MICHAEL *enter the second time the flash goes off. A third flash shows the complete family, this time in a slightly different pose. In the final flash,* MICHAEL *is holding the baby blanket in his arms. Darkness again.]*

Scene IV

The lights come up on the living room where the family has gathered. This scene has a tone of wholeness—the family is at its best.

FATHER

[Pushing the couch.] Come in. We need all hands on deck.

MICHAEL

We're moving the table? We've never moved the table before.

FATHER

Come on. Just two more feet.

MOTHER

That looks good. And now—bing! (Idea!)—the lamp table. Next to the rug. There.

SALLY

[To the furniture.] Hey, you two were meant for each other.

FATHER

[To MICHAEL.*]* Lamp! *[He runs off to get the lamp.]*

MICHAEL

Hey, dustballs.

SALLY

You can add them to your collection, Michael. *[Considering the changes.]* It's off-balance. Definitely off-balance. But, you know, there's something kind of—

MOTHER

—Thrilling about an off-centre room?

MICHAEL

I like it. It's got the movers and shakers look. Hey, my basketball. *[He starts to dribble it.]*

FATHER

[Removing a picture from the wall.] Much brighter.

MOTHER

Why, it looks brand new.

FATHER

But not too new.

SALLY

It's just . . . different!

FATHER

[Glancing at the TV.] Look. Quiet everyone. It's coming on TV. The report on the nuclear family.
[They all sit and watch the TV screen flicker. The theme from W5 plays.]

REPORTER (CHARACTER FIVE)

[At the studio podium, to one side.] This evening, direct from the capital, we have the chairperson for the Royal Commission on the Family. Our story tonight: "Family on the Fault Line." *[More theme music.]*

FATHER

"Family on the Fault Line."

SALLY

The fault line?

MICHAEL

[Wearily, ready to explain.] That means—

FATHER

[Half-speaking, half-singing, he steps to front of the stage.]
    Your fault—

MOTHER

[Stepping.]
    My fault?

FATHER

    Our fault—

MOTHER

    Their fault—
[They freeze; MICHAEL *and* SALLY *step to the front of the stage, facing each other, and chant in rounds.]*

MICHAEL

    His fault, her fault—

SALLY

    Her fault, his fault.

MICHAEL

    Our fault?

SALLY

    Their fault.
*[*REPORTER *enters the house with a microphone. The family sings the following, while* REPORTER *interjects with comments.]*

ALL (INCLUDING REPORTER)

    Family at the fault line,
    Family at the fault line,
    Shaking, quaking,
    Sleeping, waking.
    Famil-ee-hee—

REPORTER

Won't you share your comments on the family project to date?

MOTHER, FATHER, SALLY AND MICHAEL

[Singing again.]

Family at the fault line, one, two—

REPORTER

Into the mike, please.

MOTHER

All unhappy families are unhappy in the same way . . .

FATHER

No, no, you've got it wrong, honey. All unhappy families are unhappy in different ways, or something or other—how does it go?

REPORTER

Is that how you see it?

MOTHER, FATHER, SALLY AND MICHAEL

[Singing again.]

Family at the fault line,

My fault, your fault, our fault,

Family at the fault—

MICHAEL

A family is just a random scattering of genetic chips.

SALLY

A family is the basic building block of society and its most conserving agent. A family's whatever you want it to be.

MICHAEL

The trouble is, people are always trying to climb out of their families . . . then falling back in—

SALLY

A family gives you your primary wounds.

ALL

[Crooning.]
　　Fam-i-ly, fam-i-lee-hee—

REPORTER

A family gives you your primary wounds? Have I got that right? Can I quote you?

FATHER

A family is the crucible of . . . of . . . of . . . I dunno . . . the crucible of . . . hmmmm . . . whatever. And another thing . . . Now what was that other thing?

SALLY

Even an intact family can be pretty . . . tacky.

MOTHER

Every tacky family is tacky in its own way.

ALL

[Singing, clapping, including REPORTER.*]*
　　Family at the fault line,
　　Our fault, their fault,
　　One, two, three, four,
　　Salvation at the family door.
　　Family at the fault line—

FATHER

Now I remember what I was going to say. A family heals, protects its members—

SALLY

A family is like these people, you know? With nothing in common? Who sort of like live together, under the same roof kind of thing, even though—

ALL

[Singing.]
    Family at the fault line,
    Fitting in, fitting out,
    Making up, making do.
    Family at the fault line—

MOTHER

[To REPORTER.*]* A family—I hope you're getting this—helps you grow out of your silences—

FATHER

Or else freezes you in them.

MICHAEL

Families like to sit around and play . . . y'know, games and stuff. Good games. And bad games.

FATHER

Talking to each other. Or not talking.

ALL

[Crooning.]
    Fam-i-ly. Fam-i-lee.

MOTHER

Families have a way of pretending everything is just fine, and sometimes—

SALLY

Sometimes it really is. Just fine. Oh God, when that happens, it's heaven. It's like it's the only place you want to be.

FATHER

But . . . there're always these funny little pieces of family history that go—
missing.

MICHAEL

Maybe . . . that's okay—

REPORTER

Hold on, you're saying that—

MOTHER, FATHER, SALLY AND MICHAEL

[Singing.]
>   Family at the fault line—

REPORTER

Tell me, would you go through this experiment again?

MICHAEL

Wait a minute, wait a minute. I've got something to say.

MOTHER

Go ahead, no one's stopping you—

MICHAEL

You keep interrupting.

FATHER

Your turn, go ahead.

MICHAEL

I just want to say that a family—

ALL

[Singing.]
>   Family on the fault line—

MOTHER

Shhhh. Let this young person speak. Give him his moment.

MICHAEL

It's just that, well, with a family you have to take it or leave it, except you can't.

SALLY

Can't what?

MOTHER

Take it.

FATHER

[Slight pause.] Or leave it.

REPORTER

Would you recommend this family idea to others?

SALLY

There doesn't seem to be any formula.

MICHAEL

Just say—

FATHER

Say we want to test it out some more.

MOTHER

We could, you know, just carry on and sort of see what happens. We're bound to get better at it.

REPORTER

[To an invisible TV camera.] In closing, we continue to watch with interest—

MOTHER

Eyes to the future . . .

SALLY

And the past . . .

MICHAEL

Let's remember to write it down—

SALLY

Listen! What's that noise?
[A dog howls in the distance as the family freezes for a moment and listens. After a long pause, they sing softly as the lights fade. Music has segued into gospel rhythm.]

ALL

Family on the fault line.
One, two, three, four,
Trouble always at the door.
Family on the fault line,
On the fault line,
On the line, on the line,
Looking for a recipe.
Famil-ee, fami-l-ee.

Right there, right there,
On the line, on the line, on the line, line, line,
Line, line, line, line, fault line.
Carryin' on,
Carryiiin' ooooooon.
[Music and singing fades to silence as brilliant sunlight floods the stage. It slowly fades as a single dog barks. The end.]

THIRTEEN HANDS

Carol Shields

Playwright's Note

It is hoped that the open structure of the play will permit directors a measure of flexibility, so that they can omit scenes or juggle their placement. It is taken for granted that geographical references may be changed to suit particular audiences.

The play's various scenes shift back and forth between the naturalistic and the abstract mode. Suitable lighting can gesture toward, and enhance, these shifts.

Costumes are simple, a basic "slip" or "shift" is envisioned, the same colour in different styles, or perhaps the same style in differing colours. To the basic costume, a number of simple additions can be made: a string of pearls, aprons, sweaters, hats, corsages and so forth. All costume changes can be made on stage if desired.

Scenes are separated by sound, by segments of recorded music, by live music (if possible), by the impromptu and informal singing of the actors themselves, or by a tape of women's voices talking and laughing, the actual words indistinct but a mood of conviviality conveyed.

All roles are written to be played by four women actors, indicated in the text as NORTH, EAST, SOUTH and WEST. It is possible, though, to stage the play using a much larger number of performers.

The action of *Thirteen Hands* takes place at the Martha Circle and other tables, 1920–1993.

Cast
Four women, NORTH, EAST, SOUTH, WEST, who play several roles. The play can be opened up so that the various small roles are played by any number of actors.

Setting
Most of the play takes place in Clara's living room with its card table and chairs, the simplest folding sort. To the right is an open dressing room, with hooks for the various additions that are made to the austere costumes. There should also be a bench. Other spaces can be rearranged as needed in the play.

Act One

At rise: the stage is bare. A card table is folded against the back wall, as are the utterly standard wooden folding chairs. At stage left is a dressing room equipped with dressing table, mirror, rack for clothes and bench. A bicycle leans against the wall. At far stage right is a lectern.

Tape of women laughing and talking. Four women at stage left are help-ing each other pin a corsage on each other's shoulder. Tape fades to music. They look at each other approvingly. Then enter and take their places at stage front, lining up awkwardly as though not sure of their place. They speak to each other and also to the audience.

SOUTH

Ahem!

NORTH

Shouldn't we begin. *[Looks at watch.]*

WEST

Everyone . . . *[she surveys audience]* is assembled. I suggest we begin at once.

SOUTH

Allow me.

EAST

Well, actually it would make more sense if we—

SOUTH

What?

EAST

If we went alphabetically.

WEST

That puts me last.

NORTH

Does it matter to . . . *[waves in direction of audience]* who comes first or last?

SOUTH

It's critical. Once you start getting lax about rules—

EAST

—you're in a different convention.

WEST

I hadn't thought of that, but of course you're right.

EAST

Ahem. To introduce myself, then, I'm East.

NORTH

[Bowing.] North here. And you must be—

SOUTH

Right you are. South. And to my right is—

WEST

West.
[They all shake hands, murmuring polite greetings.]

SOUTH

[Impatiently.] Well?

WEST

I think that completes the formalities. Let's get right down to—

EAST

Something's missing. *[Holds up a finger—idea!]*

NORTH

[Pulling out cards, executing an in-hand shuffle.] I have the necessary . . . wherewithal.

WEST

Shall we take our places? *[Looks around for the table and chairs.]*

SOUTH

Isn't that what we're here for?

EAST

A good question.

SOUTH

I suggest we stop asking questions and get down to it.

NORTH

[Persisting.] Nevertheless, questions occur whether we ask them or not—

WEST

What questions?

EAST

Why we're here. What we're doing.

SOUTH

Is it really necessary—posing these kinds of questions?

EAST

There are those . . . who may not . . .

WEST

—comprehend who we are—

NORTH

—who doubt our . . . seriousness, our—

EAST

—our essential value, to put it baldly.

SOUTH

[Rising to argument.] There *are* millions of us, after all. No, billions. That would mean . . . as an estimate, that several hundred million hands are played every day—

WEST

Conservative estimate.

NORTH

Very.

SOUTH

Several million times each small act. *[Holds up a card.]*

EAST

Impressive. And if you multiply that by the energy requirement, you find the result—

WEST

—equals—

SOUTH

Shhhhhh, listen.
[Voices may be either live or previously recorded.]

VOICE ONE (NORTH)

[Reading in sepulchral tones.] Opening lead—seven of clubs. Some contracts are extremely difficult to make. Here is one brilliantly played some years ago in a non-championship game in Winnipeg, Manitoba, where correct

play produced twelve tricks. Six no-trump was bid, played and made by a certain Clara Wesley, widow of one Arthur Wesley, during a scheduled Tuesday night match. It was relatively easy for her to diagnose West's opening lead as either a singleton or a—*[Fades.]*

VOICE TWO (EAST)

[Overtaking previous voice, speaking in teacherly manner, perhaps with an echo.]—one spade! This may appear to be an enormous underbid, but—

VOICE ONE

A little carelessness caused declarer to blow this deal, despite a very favourable lie of cards.

VOICE TWO

South was defeated because she squandered her entries to hand. She should have . . . *[Fades.]*

VOICE ONE

. . . should have postponed the drawing of trumps while . . . *[Fades.]*

VOICE TWO

Never stall unnecessarily. You confuse your—

VOICE ONE

The coolest nerves can be shaken by—

VOICE TWO

Steady does it when a single club ruff reveals—

VOICE ONE

Before deciding which way to take a two-way finesse, declarer must—

VOICE TWO

—at other times—

VOICE ONE

South can proceed with absolute confidence.

SOUTH

[Breaking mood.] Absolute confidence? Does such a thing exist?

WEST

It's a question of keeping track of things. Lists.

NORTH

Ace, kings, queens, ten, et cetera. Lists. You know how good we are at keeping—
[The rest of the scene is played at top speed.]

EAST

[Counting on fingers.] Carrots, potatoes, ground beef, sugar—

NORTH

June, August, October, December—

SOUTH

Piano lessons, dry cleaning, fire insurance—

WEST

123 West 68th, 29 Portage Road, 935 Beverly Crescent—

NORTH

Five pounds, six ounces; eight pounds, one ounce; six and a half—

SOUTH

Emily, Roberta, Alma, Alison, Izzie—

EAST

Aunt May, Uncle Si, Grandpa Muldoon—

WEST

Symphony, board meeting, lecture series, art gallery—

SOUTH

Canasta, bunko, mah-jong, Scrabble—

EAST

Measles, chicken pox, diphtheria—

WEST

Seersucker, piqué, organdy, velveteen—

SOUTH

Chairs, umbrella, beach towels, Thermos—

NORTH

Four ninety-five, two dollars and fifty cents, twelve dollars even—

SOUTH

Someone has to keep the lists.

NORTH

Of course they do.

SOUTH

Lard, shortening, baking powder—

NORTH

Galations, Ephesians, Philippians—

WEST

Lima, Buenos Aires, Mexico City—

EAST

Peanuts, pencils, tallies, ashtrays—

WEST

Tricks, trumps, books, hands—

EAST

There are variations. Schisms.

NORTH

Better not gone into, I think. Not here.

SOUTH

Time to go. Just one more thing before you're on your way: Can you give me a hand with this?

[She points to the folded up card table. They set up the card table ceremonially to musical accompaniment. A loud beat as each leg is unfolded. There is a little fussing with the angle of the table, getting it just right, and then each places a chair in position.

Music; At stage left three women help the elderly CLARA (WEST) *get ready for her entrance, assisting her with her dressing gown, putting her glasses on her nose, applying face powder, brushing her hair. One of them puts a lace cloth on the card table. When* CLARA *enters, the other women sit on the bench.*

Light on CLARA *as she enters from left, shuffling a little in her gown. At first she can't find the card table, walks by it, looks around, confused, then sees it. She rummages in her pockets and finds, finally, a deck of cards, which she shuffles in her hand—the first sign of her mounting energy.* CLARA *then deals out cards into four hands, walking around the table as she does so, increasing her speed and energy until she achieves a sort of halting jazz rhythm.]*

CLARA

De-dum, de-dum, de-dum and . . . de-dum. With a one and two and three and a four.

[She stops, kisses the pack, blows on it for luck.]

And a little one and a big one and a little one and a big one, here we round the dum-de-dum bush on a frosty Tuesday evening.

[She stops herself, listens, then continues.]

With a one and two and three and a four, *[reversing herself]* with a four and three and a two and a one. *[Pauses.]* With a—

[She lifts the top card, looks at it, considers putting it down, then changes her mind, mixing it into the deck and vigorously reshuffling.]

For you and you . . . and you . . . and me. You, you, you and me. Ruth, Margot—ah, Margot—Doris and me. Ruthie, Margot, Doris and . . . Clara.

[She stops abruptly, dizzy, sits down at one of the chairs.]

Clara. Clar-a.

[She cuts the remaining deck and continues, dealing counter-clockwise.]

Clara. Doris, Margot, Ruth, Clar-a, Do-ris, Mar-got, Ruth-ie. Last round, ladies, for the four of us. *[Picks up her hand and briskly sorts.]* All right, gals, breast your cards. Whew. Well! And I felt lucky tonight. Just goes to show. Hmmmm.

[She puts her hand face down on the table, rises painfully and goes to pick up Doris's hand.]

Not bad at all. Not discouragingly bad. Playable. Eminently playable. With support, that is.

[She moves to Margot's chair and arranges her hand.]

Well, well! Length, strength, two queens, ace, gor-geous. *[Looks up at the audience.]* Not that *gorgeous* was a word in Margot's vocabulary. Not Margot. *[Mimics.]* Tidy little spread, very tidy.

[She reaches across the table to pick up and arrange Ruth's hand.]

Ruth. Ruth Sprague. Your luck's swung round tonight, my girl. Bid this with your usual verve, your well-tempered verve, that's what we used to say about your bidding, well-tempered, and you'll sail home tonight on spades. Gorgeous spades.

[She starts playing the hand and then stops, hearing a kettle whistle.]

The kettle, and just when we were all getting a little dry. Thistles in the throat, as Doris put it.

[She rises, shuffles off and is back quickly with a teacup, addressing the audience.]

I remember how it was when Ruth here got so sick. *[Pats back of the chair.]* She started missing our Tuesday nights, some excuse or other, or else she'd have to go home early, pass up the dainties, tell us how she'd lost her appetite. Coconut squares, cherry slices, Rice Krispies bars, marshmallow melts—oh, the peculiar things we used to make!—she passed them up, shook her head, thank you just the same. And she'd get pooped out. Couldn't concentrate. One night, we couldn't get over it, she miscarded. Played the jack of diamonds when we all knew she had trump in her hand—clubs, I think it was. Well! There was this unholy silence. We didn't know where to look. She twigged at last. "Oh, my Lord," she said, "just look what I've done, oh, for crying out loud."

She never did come right out and talk about . . . it. Just said, after she'd been to the hospital for tests, that things weren't right . . . down there. But the pain, oh the pain was something else. I saw her once, dropped in unexpectedly. She had this piece of old cloth, an old handkerchief of Rudy's, I think it was, and she was biting down on that. Of course that was toward the end.

It bothered me, seeing her like that, with a handkerchief jammed between her teeth. She was an attractive woman when she was young. Not pretty, but she could look queenly. She wore a hat well, we all agreed on that. But she shrank down. It's a fact that a human figure, seen on its own, is very small. She was the first of us to go—she would have been sixty that spring. Oh, they offered her morphine. "Here," they said, "take this." But no, not Ruthie. She didn't want to go all fuzzy and buzzy, she said. She was always one to pride herself on her brains—she'd been a stenographer for two years before she married, worked in an office, insurance. She wanted to keep alert, even when the pain was halfway to killing her. Actually, though, it was Doris Veal, to give her credit, who said something had to be done for Ruthie when she was in such pain, going through h-e-double-hockey-sticks. We're her friends, Doris said, and if the family's not going to lift a finger, it's up to us. We've got to have a word with the doctor. Oh, that doctor. He was quite the boy, but he had a way about him that cheered you. We went to see him, the three of us, Doris, Margot Hetherling and myself. We drove over in Doris's Vauxhall, a cold March day. Doris was sucking one of her everlasting peppermints, I remember. I wore my new dressmaker suit and matching hat. We told the doctor outright: "You've got to do something for Ruth Sprague," we said. He just looked at us hard, then he looked at us in a winking way, and he said, "Ladies, the only thing that'd help her is if you'd boil up a deck of cards and serve her the broth." *[Laughs.]* Anyway, he said, "She won't last long with cancer of the uterus, no one does."

It hurt me to hear it said out loud. It affected me. But that doctor was right about Ruthie, she didn't last long.

[CLARA puts away the cards, folds the tablecloth, straightens the chairs. PEAKED CAP (NORTH), wearing a peaked cap, rides to centre stage on a bicycle, ringing the bell loudly.]

CLARA

[Looking up.] Oh, it's you.

PEAKED CAP

I'm not interrupting?

CLARA

Not at all. *[Smoothing the tablecloth.]* We're all done for today.

PEAKED CAP

I brought the questionnaire.

CLARA

[Glancing at the paper.] Oh, that, I didn't know it was time for that again.

PEAKED CAP

It won't take long. A few minutes.

CLARA

Well, let's get it over with then.

PEAKED CAP

[Clearing her throat, reaching for a pencil, and reading.] Question one. Do you, Clara Wesley, consider yourself a marginal person?

CLARA

Weellll, I suppose it depends on where the centre is.

PEAKED CAP

Shall I write that down?

CLARA

I don't know. I think someone else's already said it. And anyway, it might seem . . . disrespectful.

PEAKED CAP

That's my question. Are you given to making rude, forthright or disrespectful statements?

CLARA

Well, now, I don't know.

PEAKED CAP

[Reading.] When faced with a difficult question, do you say, "Well, now, I don't know"?

CLARA

Well now—

PEAKED CAP

Well?

CLARA

Next question. Please.

PEAKED CAP

Do you, as a member of society, contribute to that society's overall stability, cultural richness and general advancement?

CLARA

Oh, hmmm.

PEAKED CAP

Yes or no. All we need to do is check the appropriate box.

CLARA

Why don't I let you decide.

PEAKED CAP

Right. Next question. What, in ten words or less, is the purpose of your life?

CLARA

I was hoping you wouldn't ask that . . . just yet.

PEAKED CAP

Shall I leave it blank then?

CLARA

I think so. Yes.

PEAKED CAP

They won't like it.

CLARA

Any further questions?

PEAKED CAP

One more. This one's voluntary.

CLARA

Go ahead.

PEAKED CAP

Have you any advice for the teenage girls of today?

CLARA

Teenagers. Oh dear, I don't know all that many teenage girls anymore. There's my granddaughter, of course, and her friends, but they don't—
[Music, loud rock, begins and interrupts conversation.]

PEAKED CAP

I'll catch you next time.
*[*CLARA *and* PEAKED CAP *retreat to the dressing room. All four women, in time with the rock music, pull winter coats, hats and scarves over their basic costumes. They enter and sprawl on the floor or platform with hands of cards. Music only gradually diminishes.]*

WOMAN ONE (NORTH)

[Shouting.] I said, one diamond.

WOMAN TWO (EAST)

What?

WOMAN ONE

One diamond. Solitaire. One. Hey, woman, wanna turn that down?

WOMAN THREE (WEST)

I can't, you know, think without music, I just can't. I can't, you know, concentrate kind-of-thing?

WOMAN FOUR (SOUTH)

How much longer before they open the box office?

WOMAN ONE

Three hours.
[They all groan.]

WOMAN THREE

Okay. *[She reaches over and turns the radio off completely.]* You've got to say something, pass or else something above a diamond. Two something.

WOMAN TWO

How about . . . two diamonds?

WOMAN FOUR

You can't say diamonds. That's ours. You can say anything else but.

WOMAN TWO

Clubs. Is that okay?

WOMAN ONE

As long as it's two. Or more.

WOMAN TWO

Hey! How do you remember all this stuff?

WOMAN ONE

Second nature, practically. I mean, it's like built into my chromosomes. I've been at it off and on for ten years.

WOMAN TWO

Huh? You must've learned in your high chair.

WOMAN ONE

Just about. I was . . . *[stops and thinks]* seven years old, maybe . . . maybe six.

WOMAN THREE

Come off it.

WOMAN ONE

No kidding. My mother? She belonged to this group? She still does. They call themselves—are you ready for this?—they call themselves *[Said in booming opera tone]* The Edge of Night Gang.

WOMAN FOUR

The who?

WOMAN ONE

The Edge of Night, you know, like the old soap?

WOMAN TWO, THREE AND FOUR

Oh yeah, sure, that thing. *[Etc.]*

WOMAN ONE

Well, they'd get together every Thursday night, only it used to be Wednesday afternoons back then, when none of them were working, just staying home doing the housewifey thing—

WOMAN TWO

Dusting the window sills—

WOMAN THREE

Wearing little aprons—

WOMAN ONE

Making lemon pies. All that stuff. So they got together Wednesday afternoons. Wednesdays were sacred, lemme tell you. They'd play for hours. Talking and getting socked on teeny little glasses of sherry.

WOMAN TWO

And pigging out on cashews.

WOMAN ONE

You've got it. Well, my mom used to get all dolled up, that's what she called it—these itty-bitty pincurls, and she'd sit under this hair dryer thing—

WOMAN FOUR

—with one of those bonnet things on her head? And the hose?

WOMAN ONE

Yeeaah!

WOMAN TWO

Far out.

WOMAN ONE

And she'd do her nails blood-red. She'd say, "Now have any of you seen my orange stick?" We didn't know what the hell she was talking about. She used to say it gave her a lift getting out like that.

WOMAN THREE

That's called a lift? Whew!

WOMAN ONE

My dad used to say, "Hey, how come you don't get dolled up for me, don't I rate? You'd think you were more in love with those gals than you are with me"—that's what he'd say, and you know something—ha—it was probably true.

WOMAN TWO

In love—?

WOMAN ONE

They got off on each other, the four of them. My mom didn't know one single human when she first moved here—it was a company move, my dad's company—and these three dames were the first people she met. This was back—hey, it must have been the fifties.

WOMAN TWO

Wow!

WOMAN ONE

You should have heard 'em talk. They never stopped. Only thing is, I can't remember what they used to talk about. They'd all talk at once, or at least that's how it sounded, and my dad had this standing joke. "Hey, who listens?" he'd ask her. Ha ha ha. Oh, she got so sick of him saying that every single week—"who listens?" It got on her nerves—she told me that after the divorce. Sort of broke the camel's back kind-of-thing?

WOMAN TWO

Yeah, well for my mom it was—

WOMAN ONE

Well, sometimes it would happen that there'd be an afternoon when one of The Edge of Nighters had to miss. Someone would get sick or go on a trip or maybe was having a baby—they were always having babies. Once they were all preg-city at the same time. Mom said it was like they were sitting there with these watermelons on their laps. Well, this once, one of them called at the last minute. She couldn't come, some emergency or something, and so my mother said to me—I was home from school eating my lunch, a peanut butter and jam sandwich probably, that's all I ate when I was a kid, I was a real brat—anyway, she said, "How'd you like to stay home this afternoon. I'll write your teacher a note, say you've got a sore throat." Then she sat me down with a deck of cards and gave me a quickie lesson. Seven years old. Jeez. It was amazing, her sitting there pumping me full of all this stuff, all those rules, it was like she was someone else, someone, you know, nicer? Like we were two women, you know? Like girlfriends or something. That's how I learned.

WOMAN THREE

I got it pumped into me, too, but I mean like literally. My mother? She used to take me with her when she played. It was hard to get babysitters in the daytime then and I was just a baby. She just stuck me in a corner in my little basket thingamajig, and if I got hungry and made a fuss, she'd whip out a boob right there at the table. Never missed a hand. A month old, two months old, and there I was, sucking up all those hearts and diamond tricks along with my mother's milk. God, I wonder what it tastes like.

WOMAN ONE

[Reflecting.] Vanilla ice cream—that's what I've heard—only melted.

WOMAN FOUR

Well, *[long dramatic pause]* you're not going to believe this, but I swear to you it's the truth. My mother came home one night from the community club. She'd had this real heavy game. And it was the first time in her life she'd made a grand slam. Ever. She was high, she was in heaven, little birds singing kind of thing. She'd finally done it, know what I mean? It was a real rush.

WOMAN TWO

And?

WOMAN FOUR

That—that was the night I was conceived.

WOMAN TWO

I don't believe it.

WOMAN FOUR

It's the truth. I swear to God. I owe my life to a good spread of hearts.

WOMAN ONE

Hey, that's beautiful.

WOMAN FOUR

My dad probably didn't even know. They didn't talk about—you know— but my mother's friends all knew. Sometimes when I'd see them, they'd give me a little pat on the head and say, "Hi there, Grand Slam." God, I used to be so embarrassed. I'd just—it was crazy, I sort of loved it, though, if ya know what I mean.

WOMAN THREE

It's going to be different for us.

WOMAN FOUR

What? Making babies? Hey, I don't know about that.

WOMAN THREE

No. Not making babies.

WOMAN TWO

Well, what then?

WOMAN ONE

We're not going to need all that stuff. Those grand slams, that other junk. Those afternoons. Setting your hair, doing your nails. Dainties. Sherry. It'll be different. Like our bullshit isn't their bullshit, you know?

WOMAN TWO

Yeah, but is it going to be better. Or worse?

WOMAN FOUR

Better. You better believe it, better.

WOMAN THREE

When I think of the exploitation.

WOMAN ONE

But, who . . . who was exploiting them?

WOMAN THREE

What I mean is, they kind of like exploited themselves, know what I mean?

WOMAN TWO

All the same—I don't know, I've got this feeling—

WOMAN ONE

What?

WOMAN TWO

I was just going to say—at least it was better than—

WOMAN FOUR

At least they were kinda looking after each other, you know?

WOMAN TWO

Let's start. Now. Let's not waste any time. We've already wasted too much time.

WOMAN ONE

What do you mean? Start what?

WOMAN TWO

[Desperately.] Let's play. Let's . . . *[she reaches for the radio and turns up the music]* let's turn up the music. Come on, you guys, let's *[she is shouting now]* let's deal.
[Lights fade; music fades. Lights come up on the elderly CLARA *seated at a table, moving cards back and forth. She looks up and addresses audience.]*

CLARA

That doctor, he was right about one thing—Ruthie didn't last long. And after she went? There was this one whole summer and fall we didn't play. Tuesday nights would roll around, and it would be like any other night, but then Margot phoned me up one day and said she'd run into Geraldine McMurtry who was a sort of cousin of hers, the *money* side of the family, and Geraldine happened to say to Margot how she liked a few hands now and then, nothing serious, and Margot said to me, you know, maybe we should think of, you know, getting started again, and so we did.

It gave me . . . it gave me pause . . . seeing Geraldine McMurtry sitting here, in this chair. I found it . . . upsetting. Well, she's very . . . she's got . . . that is, compared to the rest of us, she's very . . . comfortable. That house! And those pearls of hers, they were real pearls. That first night, she made Doris so nervous, she was biting her nails. It was her manner of bidding, I think, not so much the pearls. Ruthie, well, Ruthie had always been a firm bidder, slow, but decided. But here was Geraldine. She sort of tore into her bids, just ripped in. Sometimes she'd open with, say, three hearts. Sometimes—whew—right into no-trump. Just lunged. Like she hadn't even taken time to count her points—only, in fact, she had. She was much, much sharper than she'd let on that day she ran into Margot. She'd fooled us in a way. And I don't know how it happened, but we all got kind of reckless, too.

It changed us. Suddenly we were all playing these no-trump hands— but anyway, it was something to do on a Tuesday night. We got used to her, Geraldine. And I suppose . . . at first . . . she was getting used to us. She hated being dummy, she'd tap her fingernails on the edge of the table or else pull out her knitting . . . with a kind of jerk . . . but she relaxed after a bit. And she could make us laugh, Margot especially. It was something to see, Margot going off in, in gales.

It was a funny thing about Margot. In all those years—it was forty-three years in all, we were young women when we started out, just newly married, all of us—in all that time, Margot's husband, Ronald—Ronald thought she spent her each and every Tuesday night doing knitting for the Martha Circle. *[Long pause.]* He was a Baptist, Ronald, all his life. No drinking, no dancing, no this, no that. So we had this code word. I'd call up Margot and say, "Martha Circle's meeting at Doris's next Tuesday," or, if something came up, "Martha Circle's cancelled this week." Oh, she hated that, when we had to cancel for some reason or other. Oh my. The Martha Circle.

We used to say to her, "Tell him, face up to him. Own up to it." But the thing was, she left it too late. *[As she talks, she moves the cards about.]* It's one thing to face up to a young husband and get your way. A young girl can do pretty well anything she wants. It's something else to sneak around for forty-three years, making up lies and excuses. *[Holds up a card.]* The devil's eyelids, that's what Ronald called these—he'd been brought up in a strict household. Well, we said to Margot, explain to him there's just as much skill as chance involved, maybe more, but she just shook her head.

I think it made her ashamed, even though we made a joke about it. "Who's going to cut the devil's eyelids?" we'd say, that sort of thing. You'd think we'd get sick from laughing, oh, we'd howl.
[She picks up the cards and starts again.]

After Margot was . . . gone, about a year after, and Ronald asked me, asked me if I would do him the honour, the honour of being his wife, well,

I said I had to think about that a bit. "You'll have to give me some time," I said. He said, "Here we are, Clara, the two of us. We've known each other for donkey's years, and now we're each of us left on our lonesome, your Arthur gone to his reward, and my poor Margot. You and I, we could be company for each other." And I said to Ronald, yes, that's true enough, but I needed time to think about it.

Well, I screwed up my nerve and went and asked Doris, what did she think. Luckily I caught her on one of her good days. I said, did she think Margot would have had any objection if Ronald and I . . . and she said, Doris said, on the contrary, just the opposite, that Margot would have taken it as a compliment. Another thing Doris said was Ronald Hetherling's a good-hearted man and he's got . . . the loveliest head of hair you've ever seen on someone that age.

So I said to Ronald, yes, but on one condition, that on Tuesday nights I was . . . occupied . . . with my Martha Circle. He gave me a look. And cleared his throat. On Tuesday nights, he told me, he himself attends his adult Bible class. In the church basement, it's been going on for years and years, and they're still in the prophets. He goes out every Tuesday night, he stressed that particular point, from seven to ten o'clock, and he wanted me to go on doing what I'd always been doing, because it meant a great deal to me, he knew that.

[She gathers up the cards, stacks them slowly; the clock chimes; when it reaches ten strokes, she puts the cards in her pocket. The clock strikes fourteen times. Lights fade almost completely, then come up brilliantly. She sits up straight, suddenly younger, WOMAN ONE (WEST).

Three other women enter briskly, joining WOMAN ONE *and taking their places at the card table. They are all talking at once as the cards are rapidly dealt out and hands taken up and arranged.]*

WOMAN ONE

—so the wind started blowing like crazy—

WOMAN TWO (SOUTH)

[Simultaneously.]—dead tired, but the floors to do—

WOMAN THREE (EAST)

[Simultaneously.]—half a pound of sugar, not half a cup—

WOMAN FOUR (NORTH)

[Simultaneously.]—never could add two and two—
[Pause.]

WOMAN ONE

—Victoria Day picnic after all—

WOMAN TWO

[Simultaneously.]—swallowing an upholstery tack and—

WOMAN THREE

[Simultaneously.]—specialized in steam fitting, which I thought—

WOMAN FOUR

[Simultaneously.]—two yards of grosgrain ribbon around the border—
[Pause.]

WOMAN ONE

—the most terrible headache and his ears, too—

WOMAN TWO

[Simultaneously.]—an out and out lie, but what did I know?

WOMAN THREE

[Simultaneously.]—a sight for sore eyes, I told her, but she said—

WOMAN FOUR

[Simultaneously.]—deaf as a stone after the age of sixty-five—
[Pause.]

WOMAN ONE

Two clubs.

WOMAN TWO

Pass.

WOMAN THREE

Two spades?

WOMAN FOUR

—she said interrogatively. Pass.

WOMAN ONE

Three spades.

WOMAN TWO

—she said emphatically. Pass.

WOMAN THREE

Pass.

WOMAN FOUR

Pass.

WOMAN ONE

Dummy again. Which reminds me—
[Here she raises her hands in the air and switches into a rapid-fire recitative style.]
My grandson Trevor, you remember Trevor, oh that boy, well he scored a zero on his algebra test and not only that, he was rude to the teacher who sent him down to the principal's office, where they made him sit for two hours and twenty minutes, twiddling his thumbs and scared to death the whole time of getting expelled—now do you think that's fair? I was so burned up I just had to tell you.

WOMAN TWO

Tell away! Better to get it off your chest.

WOMAN THREE

Absolutely.

WOMAN FOUR

Why do you think we're sitting at this table—

WOMAN THREE

[Singing.]
    That's what we're here for—

WOMAN TWO

[Singing.]
    —don't ya know.

ALL

[Singing; drumming on table.]
    That's what we're here for, don't ya know.

WOMAN TWO

[Recitative.] Just between you and me and the lamppost, I can't bear to think that I am now the wife of a grandfather—with whom, if the truth were known, I sometimes have vicious quarrels about foolish things, like for instance putting too much detergent in the dishwater and not rinsing prop-er-ly, and then one of us or both of us starts in calling the other one an ungrateful, hard-hearted, insensitive so-and-so—

WOMAN ONE

Just lay it on us. Just let it go.

ALL

[Singing; drumming table.]
    That's what we're here for, don't ya know.

WOMAN THREE

[Recitative.] I feel I can't keep this to myself for one minute longer—I am

so bloody sick and tired of making things for bazaars, hideous things, things made out of orange nylon, things nobody in God's creation wants or needs or appre-ciates. Sure I know it's not worth making a fuss about, so tell me, why do I want to climb up on a soapbox and scream and rage and tell the whole wide world where to gooooo.

ALL

[Singing; drumming table.]
    Hey, tell us about it, tell us about it,
    That's what we're here for, that's what we're here for—
    Sitting at this table, sitting at this table, sitting here, sitting here—
    Don't ya know.

WOMAN FOUR

[Recitative.] So she turned around and said to me in this loud, snarky voice, "This is the express line, madam. Can't you see this is the express line? Only nine items allowed, madam, and you have at least twelve in your basket, madam. That's the rule, nine items," and I said, "Oh I'm so sorry, I guess I was thinking of something else," feeling like a complete and utter fool, and for days I've been walking around feeling lower than low—

ALL

[Singing; drumming table.]
    Let it out, just let it out,
    That's what we're here for
    Sitting at this table, sitting at this table,
    Don't ya know.

WOMAN ONE

[Recitative or speaking.] Listen, my friends, something's wrong with me, something's terribly wrong. Lately I keep forgetting things. I keep losing things, my purse, my slippers, my famous recipe for mango chutney. I've become one of those women, you know the type, who's always rummaging in her purse, rummage, rummage, and—this is the worst part—most of the time I can't remember what the hell I'm rummaging for. Oh my God,

sometimes I sit in the dark and cry for no good reason. I mean, tell me, honestly, do you think it's just hormones or what?

WOMAN TWO

[Recitative, quietly.] My husband got this statuette for working for the same company for forty-five years, and I wanted him to put it on the mantle— this is something to be proud of, I said—but do you know what he did? He put it in a green garbage bag and put a twist-tie around it—he actually went and took the darn thing to the dump.

WOMAN FOUR

[Recitative.] I'll never understand men, I'll never understand my in-laws, I'll never understand my children, my grandchildren, my grade three teacher, and as for that snarky woman in Safeway, I can't stop thinking how mad I am at, at, at—

WOMAN ONE

[Speaking.] Never mind. Just let it out.

WOMAN TWO

[Speaking.] Our ears are open.

WOMAN THREE

[Speaking.] You'll feel better.

WOMAN ONE

A helluva lot better.

WOMAN TWO

You know what they say about bottling things up.

WOMAN THREE

Just let it go.

WOMAN ONE

[Recitative.] I hate to sound like I'm complaining, but I'm so fed up with colouring my hair, tinting my hair, dying my goddamn hair. I mean my mother had grey hair. Why can't I have grey hair, grey hair done up in a teensy-weensy, itsy-bitsy bun? Do you understand what I'm saying? A little grey bun, here! With a rubber band around it, here!

WOMAN TWO

[Speaking.] Really?

WOMAN THREE

[Recitative.] If that's what you want—

WOMAN ONE

[Screams.] That's what I want.

WOMAN THREE

Go for it, as my grandson would say.

WOMAN FOUR

[Recitative.] Sometimes—sometimes I feel invisible. It started not long after my fiftieth birthday. I could feel people looking right past me, looking for someone more attractive, looking for someone more interesting to talk to. It's like I'm not here anymore—am I crazy or what?

WOMAN TWO

[Recitative.] I know juuuust what you meeeean—

WOMAN ONE

[Recitative.] The saaaame thing happens to meeee—

WOMAN THREE

[Recitative.]—and to meeeeeee *[holds high note as long as possible].*

WOMAN ONE

—and to meeee.

ALL

[In unison.]—Meeeeee.

WOMAN TWO

What can we do, what can we do?

WOMAN THREE

[Speaking, struck by idea.] Hey, if we're invisible, doesn't that mean we can do anything we want? Rude things. Appalling things. Hideous things.

WOMAN ONE

[Recitative.] Let it out, just let it out, let it goooo.
[Pause. They all sing.]

ALL

That's what we're here for, that's what we're here for,
Sitting round the table, sitting round the table,
That's what we're here for,
Don't ya know.

[The women retire to the dressing room, softly carrying on with the chorus. The music gradually fades. Light comes up on four women seated around a card table. They are wearing hats of a vaguely fifties fashion. Their postures and voices betray their nervousness. One of them has just dropped a sherry glass on the floor and broken it.]

WOMAN ONE (NORTH)

Oh! Oh, I'm so sorry, I don't know how I—

WOMAN TWO (WEST)

Please. It's nothing.
[She pats WOMAN ONE's hand comfortingly and starts to pick the pieces off the floor. The other three women dive to the floor to help with the cleanup.]

WOMAN ONE

Such a beautiful crystal glass. I don't know how I could have been so—*[To herself.]* Damn, now I've done it. Oh, damn, damn, damn, damn. At least the damn thing was empty.

WOMAN TWO

Please, please don't give it another thought. Really, it isn't at all valuable. *[To herself.]* If she only knew. Crystal, ha! Thirty-nine cents at Woolworth's.

WOMAN THREE (SOUTH)

Careful, don't cut yourself. *[To herself.]* Bad enough I overbid on that last hand. Brian warned me about overbidding.
[Women rise and take their places again.]

WOMAN TWO

[To WOMAN ONE.*]* I'll just get you another glass of sherry. *[To herself.]* I can't stand it, the way she's looking at me. Oh, no, she's going to cry. I cannot stand this.

WOMAN ONE

Oh, no, thank you, I've had enough, thank you just the same. *[To herself.]* Enough, ha. I'm drunk. I am drunk. Hee hee. I'm high as a kite, I'm flying.

WOMAN FOUR (EAST)

[Anxious to change subject.] Well. Shall I deal then? *[To herself.]* I wish she'd offer *me* another sherry. Not that I need it. Whew.

WOMAN THREE

I'm not sure, but I think, if I'm not mistaken, I think it's . . . maybe . . . my . . . deal? *[To herself.]* I wonder if I sound pushy, overbearing. But it really is my deal. At least I think it is.

WOMAN FOUR

Oh, of course, how stupid of me. *[To herself, Southern accent.]* Ah'm just sooo stew-pid. Pu-leese! The stupid part was saying I'd come here today. I'm going to kill Jonathan when I get home. Roping me into this!

WOMAN THREE

[Dealing.] Oh, sorry, misdeal. I'll start over. *[To herself.]* What's the matter with me. My hands are . . . they're sweating. This is real sweat. Wet sweat. And my underarms, I wonder if I smell. This is like being a teenager again. Worse. Why did I let myself in for this?

WOMAN ONE

About that sherry glass, I really would like to pay for it. I'd feel better.

WOMAN TWO

[To herself.] Can't she just forget it. *[Out loud.]* Honestly, I wouldn't dream of letting you.

WOMAN ONE

[To herself.] I don't know why she's serving sherry anyway. Especially sweet sherry. I could puke. My mother always used to serve tea. Orange pekoe. And date squares.

WOMAN TWO

[To herself.] I shouldn't have listened to Thurston. I knew I should have stuck with tea or coffee. I think—I think she's a little . . . drunk.

WOMAN THREE

I'm going to say . . . one heart. *[To herself.]* Well, just say it then, why don't ya. One little buttery heart.

WOMAN TWO

[To herself.] I wish I was drunk. Veddy, veddy drunk.

WOMAN THREE

Ahem. *[Repeating.]* One heart? *[To herself.]* Pretty timid bid, but I don't dare overbid again. The way she glared at me. At least I think she was glaring. How'm I supposed to know without my glasses on? Why didn't I wear them. Who cares. *She's* got glasses on. Gawd, are they hideous, too.

WOMAN TWO

Pass. *[To herself.]* I wonder if they noticed the fruitcake was underdone. They did eat it. They chewed. And they swallowed, but they swallowed in a kind of thick, cakey way. *[Whimpers.]* Maybe—maybe that's why they drank so much sherry.

WOMAN ONE

Two hearts. *[To herself.]* Do it for me, he said. It's important, meeting the other company wives. What the hell does he know about company wives?

WOMAN FOUR

Pass. *[To herself.]* Coward. And with twelve points in my hand! I wonder if anyone'll notice.

WOMAN THREE

Pass. *[To herself.]* I should go to three, but I'd better not chance it. Brian's always saying how reckless I get. We could actually have a little slam here . . . no, better not.

WOMAN FOUR

[To herself.] I'm the only one here whose purse and shoes don't match.

WOMAN ONE

[To herself.] I've got to forget that damn broken glass.

WOMAN TWO

[To herself.] I don't care what Thurston says, I'm not cut out to be the boss's wife. Charming, sweet, thoughtful. Argggh.

WOMAN THREE

[To herself.] The next time she invites us, I'm going to say I'm sick. I'll say something like, like I've got a migraine. Or I'm waiting for a long distance

call from . . . my sister or something. How's she going to know I don't have a sister?

WOMAN ONE

[To herself.] And Mother actually enjoyed this. But that was different.

WOMAN THREE

[To herself.] My nail polish. Chipped. And I just did them before I came. Brian always says—

WOMAN ONE

[To herself.] I'll send her a little hasty note, tell her how *frightfully* sorry I am about her dumb, stupid, idiotic, unspeakable, precious two-bit sherry glass—

WOMAN TWO

[To herself.] I should have served chocolate chip cookies. Why do I always listen to Thurston? What does he know anyway? Next time I'll serve—if there is a next time. If only they'd go home—

WOMAN THREE

[To herself.] I wish I was home. It's four o'clock. I could be flaked out on the couch, my feet up, watching *The Edge of Night.* I wonder if Sarah's going to tell Steve about the baby's real father today.

WOMAN FOUR

God, I'm wrecking the cards, clenching them like this. *[To herself.]* I wish this was over.

WOMAN ONE

[To herself.] I wish I was dead.

WOMAN TWO

You made it. Two hearts.

WOMAN FOUR

Well played.

WOMAN THREE

I can't believe it, what luck.

WOMAN ONE

[To herself.] When I think Mother did this every Tuesday night for . . . forty years, the four of them. Doris Veal, Auntie Doris, she was a bit scary, and Clara Wesley and Margot Hetherling. *[Out loud.]* When I think of it, my mother used to play every Tuesday night, for forty years.

WOMAN TWO

Really! That's . . . *[hunts for word]* marvellous.

WOMAN THREE

My mother, too. Only it was Saturdays. They'd start off with a potluck lunch, macaroni and tuna things, or something creamed on patty shells, and then—

WOMAN FOUR

With our family it was the back porch. In the summertime. We'd play until it got dark. Men against the women. My uncles, my grandfather, cousins. There'd be mosquitoes buzzing like mad in front of our faces, but we'd keep—

WOMAN ONE

I used to lie in bed and listen to them downstairs in the living room. I could smell their cigarette smoke drifting up the—of course they all smoked like chimneys—

WOMAN TWO

Well, people did then.

WOMAN ONE

[To herself.] God, I could use a fag right now. Doesn't this woman own any ashtrays?

WOMAN THREE

[Desperately.] Good heavens, I just noticed the time, I hate to break this up, but I've got to get on my way. *[To herself.]* Oi, oi, now that was pretty smooth!

WOMAN FOUR

Me too. Jonathan likes me to be there when he comes in the door. He likes dinner waiting, likes to walk in and smell dinner cooking. He says it's the best part of his—*[To herself.]* My God, I'm babbling, stop it, stop it.

WOMAN TWO

I'll just get your coats.

WOMAN ONE

[Rising.] My mother was only fifty-nine when she died. Cancer. Of the uterus. The rest of them, they went on for years. One of them, Clara Wesley, she phoned me specially and asked me if I minded that they went on, if I'd mind. As if I, as the daughter, would be offended that my mother's friends were carrying on. Isn't that amazing? They were like these strange extra aunts, coming in through the door, winter nights in their heavy coats, summertime in cotton dresses, all the time I was growing up.

WOMAN FOUR

My mother died of cancer, too. It was all through her.

WOMAN THREE

My mother still plays, every Saturday. There were eight of them back in the old days. Now they're down to four. I don't know what they'll do when—

WOMAN ONE

When my mother died, afterwards, I was going through her things, sorting through her gloves and her purses, all those things, and her hats—she loved hats. Oh, not little pie plate things like we wear today. Big hats. They meant something. Well, I was emptying out one of her dresser drawers, and what should I come across but a bunch of old card-party tallies. Oh, I can't tell you, they were lovely. *[Her voice breaks.]*

WOMAN FOUR

Here. *[Hands tissue.]*

WOMAN ONE

They had these . . . little silk tassels on them.

WOMAN TWO

You mustn't upset yourself.

WOMAN ONE

[Dry-eyed now.] They were always laughing. Laughing to beat the band, as they would have said. One of them, Doris I think, she used to tell . . .

WOMAN FOUR

What?

WOMAN ONE

Well . . . stories. Maybe a tiny bit off-colour. I couldn't hear very well, but that's what it sounded like, from the way they were laughing. I couldn't believe it was my mother. I never heard her really laugh except on those Tuesday nights. They were so . . . gay.

WOMAN TWO

My mother, she didn't have much chance for a good time . . . we were out on this godforsaken farm, eight of us kids—

WOMAN FOUR

Well, thank you so much. It's been—

WOMAN ONE

Their voices would come up through the hot air register. I tried to listen, but I couldn't make out exactly—

WOMAN THREE

A very pleasant afternoon. Thank you for asking me. I appreciate—

WOMAN TWO

Maybe we could do it again. I don't actually know all that many people here—

WOMAN FOUR

I don't know a soul.

WOMAN THREE

Well, I'm not sure, I'm pretty busy, and my sister might be—

WOMAN ONE

Maybe you'd like to come to my place next time.

WOMAN TWO

Well—

WOMAN ONE

Only thing, we haven't got around to getting a card table yet, and the dining room table's too big, but maybe, there's always the kitchen table—

WOMAN FOUR

That's no problem, the kitchen table.

WOMAN ONE

And another thing, we're having our floors sanded and it's pretty dusty. Maybe you could come in something—

WOMAN FOUR

Casual?

WOMAN TWO

We could wear . . . *[as though struck with inspiration]* sports clothes.

WOMAN FOUR

Should we set a date?

WOMAN THREE

If we could make it a little earlier? I always watch, well . . . *The Edge of Night.*

WOMAN TWO

Oh, so do I.

WOMAN FOUR

Me too. As a matter of fact, I was just wondering, if Sarah and Steve were going to—

WOMAN ONE

How about next week, next Wednesday. A few hands, and then we'll put the TV on. We can, you know, just see how it goes.
[Lights dim and give way to a tape of women talking and laughing. Three women exit to the dressing room, leaving CLARA behind. Light softens. Clarinet music. FLOWERY HAT (SOUTH), wearing a large flowery hat, mounts a bicycle, rides to centre stage, ringing the bicycle bell importantly.]

FLOWERY HAT

You must be Clara. Clara Wesley.

CLARA

[Rummaging in her purse.] Actually, it's Clara Hetherling now. Now what did I do with those keys of mine?

FLOWERY HAT

Of course. Mrs. Hetherling. That's the name I have on this form.

CLARA

There they are, my keys. I knew they were there. Now, if I can just put my hands on my specs . . .

FLOWERY HAT

I see you're still rushing around, getting ready to go out, getting ready for an evening with your friends. I see you've become the kind of person who's always rummaging in her purse. I see you're a little older.

CLARA

Older? Well, yes, I suppose. We all get older, don't we? Now if you'll excuse me, I really must—I can't see a thing without my specs.

FLOWERY HAT

I see you're still going on with your life, Clara. That is, I see your life is going on with you.

CLARA

Well, I suppose you could say—

FLOWERY HAT

I find it strange, don't you, the way a human life drains down toward one thing, just one little revealing thing.

CLARA

What thing? What do you mean, thing? Now I really must concentrate. Where did I put those—

FLOWERY HAT

This game you play, this Tuesday night game the four of you *hurl* yourselves into—

CLARA

[Finding specs.] Here they are, thank the Lord. *[Rushing away.]*

FLOWERY HAT

[Calling after her.] This game of yours. Can you tell me about this game?

CLARA

[Turning impatiently but politely.] I'm terribly late.

FLOWERY HAT

This game.

CLARA

Oh, for heaven's sake. *[Laughs.]* For heaven's sakes. *[Quietly, puzzled herself.]* It isn't—it isn't just a *game*, you know.
[Music. Lights fade. End of Act One.]

368

Act Two

Song: to be sung in the lobby during the last three or four minutes of inter-mission or on the stage as the opening of Act Two. Four women wearing beads and long white gloves take their places at the card table. The song is operetta style, sung with Gilbert and Sullivan lightness.

ALL

It's not a sin—no it's not a sin—
It's not a sin, sin, sin, sin, sin,
To want to win, win, win, win,
Competi-tion is not necessar-ily
a sin.
It's only nat-ural, it's o-nly fair,
To come up breathing—na-tural com-pet-i-tive air.
To want to win, win, win, win,
Is not a sin, no, no, it's not a sin.
So let's be-ginnnnn.
[Piano repeat.]

SOUTH

A very fine hand
Is all I ask, it's all I ask,
A decent hand is what I require
To make the e-vening catch fire.

ALL

A very fine hand
Is all she asks, is all she asks,
A decent hand is what she requires
To make the e-vening catch fire.
It's not a sin—you know, you know—to want to win.

EAST AND WEST

A run of spades will bring us luck,

Will bring us luck, will bring us luck,
With King and Queen—and Ace and Jack—
It's all we need—a little luck.

ALL

A King and Queen and Ace and Jack
It's all they need, a little luck.
A little luck, a little luck,
Or a little more than a little luck,
A little more than a little luck.
It's not a sin—you know—to want to win,
It's not a sin, no, no, it's not a sin.
So let's be-gin.

SOUTH AND NORTH

It's not a crime to take your time,
No, it's not a crime to take your time,
Their reason's sound, they're off the ground,
They'll bring the e-vening around.

ALL

We'll bring the e-vening around,
Oh, we'll bring the e-vening around.
It's not a sinnnn
To want to winnnn
So breast your cards, my friends,
And we'll begin.

NORTH

We'll counter with—our sturdy hearts,
Our mighty hearts, our bleeding hearts,
With length and strength in bloody hearts
We'll bring a crushing bid to start.

ALL

Ooooo-oooo-oooo,
Trump, trump, trump, trump,
Trump, trump, trump, trump.
Taking in those gorgeous trumps,
It's not a sin, to want to win.
We're on our way—to victory.
Trump, trump, trump, trump.

EAST AND WEST

One, two three, four five six, seven,
Trump, trump, trump, trump,
Trump, trump, trump, trump.
[Carry on beat through next chorus.]

SOUTH AND NORTH

We'll open with a lead to trump.

EAST AND WEST

We won't be stumped by a lead to trump.

SOUTH

We'll open low, then third hand high
And that will be our strat-ta-gy. *[Pronounced: strat-e-gye.]*

ALL

They'll open with a lead to trump.
They'll thump them hard with a lead to trump,
They'll open low low low,
Then third hand high high high,
That is to be—their strat-ta-gy. *[Strat-e-gye.]*

SOUTH AND NORTH

Trump, trump, trump, trump,
Trump, trump, trump, trump.

EAST AND WEST

And now the tricks come rolling in,
Come rolling in, come rolling in,
We'll make our bid or go down low,
This is the way—the game will go.

SOUTH AND NORTH

We must confess—a bold finesse,
We must confess—yes, yes, yes, yes,
A bold finesse.
It's not a sin—you know, to want to win.

ALL

Club and diamond, hearts and spades.
And tricks and trumps—and masquerades—
With luck and cun-ning, we'll raid and trade—
This isn't—you know—the Ladies' Aid.
No, no, no, no, it's not a sin
To want to win.

[All rise from the table, repeat.]

Club and diamond, hearts and spades
And tricks and trumps—and masquerades—
With luck and cun-ning, we'll raid and trade—
This isn't—you know—the Ladies' Aid.
No, no, no, no, it's not a sin
To want to win
So let's begin.

[Lights come up on the card table. The women are The Edge of Night foursome, a few years older.]

WOMAN TWO (WEST)

And we were so close to making it! If we'd just made that club trick, it would have been ours.

WOMAN FOUR (EAST)

Oh God, I'm sorry.

WOMAN ONE (NORTH)

Hey, hey, hey, since when did we start apologizing?

WOMAN FOUR

My second boob this afternoon. What's the matter with me?

WOMAN TWO

Anyone can have a bad day.

WOMAN THREE (SOUTH)

Don't I know it. Remember last week? My God, I bombed with my diamonds. Twenty-one points and I took a royal nose-dive. Sheesh.

WOMAN FOUR

[Shuffles the cards, which suddenly slide out of her hands.] Oh, no, look what I did now.

WOMAN ONE

Maybe we should quit. There's not really enough time for another game.

WOMAN THREE

We could have a quickie—

WOMAN TWO

Okay, one more hand.

WOMAN FOUR

[Taking a deep breath.] Listen, maybe we'd better . . . not. I've got . . . something to say. An announcement, sort of. I've been putting it off and putting it off—oh look, but maybe I should just say it fast and get it over with.

WOMAN ONE

What gives? You sound . . . serious.

WOMAN FOUR

I am . . . serious.

WOMAN THREE

Go on.

WOMAN FOUR

I don't know how to tell you this. All of you. I meant to tell you right away, when we first got here this afternoon, but—

WOMAN TWO

You can't—you can't be—

WOMAN THREE

Not at your—I mean, you had your tubes—

WOMAN FOUR

No, no, no, it's, well, oh, this is harder than I thought—

WOMAN TWO

You haven't got a brain tumour.

WOMAN ONE

A brain tumour! What made you think of a brain tumour?

WOMAN TWO

I dunno. I guess I was thinking of that time way back when Steve on *The Edge of Night*—

WOMAN FOUR

It's nothing like that. It's something . . . completely different. It's just that—
I've—

WOMAN ONE

Come on, take it easy. You're going to feel a whole lot better once you've got whatever it is off your—

WOMAN FOUR

It's just that I've, well, I've come to . . . a decision.

WOMAN TWO

I can't stand this.

WOMAN FOUR

It was a very, very tough decision to make, for, for all kinds of reasons.

WOMAN ONE

Oh my God, no. I knew it. My sixth sense. You're leaving—

WOMAN THREE

You're leaving Jonathan.

WOMAN FOUR

I, actually I—

WOMAN TWO

I saw this coming. I saw it coming for a looooonng time. I never said anything, but I did see—

WOMAN ONE

Listen, listen, you've got to get this in proportion. Okay, so it's a major decision, but it's not the end of the world. And, who knows, it just might be the best decision you've ever made. You may just—

WOMAN FOUR

I—

WOMAN TWO

You've put up with a lot.

WOMAN THREE

That's for sure.

WOMAN ONE

We know Jonathan hasn't exactly been—

WOMAN FOUR

Look, I'm—

WOMAN ONE

You're going to be just fine. You'll come through this. And we'll support you—

WOMAN THREE

—every inch of the way.

WOMAN TWO

I just wish I had the courage. I look at Thurston and I think, Is this the same man I married? Sometimes he's such a, such a—

WOMAN ONE

Jerk. Even Brian says—

WOMAN THREE

Precisely. And Jerry says exactly the—

WOMAN FOUR

Actually—

WOMAN TWO

I was serving this salad? Oooooo! A new recipe—you take cracked wheat, olive oil, green onions and, just before serving, you add a handful of currants.

WOMAN THREE

Currants? You mean like raisins?

WOMAN TWO

It's supposed to be Mediterranean.

WOMAN ONE

Sounds really . . . interesting.

WOMAN TWO

Well, I was right in the middle of serving it, there were eight of us at the table—

WOMAN ONE

Clients, I suppose. Trust Thurston.

WOMAN TWO

As a matter of fact, it was my sister-in-law Edna and her family. We were eating this salad, and do you know what Thurston said?

WOMAN THREE

I can't stand it. What?

WOMAN TWO

He said, "What exactly are these rabbit droppings doing in the salad?" He was just . . . being . . . funny, his little joke, ha ha, but something, something awful came over me. Like my scalp was freezing. And burning at the same time. Rabbit droppings. Doo-doo in my Mediterranean salad. I wanted to reach across the table and . . . tear his ears off.

WOMAN FOUR

Never mind his ears, you should've gone for his—

WOMAN ONE

You don't have to sit there and take what Thurston dishes out—

WOMAN THREE

You know something, I've got a pretty good idea what Jerry would do if he saw currants in one of my salads. He wouldn't say anything, but he'd roll his eyes. Oh boy, that gets to me, when he rolls his—

WOMAN FOUR

Look, I want to—

WOMAN THREE

In eleven years, I don't think there's been one day when he hasn't . . . rolled his—

WOMAN ONE

[Sympathetically.] Jesus, that's—

WOMAN THREE

I'll do something or I'll say something, some little thing, and up go his—zoom. They go right *through* me, right . . . through my heart.

WOMAN TWO

And you put up with that?

WOMAN THREE

I've thought seriously about leaving him. But what am I supposed to tell people, that I'm leaving my husband because he rolls—?

WOMAN TWO

Listen, you don't have to explain anything to anybody. You just have to get up and go.

WOMAN ONE

Or tell him to go. That's what I'd say. Out. Here's the door, there's the door-
knob—out! Only before he left I'd show him the Eaton's bill. Get a gander
at this, I'd say. A hundred and fifty dollars. A hundred and fifty smackers
paid out to Eaton's. A cosmetic item. Perfume. French, no less. Explain that
if you don't mind.

WOMAN THREE

What are you talking about? What Eaton's bill? What perfume?

WOMAN ONE

What perfume—that's what I wanted to know. There it was on February's
statement, a $150 charge. Does he honestly think I'm not going to phone
the store and ask what's what?

WOMAN TWO

I had no idea he was the type to—

WOMAN ONE

And believe me . . . believe me, it isn't . . . the first time.

WOMAN TWO

Why on earth have you stayed with him?

WOMAN ONE

I've thought about it a lot. Especially lately. I mean, the kids are old enough
to understand. He could get an apartment downtown, see them on weekends,
not that he takes all that much interest in them anyway. The last time he—

WOMAN THREE

And you'd keep the house?

WOMAN ONE

I could rent out the basement to a couple of university students. The
money would help. And, well, to tell you the out and out truth, I wouldn't

mind the company. Someone to, you know, chew over the day with—What did you do? What did *you* do?—that kind of thing.

WOMAN TWO

Why not? We all need—

WOMAN THREE

You might be lonely. You know, at night.

WOMAN TWO

I don't know about that. When Thurston's away on business trips, I just love it. You know what I do? I eat peanuts. I just sit in front of the TV and eat peanuts, and no one ever says, "Hey, what about those saddlebags of yours."

WOMAN ONE

Talk about the pot calling the kettle—

WOMAN TWO

Exactly.

WOMAN THREE

I think, if I was on my own that is, I think I'd probably become a vegetarian. Jerry hates salad, but I could eat it three times a day. I could really get into the whole holistic thing—

WOMAN FOUR

Well, I—

WOMAN ONE

You've got to be careful about your lawyer. Really check it out, get hold of someone who's got a few progressive ideas about—

WOMAN TWO

As a matter of fact, I have the name of an excellent—

WOMAN THREE

The best thing to do, once you've made the decision, I mean, is go to a completely different city. If Jerry ever—

WOMAN TWO

A clean break. Absolutely right.

WOMAN THREE

Now, I've always—well, the fact is—I've always loved Montreal.

WOMAN ONE

Your French is terrific—

WOMAN THREE

Not exactly terrific, but I could brush up—

WOMAN TWO

I've got a line on a marvellous French course that's being offered—remind me to drop this brochure off for you.

WOMAN THREE

Why thanks, I'd appreciate that.

WOMAN ONE

I've said to him, one more time and it's over.

WOMAN TWO

I think I'd probably get myself a little puppy for company. Or maybe a *big* dog. Springer spaniels are nice. I've always wanted one. Thurston hates dogs, but—

WOMAN THREE

Jerry too, can't abide them.

WOMAN TWO

—but if . . . if I was on my own, if Thurston wasn't . . . around, well, a dog can be excellent company. Better than—

WOMAN ONE

I think you should definitely go for a dog.

WOMAN THREE

I'd redo the living room. If I was on my own. Go in for a, you know, a Mediterranean look.

WOMAN ONE

What I'd do is sell the piano. Definitely.

WOMAN TWO

I'd put a skylight in the bathroom. Right away. Thurston says they're useless in this climate, but—

WOMAN THREE

Jerry says they're a drain on the heating system.

WOMAN TWO

But they do let in a lot of light. And if it was up to me—

WOMAN THREE

If Thurston wasn't there—

WOMAN ONE

Why not. You need a change now and then. I've only hung on to that dumb piano because it belongs to *his* side of the family. Left on my own I'd—

WOMAN TWO

No one could blame you for a minute.

WOMAN FOUR

I—I—

WOMAN ONE

I just, just . . . *[close to tears]* I just want to get out while I still have a shred of dignity left.

WOMAN THREE

Listen, we'll stand by you. You know that, don't you.

WOMAN TWO

The problem is—

WOMAN ONE

The problem is, well, doing it.

WOMAN THREE

What do you mean?

WOMAN TWO

I know what you mean.

WOMAN ONE

Sometimes I think, I think it takes more courage than I've got.

WOMAN TWO

Me too. I say, hey, I'm comfortable enough. In some ways. Sometimes I'm even—

WOMAN THREE

Once I wrote him a note. A goodbye, this-thing-is-over note. I left it on the fridge.

WOMAN TWO

Really? You did?

WOMAN THREE

I thought, he'll sneak down in the middle of the night and make one of his revolting mayo and raspberry jam sandwich combos and he'll see it.

WOMAN ONE

And what did he say?

WOMAN THREE

I tore it up at the last minute. I just didn't have . . . the courage.

WOMAN ONE

[To WOMAN FOUR.*]* That's why, that's why I admire you for the decision you've taken. It takes real guts.

WOMAN TWO

And then you've got to bear in mind that Jonathan's going to recover in time, and you'll heal, too.

WOMAN THREE

You'll look back and think that leaving Jonathan was the best decision you've ever made.

WOMAN FOUR

But I'm not.

WOMAN ONE

Not what?

WOMAN FOUR

Not leaving Jonathan.

WOMAN TWO

You're not—?

WOMAN ONE

You're not leaving Jonathan?

WOMAN FOUR

I'm getting a job.

WOMAN THREE

A job.

WOMAN FOUR

It's in personnel. It's perfect for me, tailor-made, you might say.

WOMAN THREE

But Jonathan—?

WOMAN FOUR

Well, it was Jonathan actually who happened to hear about this job. He's been encouraging me to go back to work for years. But it's been a god-awful decision. It means—well, it means I have to give up . . . our Wednesday afternoons.

WOMAN ONE

Jesus Christ.

WOMAN TWO

My God.

WOMAN THREE

I can't believe it. A job!

WOMAN TWO

Actually . . . I was thinking . . . myself, of maybe, looking around for a . . . something part-time maybe . . .
[They all begin talking at once.]

WOMAN FOUR

Personnel can be the key in an up and coming firm—

WOMAN ONE

I'd need to brush up on my skills, do some kind of refresher course—

WOMAN TWO

I'd have to think seriously about how I'd handle myself in an interview and—

WOMAN THREE

I've had this gnawing feeling, you know, a kind of empty feeling, and maybe what I should do is—

WOMAN FOUR

Of course I'll have to modify my routines and work out—

WOMAN THREE

I could do one of those aptitude tests that point out the important—

WOMAN ONE

You have to consider the full range of options—

WOMAN TWO

When you think of self-fulfillment and all that—
[A musical tape plays while the women in the dressing room change—one into an apron, three into rather matronly dresses.

The MAID (SOUTH) *enters centre stage with a feather duster, jabbing at the chairs and table and putting cards on the table along with little dishes of nuts. Finally she looks up at the audience].*

MAID

I'm the maid. The *[pause]* maid. *[Speaking a little ironically.]* And today—tonight I should say, is Mrs. McMurtry's evening to have her *[flicking at the table]* ladies in. *[She dusts some more.]* They take turns, first one house then the next. Ring around the rosy. Every Tuesday night. They've been at it for years. But you better believe me, this is the only house that has . . . a maid. *[Mock curtsy.]*

Very la-dee-da, Mrs. McMurtry. Likes everything spotless, polished to the nines, but she says to me, "Keep the refreshments simple, I don't want to look like I'm showing off. The other ladies just serve something real simple, like homemade date squares. They'd die of shame before they'd go into a bakery and buy something ready-made. And," she says to me, "bring in the tea, but let me pour myself, otherwise it looks high and mighty, like I'm putting on the dog."

Well, now, let's see. The cards, the tallies, pencils, one dish of salted nuts and one of peppermints. "Don't use the silver nut dishes," she says. "That looks like I'm being posh. Just the glass ones." That's it. Lord, will you look at the time, here they come now.

[The rest of the scene is narrated by the MAID and the others operate in mime, as though they can't hear her; two women enter and are greeted by GERALDINE MCMURTRY (NORTH) with a hug and kiss. They give their coats to the MAID.]

"Take the coats," she says, "but don't make a big fuss about it—just hang them up quietly. In fact do everything quietly, no need to draw attention to—"

[The three women sit at the table. They can be observed chatting and looking at their watches, obviously waiting for the fourth. The MAID observes them from the side of the stage, flicking with her duster now and then.]

Now that's really strange. They're usually right on time, all four of 'em. On the button. Must be nice, nothing to do but trot around to each other's houses and have a high old time. Well, why not? I wouldn't mind it myself. Wonder what's keeping Mrs. Veal tonight. Sick or else maybe this weather or else—

[The three women at the table start to deal.]

Will you look at that. They're going to play three-handed. Well, I suppose they might as well while they're waiting. Terrible game, three-handed, dull as ditch water. It's funny—it just doesn't work. You gotta have four to make it work. But still, in a pinch—*[She works her way around so she can see over one shoulder.]*

Whew—what a hand. Nice hearts, a good string. Hmmm.

[She disappears and returns with three glasses of water on a tray.]

"The ladies like a glass of ice water while they're playing," she says to me. But not the best glasses, the second best. She doesn't want to put them in the position of, you know, feeling awkward—*[She looks over another shoulder, calculates.]* My, that's a real deadbeat hand. Can't do much with that—althooough she could reply in clubs just to let Mrs. Hetherling know what's what. Mrs. Hetherling used to be Mrs. Wesley, I have to be careful not to call her by—pass! She goes and passes, I knew it! No spunk, at least Mrs. McMurtry has a little—Will you look at the time, that Mrs. Veal, she's really late tonight. Maybe she forgot, though it's not very likely. You'd have thought she'd telephone if she was going to be late. That last family I worked for, they had cocktail parties just about every week, sometimes twice, and I was forever in the kitchen making these little fancy thingama-jigs. Little bits of something sitting on something else. A mouthful, they tossed them down just like that, never so much as a thank-you or even a look—at least these old biddies have some manners. Christ, I don't believe it, she's going into four hearts—well, why the hell not? What's she got to lose? *[She works her way around the table.]*

Hmmm, nice spread of spades, but I suppose she'll underplay it, she always does, she doesn't seem to have any notion of—of course she can't see what I can see. She really should set up a cross-trump. Will you look at that? She's got her cards arranged wrong, she's got the king with the clubs, out of order. Mrs. Hetherling, whew, she's in for a surprise. Oh well, it's none of my business.

[The MAID hovers around the table, glancing into card hands as the women continue to play, looking occasionally at their watches.]

"Keep an eye on the time," she says. She doesn't want to ring for me when it's refreshments time, says it looks real hoity-toity, ringing for a maid. Suits me. "Nine o'clock," she says. "The other ladies serve just after nine o'clock. Never later than nine-thirty." Well, it's about that time now. Just three cups for tonight. Might as well serve. *[She carries in a tray.]* Nothing wrong with their appetites, I'll say that much. *[She peers over a shoulder.]* Nice, very nice. Too bad she doesn't know what to sluff. Or when to sluff. She could have played that ten, it's just sitting there waiting to be—

[She reaches over and points to a card in CLARA'*s hand;* CLARA (WEST) *looks up, catches her eye and triumphantly plays the card.*

The women at the table look at each other, then at their watches, then at the MAID. *They discuss, then shrug.* GERALDINE MCMURTRY *shrugs and gestures to the* MAID. *The* MAID *shrugs, removes her apron, and looks around for a place to put it, finally draping it over the back of a chair. She takes her place at the table, and* CLARA *deals out four hands. Play begins.*

The telephone rings. The MAID *starts to rise, then sits down again.* MRS. MCMURTRY *starts to rise, then sits. The* MAID *finally rises, tying on her apron. She crosses the stage and picks up the telephone.]*

McMurtrys. *[Pause.]* Yes? *[Pause.]* Well, to tell the truth they were wondering where she'd got to—Oh! Oh! Lordy, lordy, lordy. *[She crosses herself.]* Well, that's a blessing at least, it isn't always that quick. You have to count yourself among the blessed if—Yes, I'm still here, I'm just catching my breath. I heard ya, yes. Yes, they're here. They're—we're in the middle of . . . Yes, sure, sure, I'll . . . be sure to . . . tell them . . . everything. *[She puts down the phone and turns to face the audience. She crosses to the table, speaking to the audience.]*

My ma—or maybe it was my gran, I can't just remember—she used to say—and I've heard Mrs. McMurtry here say the same thing—she'd say, "Good news travels fast, but"—*[she takes off her apron and takes her place at the table, picks up a hand, and turns to the audience]* "but bad news can wait." *[A tape of the women talking and laughing plays while the women change; this scene, gesturing at the commonalty of women, is played with the women wearing only their slips, triple strings of pearls and large pearl earrings. Their demeanour is of women fully and formally dressed.* CLARA (WEST) *takes her place at a lectern, with a microphone if available, at stage right. Two other women,* ALICE (EAST) *and* BUNNY (NORTH), *sit at the card table, and the fourth woman,* FUR STOLE (SOUTH), *wearing a fur stole over her shoulders, takes a seat in the front of the theatre. Lights on* CLARA.*]*

CLARA

[Speaking from lectern.] Good evening, ladies and gentlemen. It is my pleasure to introduce to you a group of . . . friends, dear friends, who have been together for . . . *[she consults her notes]* for years and years. And years.

Decades. What I mean to say is, generations. Yes, I know it's hard to believe, but this group has become a Tuesday night institution. A veritable institution. Together through a major depression, a world war, yes, way back then. Elections, spirals of affluence, miraculous inventions, death, illness, birth—*[Pauses, looks at her notes.]* I did say death, didn't I? Well, I haven't come here tonight to bring gloom and doom, I'm here to present to you—and here they are—the Martha Circle!

[FUR STOLE applauds lustily from the front row of the theatre. Light goes up on the card table.]

ALICE

[Briskly dealing out four hands, she looks up in surprise, then begins to speak very rapidly.] Oh! Hello there. My name is Alice Evans, long-time member of the Martha Circle, going back to . . . since . . . well, it feels like forever, I can't just . . . quite remember when . . . it must be twelve years now, something like that. I'd just moved here from Kenora, and someone I ran into said, would I like to sub one night. It seemed one of the group, Geraldine her name was, who'd replaced someone called Ruth something-or-other from way back, well, this Geraldine person, she'd moved to the coast, reasons of health, asthma, and they needed a fourth. That first night, ha, I felt like I was on trial. I was pret-ty rusty, it'd been a few years since I'd picked up a deck of—*[Slows down.]* A funny thing—that first night, I felt like I was in someone else's skin. Yeah. Not what you'd call a bad feeling, just like the way you feel, you know, when you maybe go down a long hallway and pop open the wrong door by mistake? Like you're all of a sudden in this different room where you hadn't intended to be? But it doesn't seem to matter, if you see what I mean, it's like where you wanted to be . . . *[pause]* all along sort-of-thing?

CLARA

Thank you so much, and now—*[Gestures at BUNNY.]*

BUNNY

[Briskly.] Right. How did I become a member of the Martha Circle? Well, I replaced Cora Fadden exactly two years ago. Cora, as everyone knows, was with the Royal Bank, still is, as a matter of fact, and they asked her if she'd

accept a transfer to Toronto. She hated like anything to go. She'd been a Martha Circle regular for, oh, I'd say seven or eight years. She took over, if I've got this straight, from a gal called Marcella Henry who fell out of a window. She was watering some geraniums, this huge big window box she had. Marcella, of course, replaced Doris Veal, one of the originals if I'm not mistaken. You might say I'm sort of the replacement for the replacement for the replacement—ha! Well, that's my story. Any questions?

CLARA

[Into the microphone.] Yes, are there any questions?

FUR STOLE

[Rising.] I was just wondering, well, this is getting into ancient history, I suppose, but I was wondering what ever happened to Clara. *[Clears throat.]* Clara Wesley. *[Sits.]*

CLARA

[After a long pause.] Well, the fact is, maybe I should have said so in my introduction. I'm . . . *I'm* Clara Wesley. I go right back to the beginning. Doris Veal, Ruth Sprague, Margot Hetherling and myself, Clara Wesley. Except now, of course, it's Clara Hetherling.

FUR STOLE

Hetherling? What do you mean, Hetherling?

CLARA

Well, I thought everyone knew. You see, when Margot died leaving Ronald—there I was. My poor Arthur had been gone for years, and so he and I, Ronald and I—

FUR STOLE

—got together.

CLARA

Married, yes. He wanted me to take his name and I thought, well, why not?

FUR STOLE

[Speaking very deliberately.] So you replaced Wesley . . . with Hetherling?

CLARA

It took a little getting used to, but—

FUR STOLE

And then, I suppose, you moved into . . . Margot Hetherling's old house.

CLARA

It seemed the best idea, they had this almost new furnace and that wonderful deep backyard, and the rose bushes Margot'd put in and the lilacs—

FUR STOLE

And I imagine you . . . you moved into Margot's old bedroom, too.

CLARA

Well—

FUR STOLE

Her own bed even.

CLARA

That did feel . . . a little . . . odd. At first. Sometimes I'd be lying there and I'd start to think, these same sheets, this same blanket. I'd think, Margot used to lie under this same blue woollen blanket, with the same satin binding touching her lips—

FUR STOLE

And?

CLARA

And, well . . . Ronald, too, of course.

FUR STOLE

Yes, Ronald, of course.

CLARA

Sometimes . . . there were moments . . . well, perhaps I should explain that Ronald . . . took me by surprise . . . in the beginning, that is. He turned out to be a . . . a . . . a very romantic man. For his age. And considering his background. Really quite . . . very . . . hmmm . . . passionate.
[All the women nod.]

    Sometimes, I can't explain it, but I used to get the feeling, at those moments . . . I'd start to wonder if he wasn't maybe thinking about Margot. Touching me, my . . . body—oh, he was gentle, oh my—but all the time thinking about Margot. I was sure he was thinking of her. I was positive. And I kept thinking, one of these . . . nights . . . he'll say it, say it out loud, her name . . . Margot.

FUR STOLE

And? Did it ever happen?

CLARA

No. It . . . didn't happen quite that way.

FUR STOLE

What then?

CLARA

It was me . . . one night. Instead of Ronald, it was me. I don't know what I was thinking. Well, I wasn't really thinking at all, I was, well, a long way off . . . [gives an embarrassed laugh] and it just came out of my mouth, sliding out on top of my breath somehow—Arthur. Just like that. Arthur, Arthur. Like a kind of cry. Like I was calling him back, only I wasn't, not really. Oh, I felt awful. I thought, Oh, how I've hurt him, dear Ronald, how could I?

BUNNY

And what did he say?

CLARA

[Rattled.] Who?

ALICE

Ronald. What did Ronald say?

CLARA

[Laughing a little.] Well, he said . . . he said . . . now, Ronald was a passionate man, as I mentioned, almost . . . almost wild . . . at times . . . but he never said a great deal. Some people, you know, are like that.

FUR STOLE

[Rising, approaching CLARA *and letting the fur stole slide down.]* That's true enough. Some people are like that, not given to saying what they're feeling.

CLARA

But on this particular night, when I lost my head and came out with . . . well, there I was, ready to die of shame, but Ronald, he—
[The four women take their places at the table and pick up their cards.]
But Ronald, he just held me . . . held me in his arms, oh so tight-like, and he said, "I love you, Clara." Hmmm. *[Remembering.]* He said, "I love you, my only, only Clara."

FUR STOLE

[Folds stole over the back of the chair and holds out her hand to be shaken.]
Angie Peterson. Filling in tonight for Rosie Elwood, she's in Hawaii.
[The women move to centre stage and gather around the microphone. The following song, lyrics provisional, is to be sung with a gospel rhythm and blues feel.]

ALL

Refrain:
    Hands, hands, hands, hands, (do mi so do)
    Thirteen hands, I got thirteen hands,
    Thirteen hands waving at me,
    Holding down the fam-i-ly tree.

[With variations: "Holding firm to the fam-i-ly tree," "Counting the twigs on the fam-i-ly tree," "Keeping track of the fam-i-ly tree," "Propping up the fam-i-ly tree," "Singing 'round the fam-i-ly tree."]

Hands of diamonds, hands of clubs,
Hands rinsed rough in washing tubs,
Hands of hearts and hands of spades,
Hands whose girlish beauty fades.

Hands be-gloved, hands beloved,
Women's hands with wedding bands,
Hands that raise themselves in doubt,
Hands that count the money out
(dishing out the sauerkraut).
[Refrain.]

Shaping hands and knowing hands,
Crocheting hands and sewing hands,
Bedside hands and birthing hands,
Hands alight and cooling hands.

[The following verse is recited.]
Hands unkissed or in a fist,
Hands that salute the absolute,
Counting hands and praying hands,
Hands that take a public stand.

Hands that feed and hands that fill,
Hands at rest and hands grown still,
Hands that hammer, hands that hack,
Hands that hold the thunder back.
[Refrain.]

Erotic hands, exotic hands,
Travelling-round-the-worldly hands,

Caressing hands and blessing hands,
Ring-around-the-rosy hands.
Hands that reach and catch the rain.
Hands that take the sting from pain.
Wheeling, dealing, reeling, hands.

Hmmm mm mmm mmm (do mi so do)
Thirteen hands, we need thirteen hands,
Hands held tight through thick and thin
(hey, make that thin and thick),
Hands held tight through thin and thick.
It takes thirteen tricks to make a hand,
And thirteen hands to do the trick.

[The women enter the dressing room and change for the next scene into tie-on skirts—micro-short, short, longer and very long—that reflect their different ages: great-grandmother, grandmother, mother and daughter.

The stage is dark. Sound of loud creaking. Large shadows on the walls. Light comes up on CLARA, *as a great-grandmother in wheelchair, entering from one side of the stage; she stops and composes her hands; light comes up on* CLARA'S DAUGHTER (EAST), *sixty. Exaggerated sound of footsteps: two women, one about forty,* CLARA'S GRANDDAUGHTER (NORTH), *the other a teenager,* CLARA'S GREAT-GRANDDAUGHTER (SOUTH), *enter talking to each other.]*

GRANDDAUGHTER

[To GREAT-GRANDDAUGHTER.*]* It'll just be an hour or so, I promise.

GREAT-GRANDDAUGHTER

A whole hour!

GRANDDAUGHTER

Shhhh. She'll hear you.

GREAT-GRANDDAUGHTER

You've got to be kidding. You'd have to put a bomb under her to—

GRANDDAUGHTER

Shhhh. She's got her new hearing a-i-d on.

DAUGHTER

[To everyone, in a false-cheery voice.] Isn't it wonderful! *[Wheels the wheelchair up to the card table.]* Granny Clara's got a new hearing aid.

GRANDDAUGHTER

Very attractive, Granny Clara. *[Louder.]* I said, it's very attractive.

CLARA

What?

GRANDDAUGHTER

I said, "It's very attractive."

CLARA

I heard you. *[Pause.]* What's attractive?

GREAT-GRANDDAUGHTER

[Gives CLARA *a kiss, then shouts.]* Your hearing aid, Gran. Very nice.

CLARA

And what's so nice about it? *[Starts dealing out hands.]*

DAUGHTER

It's, it's not as, as noticeable as your old one.

GRANDDAUGHTER

The one you refused to wear.

GREAT-GRANDDAUGHTER

[Whispering.] The one you kept hiding in the cutlery drawer. Under the spoons.

CLARA

The moon? What about the moon?

DAUGHTER

We were just saying, there's a full moon tonight. The moon is made of blue cheese.

GREAT-GRANDDAUGHTER

Green cheese. The moon. That's what you always used to say, Mom.

GRANDDAUGHTER

[Picking up hand.] Did I? Two hearts.

CLARA

What was that?

DAUGHTER

Two hearts, Mother. Your bid.

CLARA

Two hearts?

GREAT-GRANDDAUGHTER

I can't stand this, we're never going to get done here. I've got this essay to finish, and there's a movie on channel—

GRANDDAUGHTER

[Whispering.] One hour. Is that too much to ask? A few hands with your mother and grandmother.

DAUGHTER

And your great-grandmother. It does her the world of good. Keeps her alert.

GRANDDAUGHTER

Good therapy, best there is.

                              CLARA
Two spades.

                              DAUGHTER
Th—ree hearts. *[Louder.]* Three hearts.

                    GREAT-GRANDDAUGHTER
Four spades.

                              DAUGHTER
You only have to go to three, dear.

                    GREAT-GRANDDAUGHTER
Four.

                         GRANDDAUGHTER
Are you sure? You don't really have to . . .

                              CLARA
If she said four—

                         GRANDDAUGHTER
Pass.

                              CLARA
Five spades.

                              DAUGHTER
Five! Pass.

                    GREAT-GRANDDAUGHTER
Pass. And I mean pass. Do I ever mean pass.

                         GRANDDAUGHTER
Pass.

GREAT-GRANDDAUGHTER

We've had it. We've goofed, Granny Clara. We're into the primordial—
[The four women play the hand out as they talk.]

CLARA

I remember one night, oh, I think it was during the war, one night, summer, I think. Margot had just dealt out the nicest spade hand—

GREAT-GRANDDAUGHTER

Which war was this?

DAUGHTER

Shhhh.

GREAT-GRANDDAUGHTER

I've gotta do this essay about the Treaty of Versailles, and I was just wondering if maybe Grandma was there.

GRANDDAUGHTER

Trump.

DAUGHTER

Rot-ten split.

CLARA

It was toward the end of the war, not that we knew it was toward the end—
how would we know that?

DAUGHTER

Another spade! I do not believe it.

CLARA

Everything was rationed, butter, sugar, the lot. Coffee even. We'd get
together, Tuesday nights as usual, Doris, Margot, Ruth Sprague, and what'd
we serve? A slice of Spam on a cracker *[laughs]*, and we used to make this

concoction called eggless chocolate cake. We'd put something in it to make it rise, what was it now?

                    GRANDDAUGHTER

Was it good?

                         CLARA

I can't remember. It didn't matter. We didn't think about it.

                GREAT-GRANDDAUGHTER

[Whispering.] Well, you're thinking about it now.

                    GRANDDAUGHTER

Shhhh.

                         CLARA

Vinegar, I think. A couple of tablespoons of white vinegar—

                        DAUGHTER

Down one!

                         CLARA

There we were, 1944, or maybe 1943—I wish I could remember—

                        DAUGHTER

It doesn't matter, Mother.

                         CLARA

Margot had just dealt out this beautiful hand, that is to say I had the most beautiful hand, a nice run of spades—and my diamonds were pretty good, too.

                GREAT-GRANDDAUGHTER

I don't believe it—we did it, Gran, five spades. Hee! We actually made five spades. And the crowds go wild—

CLARA

—and all of a sudden Ruth Sprague, you remember, Ruth Sprague, dear—
[Dialogue from this point goes at top speed.]

DAUGHTER

As if I could forget. That wonderful black hair, the way she parted it down
the middle and wore it in these coils over her ears. Like little earphones.

GREAT-GRANDDAUGHTER

There's this girl in my class, Rosalie Spiers, who wears her hair in—

DAUGHTER

Rosalie? Spiers? Would she be the one whose sister married the Hungarian
labour organizer and went—

GREAT-GRANDDAUGHTER

Her cousin. Remember? The one with the thing on her forehead? Right in
the middle of the forehead? Rosie's sister is the one who got so sunburned
that time she had to—

DAUGHTER

Ruth Sprague, she really did have hair that—

CLARA

You're thinking of Doris. It was Doris Veal who had the—

DAUGHTER

That's right, Doris had the hair. And the Vauxhall. Her own car, and that
was something in those days, a woman having her own car. Oh, I remember Doris Veal. I remember that uproar about her son—

GRANDDAUGHTER

—her grandson—

CLARA

Lovely boy—

GREAT-GRANDDAUGHTER

Teddy? Teddy Veal? The same one who got what's-her-name pregnant. Charlene Windsor.

DAUGHTER

They both sang in the same choir, too. That's the whole point. Charlene Windsor's father, he voted Liberal—

GREAT-GRANDDAUGHTER

Wasn't he the one—

GRANDDAUGHTER

Exactly. It was on Valentine's Day, he was courting Eleanor McMurtry who was related, very distantly of course, to—what was her name anyway?

CLARA

Geraldine. She had trouble with asthma, always did, more or less ran in the family. Judge McMurtry, you remember poor old Judge McMurtry—

DAUGHTER

They were cousins or something.

CLARA

By marriage only. I think it was Judge McMurtry who—

GRANDDAUGHTER

Do you mean *the* Judge McMurtry? I think you mean his half-brother, what was his name, Foster. Long bushy beard. Big black boots? Remember when he played Santa Claus for the Lions and his beard caught fire. Ed Kroger came running over with a fire extinguisher—

DAUGHTER

He was married three times, Ed Kroger, imagine, and he was not what I would call an attractive man either, and his third wife—was it Bessie?

CLARA

No, I don't think it was Bessie. Lizzy maybe.

DAUGHTER

Lizzy, she was the one, I'm sure she was, who had to have her gallbladder out while she was in Victoria attending a teachers' convention, and her sister-in-law—

GRANDDAUGHTER

That would be Marguerite. I was a friend of hers before she married Bob Hartley, his mother was Doris Veal's cousin, the one who married the youngest Spicer boy—his sister married into the Hartwells. It was his brother, Grover Spicer who beat his wife and went to jail for it and later converted to Catholicism. Remember that priest, Father what's-his-name, came from Quebec and spoke with that—where was I?—Marguerite, this will amaze you, but Marguerite got the silver medal the year we graduated. She had these pathetic bowed legs—

CLARA

That was the polio. Her mother was in a state—

DAUGHTER

Never the same after—

CLARA

True.

GRANDDAUGHTER

Sad.

DAUGHTER

Tragic.

CLARA

Couldn't be helped, of course. Not in those days.

GRANDDAUGHTER

Not with that family background. Her uncle—

CLARA

He was, well this was later, he was—what's the word?

DAUGHTER

Eccentric. Ha. He had himself a permanent wave, yes, really, a perm, and he wore cologne. "Evening in Paris" if I'm not mistaken—

GREAT-GRANDDAUGHTER

Was he the guy they found in the park with the fishing rod and the sack of oranges and the—

CLARA

No, that was Myron Bell. His mother and my mother went to school together. She was an Ambrose, fine family, St. George's, very active, but they did things differently, that family. We used to say it was because they were from Newfoundland.

DAUGHTER

[Musing.] But aren't we all? From Newfoundland. Metaphorically, I mean.

CLARA

Just to give you a for instance, they believed in using their silver every day, sterling silver, and then she married a Bell, one of the Selkirk Bells, and that was the end of the silver—all of it got sold—and the start of, what was it now? Nine children, ten maybe. This was before the days of—Myron was the last of the lot, a strange child. He talked to animals, birds and so on. So the episode in the park didn't really surprise us.

GREAT-GRANDDAUGHTER

Is it true he took his fishing rod and the—

GRANDDAUGHTER

Good heavens, now how do you know about Myron Bell in the park with the oranges and the fishing rod? You weren't even born then.

DAUGHTER

You weren't born either. And don't forget the grapefruit. What he did with the grapefruit.

GRANDDAUGHTER

That's right. And I haven't forgotten the grapefruit, how could I?
[All four laugh hysterically.]

DAUGHTER

I guess it's history more or less. Real history!

GREAT-GRANDDAUGHTER

This essay I'm writing—

CLARA

And so . . . on this night, I remember it as though it were . . . minutes ago . . . Ruth Sprague looked at her hand, these lovely spades and said right out loud . . . now, what was it she said?
[There is a long pause.]

DAUGHTER

You feel up to another hand, Mother?

CLARA

I wish I could remember things. Not everything, but I wish I could remember what we talked about all those years. Margot and Ruth and Doris and—

GRANDDAUGHTER

Whose deal is it? I've lost track.

DAUGHTER

Yours, I think.

GREAT-GRANDDAUGHTER

Gossip.

GRANDDAUGHTER

[Sharply.] Gossip? What do you mean, gossip?

GREAT-GRANDDAUGHTER

Well, Granny Clara was wondering . . . what she and her cronies used to—

GRANDDAUGHTER

Oh, they weren't cronies, cronies isn't the word. They were—

DAUGHTER

It wasn't really gossip, not the way you're thinking of.

GREAT-GRANDDAUGHTER

[Shouting.] What'd ya talk about, Gran, if you weren't dishing the dirt? Your old boyfriends? Your beaux?

CLARA

No, I don't think so. I don't remember—

GRANDDAUGHTER

Your husbands probably. Your hubbies and your kids.

CLARA

Well, maybe now and then, but—

DAUGHTER

What you were gonna fix for dinner. Recipes.

CLARA

I suppose we did. From time to time, but most of the time—now I remember! What we talked about. *[Pause.]* We talked about our mothers.
[Lights dim. Tape of women talking and laughing. Fade. Lights come up immediately on CLARA *at centre of darkened stage in her wheelchair. She rises suddenly to her feet, facing audience directly.]*
[Repeating in exactly the same tone she used previously.] Now I remember. We talked about our mothers.
[While CLARA *listens, other women speak from various positions on stage.]*

WOMAN TWO (EAST)

My mother, she used to put thirteen egg whites in a cake. The recipe called for twelve, but no, that wouldn't do. She always put in thirteen—for good luck, she said.

WOMAN THREE (SOUTH)

Not my mother, no siree, if it called for twelve eggs, she put in eleven. Waste not, want not—

WOMAN FOUR (NORTH)

Well, when it came to children, bringing them up, my mother had this saying. One is one, she said, but two is ten. That's a kind of proverb, I think. Icelandic. Or else she made it up, she was like that—

WOMAN THREE

When bad things happened, sickness, death, tragedy, she used to say—oh, she knew her Bible backwards and forwards—she used to say, tares among the wheat, tares among the wheat—

WOMAN FOUR

Become a nun, she said, and you get none. Ha.

WOMAN THREE

A mother needs a dozen eyes and thirteen hands, that's what my mother used to say—

WOMAN TWO

Of course she always called my father "her better half." But the way she said it, her tone of voice, it was, like a private joke she had—like she was sucking on a pickle.

WOMAN FOUR

Shabby underwear, she'd say, is the sign of a shabby—

WOMAN TWO

Never skimp on baking chocolate. Or good wool gloves or—

WOMAN THREE

—there she'd be out in the back garden. Early in the morning. She loved the early morning, especially in the summertime. She'd be out there picking raspberries, she'd have a whole bowl picked by the time the rest of us—

WOMAN TWO

Indisposed, she used to say. Or my granny's come calling. Or I fell off the roof. Well, we knew what that meant.

WOMAN FOUR

—of course she was excommunicated when she married, but sometimes we'd catch her, standing at the window, making the sign of the cross—

WOMAN THREE

—that's what she said. She said it only once, but it . . . [pause] stuck with me. That she'd wanted to be an opera singer when she was a girl, go away to Europe and have her voice trained. And she couldn't carry a tune in a basket.

WOMAN FOUR

—my father used to say it shamed him, seeing her chop kindling, but she loved it, loved getting outdoors—

WOMAN TWO

—well, they didn't have running water, but she had this saying, "A lady can take a bath in a teacup." And she could—

WOMAN THREE

—mysterious aches and pains especially in her legs. Of course the doctors didn't know anything then about—

WOMAN TWO

—hid in the closet during the electric storms. She used to take us with her, we could feel her trembling in the dark.

WOMAN FOUR

Well, when there was thunder, she'd say, "It's just the angels moving their furniture." Her voice bright as—

WOMAN TWO

She'd launch into this story about her cousin Aaron, struck by lightening, standing there between the house and barn. The tears would roll down her face. And this happened maybe fifty years back.

WOMAN THREE

She smacked us on the back of the hand. Hard. With anything she happened to have in her hand, a wooden spoon, whatever. Her mean streak. We learned to keep out of her way when she was in one of her moods.

WOMAN TWO

—used to say how her idea of paradise was sitting in front of the wood stove with her feet up on a chair. She had this problem with her veins, her mother had had the same thing, and now I—

WOMAN FOUR

—my father's shirts. It's the least I can do for him, she used to say, send him out in the world every day with a properly ironed shirt and collar.

WOMAN THREE

[Counting on fingers.]—never rode a bicycle, never went ice-skating, not once, never had a real engagement ring—

WOMAN TWO

Well, you know how it was then, spring cleaning began the first day of April, but she liked to get a head start. She'd get my father to carry out the carpets—there'd be snow on the bushes, but she'd get going. It was like a *[harshly]* sickness she had.

WOMAN FOUR

—saved every letter and postcard she ever got. She had boxes and boxes of them, and after she died we found—

WOMAN TWO

—saved wrapping paper, string, she even saved her basting threads and used them over again.

WOMAN FOUR

—hoarded the little stumpy ends of candles, saved orange peels to make candy out of—

WOMAN TWO

—saved this postcard of Niagara Falls where—

WOMAN THREE

—saved a lock of my father's hair, from when he was a young man, courting, smitten to the heart, and years later when he was bald as a—well, she'd
show us kids this little piece of hair, tender like a baby's hair. She had it all
tied up with a billy piece of ribbon. She'd get it out and show it to us and
say, "Your father, he was a prince."

WOMAN TWO

Oh, oh, she started one night—coughing up blood—
[WOMAN TWO rises from the table and moves toward the bicycle.]

WOMAN THREE

—a tumour in her stomach the size of two fists—

WOMAN FOUR

—broken hip, her bones were like finest china. Shattered. Oh dear God,
that was the beginning of the end—
*[A change of light indicates a change of mood. SCARF (EAST), mounted on the
bicycle, approaches CLARA, ringing the bell. She has tied a scarf around her
head.]*

SCARF

[She is not so much angry as emotionally on edge, close to tears.] Pardon me.
Pardon me? It's none of my business, but I wonder, has it ever occurred to
you that you could have been knitting wool socks for our fighting men, the
four of you? Did you ever stop to think of that? You could have been rolling
bandages. But, no, there you were, playing hand after hand every Tuesday
night when our Christian missions in Africa and China were begging for
flannel nightgowns and bibles and warm blankets. You could have saved
lives. Yes, you could have. You could have been—useful.

CLARA

[Taken aback.] Well, the fact is . . . you see . . . we never thought—we felt
we needed a little—

SCARF

[Tearful.] At least, at least you might have talked about something interesting? The history of the Commonwealth? Russian novels? Medieval art? Now that's a very interesting subject, medieval art. You could have been learning a foreign language on those Tuesday nights. You could have looked into philosophy, economics, investment opportunities. Oh, there were so many useful—

CLARA

[Wonderingly.] Investment opportunities?

SCARF

Or you could have been, you know, out fighting for political change, for the extension of women's rights. You could have bettered your conditions, enriched your lives. Do you know what? You could have . . . you could have made something of yourselves.

CLARA

It was . . . not at our disposal. We did not have at our disposal—

SCARF

How could you have thrown away all that time.

CLARA

[Merrily.] I don't know . . . but we did.

SCARF

And there's one thing I'll never be able to understand.

CLARA

Why, I know you, you're Doris Veal's oldest girl.

SCARF

Remember how at the funeral you came up to me, all teary-eyed—oh, it made me sick—and said you felt like you'd lost a sister.

CLARA

She was. We were all of us—

SCARF

Oh, when I think about it. Those Tuesday nights of yours. Sitting there. The blue-rinse girls. The white-glove ladies. Shuffling cards. Killing time. Running away from reality.

CLARA

Well, reality now, that's a good point. Who knows what it really is. It's a *funny* thing. Sometimes it—reality I'm talking about—shrinks down so small it's no bigger than that card table over there.

SCARF

I can tell you about reality if you want.

CLARA

You see, we thought—

SCARF

My mother, your friend Doris Veal, was sober one day out of the week, Tuesday. On Tuesday she got up sober and went to bed sober—so she'd be fit to go to Martha Circle. The rest of the time, well. It went on for years. You could have done something, helped her. But you didn't even know.

CLARA

That's not—true.

SCARF

None of you lifted a finger. You didn't do one thing.

CLARA

I can't tell you—we wanted more than anything—

SCARF

You turned a blind eye. *[Voice breaking.]*

CLARA

Yes. *[Slowly.]* A blind eye. I suppose you could call it that.

SCARF

You just let her be. Just let her *[pause]* be.

CLARA

[Softly.] That's what we did. Yes.

SCARF

You let her be.
[Her voice breaks. The two women take each other's hands, a sudden open embrace of understanding.]

CLARA

[Pulling away.] And, you know, sitting there, the four of us, we were as close together as people can get.

SCARF

Close . . . close.

CLARA

When people think about being close, they think of two people in bed together, a husband and wife, a man and a woman, but this was closer. At that card table we were closer, you know, than families are sitting at a dining table, sitting with your own flesh and blood, eating a Sunday dinner. I'm talking about inches away, real distance as we measure it.

SCARF

And the things you talked about—

CLARA

It was as if our brains were so busy, counting points, planning the next move, trying to guess what was in our partner's head, and you know, we got so we could do just that. It was like a kind of enchantment—well, there we were, thinking so hard about what we were doing that our tongues just went and did what they wanted to do, said things that seemed to come out of nowhere, came right up out of foreign parts of us. Oh, it was a strange thing, those cards slipping out of one hand into another.

[SCARF nodding, understanding.]

It was like we were making something, a kind of handiwork, and everything else falling away. It was like a little planet we'd put together, and it was us who'd written the rules and bought the furniture and the curtains and the carpets, and we'd set it whirling out there in the darkness. At that table, I knew exactly where I was.

SCARF

[Quietly.] And where exactly *[pause]* were you?

CLARA

I was . . . I don't know . . . at home! At home in the world. Ruth. Margot. Doris. Oh my, the four of us around that table, dealing out hands. I know it's hard to believe, but we were young then. Young as . . . girls! Starting out our lives. Every Tuesday night. Oh, my! We couldn't see into the future, of course we couldn't. The future was too far away. But we could see as far as Tuesday night. And that was enough. We'd get together in each other's houses, those little living rooms, all dusted, the table set up, everything ready. *[Expository tone.]* On Tuesdays, for once, we'd leave the dishes in the sink. We'd try to start as soon after supper as we could get away, oh, I'd say about seven-thirty or thereabouts, it would just be getting dark, twilight— *[Clarinet music. Lights fade, then come up again in the form of flickering silent-movie lighting. Clarinet music fades to nickelodeon music. A* YOUNG WOMAN *wearing a vaguely twenties outfit carries on stage a flip chart or electronic substitute if possible, on which are written the titles that accompany the silent film sequence that follows. The first title reads "The Card Party," and she immediately flips this so that the card reads, "Waiting for Clara." She is joined by two others, similarly dressed. The three of them go to an imaginary window, gesturing broadly. One returns to the flip chart, and turns the leaf to reveal the title: "Where, oh, where is Clara?"*

The three women gesture broadly at each other, shrugging, questioning. Nickelodeon music grows louder. They go again to the window and look out. One goes to the chart and turns to the next title: "This is very mysterious." One woman rushes offstage and returns with a tea tray; she mimes an offer of tea, but the others shake their heads.

The three women sit at the table: one holds up a deck of cards: all look agitated. One goes to the flip chart and turns to "Where, oh, where is Clara?" and flips immediately to the next title, which says, "What can be keeping her?"

One woman goes to the window again. She peers out and begins to mime wildly. The other women run to the window, gesturing wildly, then run to flip chart revealing "At last."

The young CLARA *enters, running from stage left. The others embrace her and lead her to the table. They sit at the table, pick up their cards. A warm, golden, steady light replaces the black and white film flicker; nickelodeon music fades to recorded music. The women freeze. Light slowly fades. Very gradual introduction of tape of women talking and laughing.*
The end.]

Carol Shields

Carol Shields is an internationally known author who has won many awards for her novels and short stories. *Larry's Party* won the Orange Prize and was shortlisted for the Giller Prize. *The Stone Diaries* won the Pulitzer Prize, the Governor General's Award and the National Book Critics' Circle Award, and was shortlisted for the Booker Prize. Ms. Shields has also written eleven other novels and short-story collections, three books of poetry, numerous plays and a biography of Jane Austen. She is also co-editor, with Marjorie Anderson, of *Dropped Threads: What We Aren't Told.* Her latest novel, *Unless,* reawakens the voice of Reta Winters, from her story "The Scarf," included in *Dressing Up for the Carnival.*

Catherine Shields

I am the product of an extremely happy childhood; the bar was set high to work hard and be thankful. And not to take oneself too seriously. During an internship with UNESCO, I discovered the ordered world of information management. I was attracted to these shiny tricks to organize ideas and this lead me to jobs in museums, art galleries and universities. At present, I manage libraries at Parks Canada, for the West. I have two fine sons and a brilliant husband. I now live in Winnipeg.

Dave Williamson

Dave Williamson is the author of four novels, *The Bad Life, Shandy, Running Out, Weddings,* and a collection of short stories, *Accountable Advances.* His most recent book is the memoir, *Author! Author! Encounters with Famous Writers,* which includes a chapter about his collaborating with Carol Shields on the play *Anniversary.* He is also co-editor of an anthology of fiction, essays and poetry, *Beyond Borders.* For many years, he was Dean of Business and Applied Arts at Red River College in Winnipeg. He presently heads up the academic planning for Red River's new downtown campus.